Dear Brandon
Love DAD
1996

EYEWITNESS

LIVING
EARTH

EYEWITNESS

LIVING EARTH

Written and edited by
MIRANDA SMITH

A DK PUBLISHING BOOK

Senior editor Miranda Smith
Senior art editor Andrew Nash
Designer Joseph Hoyle
Senior managing editor Gillian Denton
Senior managing art editor Julia Harris
Production Catherine Semark
Editorial consultant Barbara Taylor

First American Edition, 1996
10 9 8 7 6 5 4 3 2 1

Published in the United States by
DK Publishing, Inc.,
95 Madison Avenue,
New York, New York 10016

Distributed by Houghton Mifflin
Company, Boston.

A catalog record is available from the
Library of Congress.

ISBN 0-7894-0644-6

Color reproduction by
Colourscan, Singapore.
Printed and bound by
New Interlitho,
Italy

CONTENTS

INTRODUCTION

THE EARTH IS HOME to millions of species, all with different characteristics and needs. How these species behave and how they interact with their environment and with one another is a source of endless fascination. They survive in a variety of habitats and climates – from the frozen wastes of Antarctica to the tropical swamps of Southeast Asia, from the teeming Australian barrier reef to the arid sands of the Namibian desert. The life cycles of these animals and plants have been captured in superb detail by the photographers of the Eyewitness series, providing a unique insight into the living Earth.

FIRST FOSSILS

Fossils are the remains or impressions of living things that have hardened in rock. They tell scientists a great deal about the past, and the animals and plants that lived millions of years ago. The oldest fossils found so far are 4.5 billion years old and are of single-celled, bacterialike organisms. It was another million years before an oxygen-rich atmosphere developed on Earth, allowing more complex organisms to survive.

Fossil of rugose coral

Fossil of trilobite

Fossil of ammonite

FIRST STEPS

Four-legged animals took a major step forward when reptiles appeared. Unlike their amphibian ancestors, reptiles did not rely on an aquatic environment for survival. The land invasion from the swarming prehistoric seas that had begun with plants, arthropods, and amphibians was complete. Today's lizards, such as this tegu lizard from tropical South America, are not very different in shape or characteristics from prehistoric reptiles.

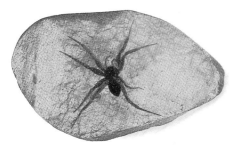

Spider preserved in amber

CHAPTER 1

FIRST LIFE

LIFE IS ONLY KNOWN here on Earth, and Earth's rocks contain fossils of past life. Paleontologists use these fossils to construct the story of that life. The first fossils date back to 4.5 billion years ago, when very diverse forms of life began to develop, eventually including reptiles, dinosaurs, and early mammals.

The Sun

A close-up view of the Sun, showing a violent storm erupting at the surface

THE SUN IS THE STAR at the center of the Solar System. It is 875,000 miles (1.4 million kilometers) in diameter and consists almost entirely of hydrogen and helium. The heat and light of the Sun sustain life on Earth. Without the Sun, there would be no weather. Because the Earth's surface is curved, the Sun's rays strike different parts at different angles, dividing the world into distinct climate zones, each with its own typical weather. Light from the Sun is the energy that fuels the world's great weather machine – its heat keeps the atmosphere constantly in motion.

Young stage of crab larva

Sample of zooplankton collected from northern Atlantic coast of Scotland

Shrimp

LIFE IN THE SEA
Zooplankton are tiny animals that drift in the oceans. They eat phytoplankton, minute, single-celled plants that use nutrients in seawater and sunlight to grow. Zooplankton in turn are eaten by larger fish, such as the dogfish, which are, in their turn, eaten by still larger fish or other predators such as dolphins. Some larger ocean animals (whale sharks and blue whales) feed directly on zooplankton.

Shaving brush tree
Pachira aquatica

ANIMAL LIFE
All life on Earth needs the Sun to survive. A lizard makes a dramatic example because it is cold-blooded. This does not mean that its body is always cold, but that its temperature rises and falls with that of its surroundings. A lizard needs to be warm to move around, and it heats up its body by basking in sunshine. If it gets too hot, it retreats into shade. Butterflies also adjust their body temperature in this way.

PLANT LIFE
The incredible variety of plant life on Earth relies on its ability to convert the energy from sunlight into food (pp. 46–47). In shape and form, leaves are adapted to the task of capturing light; pigments such as chlorophyll and carotenoids absorb the light energy. However, only a tiny fraction of the Sun's energy that reaches the Earth is actually used to create plant material.

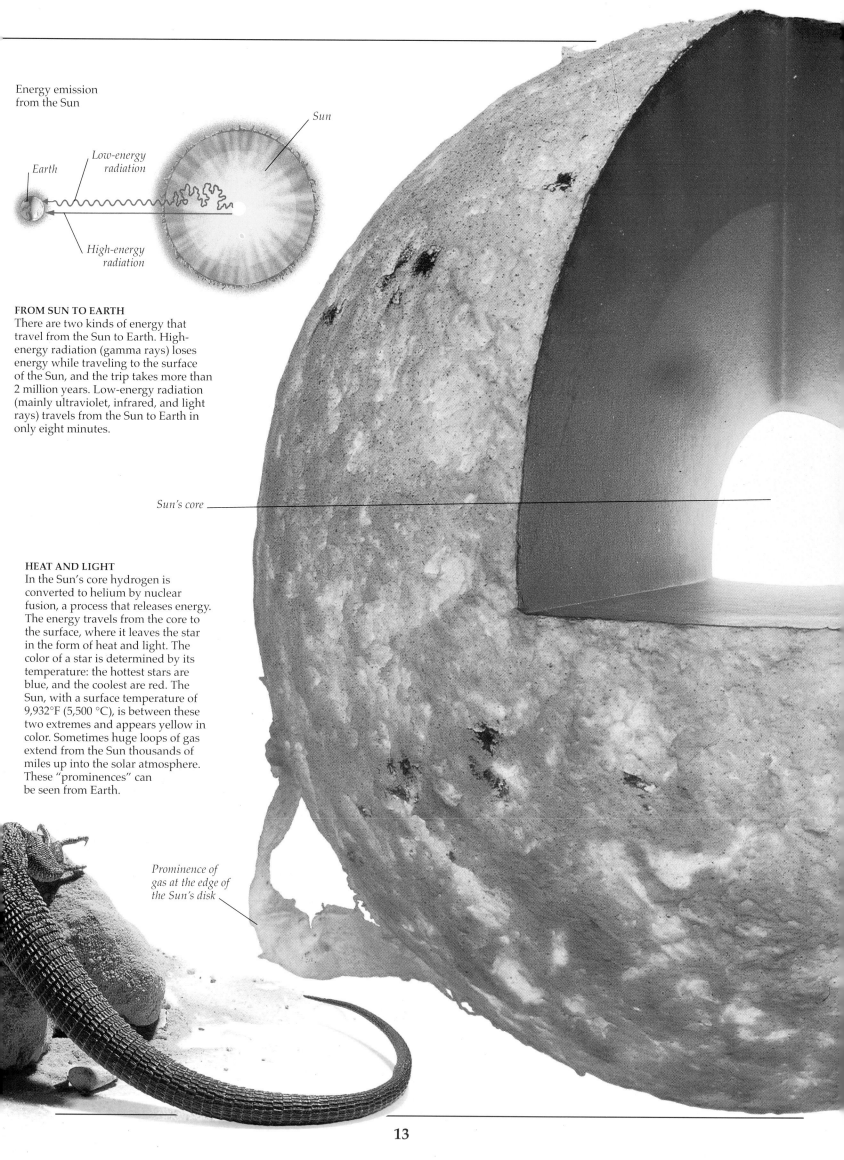

Energy emission
from the Sun

Sun

*Low-energy
radiation*

Earth

*High-energy
radiation*

FROM SUN TO EARTH
There are two kinds of energy that travel from the Sun to Earth. High-energy radiation (gamma rays) loses energy while traveling to the surface of the Sun, and the trip takes more than 2 million years. Low-energy radiation (mainly ultraviolet, infrared, and light rays) travels from the Sun to Earth in only eight minutes.

Sun's core

HEAT AND LIGHT
In the Sun's core hydrogen is converted to helium by nuclear fusion, a process that releases energy. The energy travels from the core to the surface, where it leaves the star in the form of heat and light. The color of a star is determined by its temperature: the hottest stars are blue, and the coolest are red. The Sun, with a surface temperature of 9,932°F (5,500 °C), is between these two extremes and appears yellow in color. Sometimes huge loops of gas extend from the Sun thousands of miles up into the solar atmosphere. These "prominences" can be seen from Earth.

*Prominence of
gas at the edge of
the Sun's disk*

Single-celled life

MOST FORMS OF LIFE consist of a single cell that carries out all the tasks involved in staying alive. With a few exceptions, single-celled organisms are so small that they cannot be seen with the naked eye. Until the 17th century, no one knew that they existed. The invention of the microscope revealed that single-celled creatures live almost everywhere, from pond water to household dust. Many exist on or in the human body. During the 20th century, scientists discovered that the many different forms of single-celled life fall into two distinct groups. Some cells have a nucleus and a range of special internal structures called organelles that harness energy and put it to work. Other cells are smaller and simpler, with very few internal structures. These organisms – the bacteria – are the most abundant life form that exists. It is estimated that the combined weight of all the bacteria in the world would be 20 times greater than the weight of all other living things put together.

EXPLORING A HIDDEN WORLD
The pioneering Dutch scientist Anton van Leeuwenhoek (1632–1723) designed and built this small single-lens microscope. In 1683, he used it to become the first person to see bacteria. He made these sketches of the movements of bacteria that he found living on his teeth.

ANCIENT LIFE
These wormlike strands, photographed in ultraviolet light, are clusters of single-celled organisms called cyanobacteria. They make their food by using sunlight, and are the oldest living things to be found on the Earth. Geologists have discovered huge fossilized mats of cyanobacteria, called stromatolites, that are more than 3 billion years old – almost three-quarters as old as Earth itself.

THE RACE TO REPRODUCE
A bacterium reproduces simply by dividing to make two new cells. Under ideal conditions, each bacterium can split in two every 20 minutes. Each of these two will then do the same, and so on. Within just a few hours, a single bacterium can produce a teeming colony of millions, like the one below.

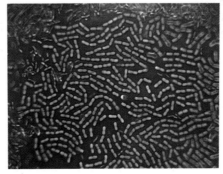

MICROBES AND DISEASE
Research by the German bacteriologist Robert Koch (1843–1910) helped prove that bacteria are one of the causes of disease. He found that certain bacteria cultured in the laboratory could produce the deadly disease anthrax when introduced into cattle.

Fossilized plant-like organisms known as diatoms

LIFE IN A SILICA CASE
The circle below is a collection of fossilized diatoms, tiny plantlike organisms that are far smaller than the period at the end of this sentence and invisible to the naked eye. A diatom's single cell is supported by a delicately sculpted case (right) made of silica, a glasslike material found in sand. The case consists of two halves that fit over each other, and each species has a case of a slightly different shape. In the 19th century, arranging diatoms became a fad. One microscopist managed to squeeze all the diatoms then known – more than 4,000 species – into a square less than 0.3 in (7 mm) across.

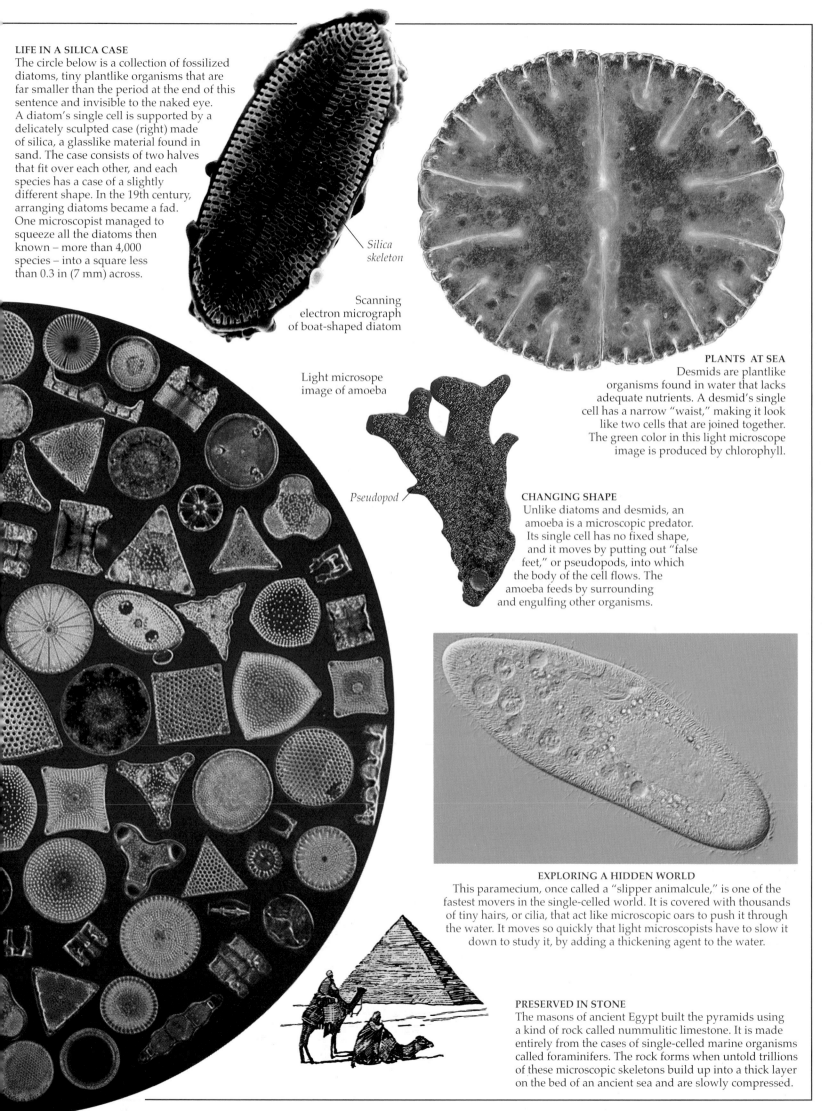

Silica skeleton

Scanning electron micrograph of boat-shaped diatom

Light microsope image of amoeba

Pseudopod

PLANTS AT SEA
Desmids are plantlike organisms found in water that lacks adequate nutrients. A desmid's single cell has a narrow "waist," making it look like two cells that are joined together. The green color in this light microscope image is produced by chlorophyll.

CHANGING SHAPE
Unlike diatoms and desmids, an amoeba is a microscopic predator. Its single cell has no fixed shape, and it moves by putting out "false feet," or pseudopods, into which the body of the cell flows. The amoeba feeds by surrounding and engulfing other organisms.

EXPLORING A HIDDEN WORLD
This paramecium, once called a "slipper animalcule," is one of the fastest movers in the single-celled world. It is covered with thousands of tiny hairs, or cilia, that act like microscopic oars to push it through the water. It moves so quickly that light microscopists have to slow it down to study it, by adding a thickening agent to the water.

PRESERVED IN STONE
The masons of ancient Egypt built the pyramids using a kind of rock called nummulitic limestone. It is made entirely from the cases of single-celled marine organisms called foraminifers. The rock forms when untold trillions of these microscopic skeletons build up into a thick layer on the bed of an ancient sea and are slowly compressed.

Carbon on the move

ALL LIVING THINGS contain the element carbon.
It is also found in the oceans, in the air, and in
the Earth itself. Carbon combines with other
substances to take different forms. In the
atmosphere, with oxygen, it exists as carbon
dioxide (CO_2). In the ground and in the bones
and shells of animals, carbon takes the form
of chalky calcium carbonate. Carbon is passed
around the biosphere, with plants as the
main point of exchange. They convert
atmospheric CO_2 into carbohydrates,
a source of energy used to
maintain their existence, through
photosynthesis (pp. 40–41).
When living things die, they are
broken down by bacteria known
as decomposers. The carbon
that they needed to live is
released back into the
atmosphere to be used
by other forms of life.

STORES OF CARBON
As plants grow, they absorb carbon
from the atmosphere. Some is used
immediately by the plant, but some is
stored by being incorporated into the
plant's structure, for example, as
starch (p. 40). Every tree trunk is
a store of carbon. If the tree is
burned, its stored carbon is
released back into the
atmosphere as
carbon dioxide.

THE CARBON CYCLE

Less than 1 percent of carbon on Earth is in active circulation in the biosphere. The rest is locked up as inorganic carbon in rocks and as organic carbon in fossil fuels. As growing plants take in carbon dioxide from the atmosphere and incorporate it as carbohydrates, carbon passes into the food chain. The plants release stored energy by breaking down the carbohydrates in a process called respiration. This releases energy and produces carbon dioxide as a waste product.

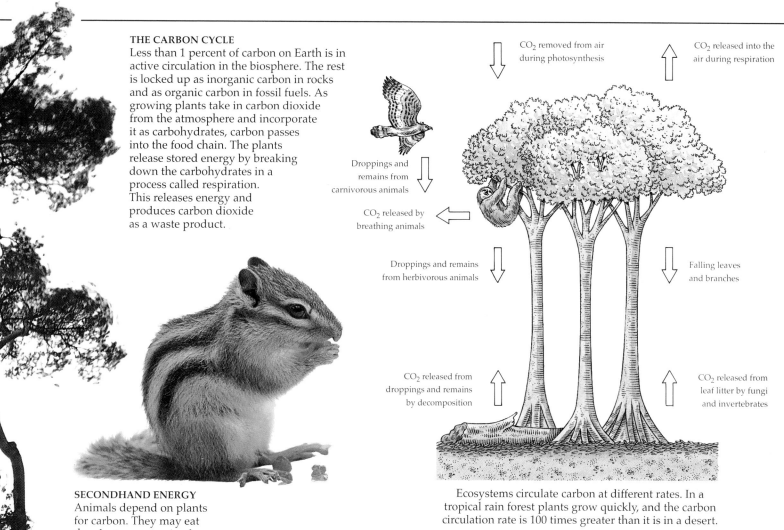

CO_2 removed from air during photosynthesis

CO_2 released into the air during respiration

Droppings and remains from carnivorous animals

CO_2 released by breathing animals

Droppings and remains from herbivorous animals

Falling leaves and branches

CO_2 released from droppings and remains by decomposition

CO_2 released from leaf litter by fungi and invertebrates

Ecosystems circulate carbon at different rates. In a tropical rain forest plants grow quickly, and the carbon circulation rate is 100 times greater than it is in a desert.

SECONDHAND ENERGY

Animals depend on plants for carbon. They may eat the plants or eat animals that have fed on plants. The nut this chipmunk is eating is a carbohydrate that the tree converted from carbon dioxide by photosynthesis and stored. All animals are living stores of carbon. However, they release some of this as carbon dioxide in each breath they exhale.

FEEDING THE YOUNG

When the adults of some species of salmon have migrated upriver and spawned, they are so exhausted that they die. Their decomposing bodies can glut the river's headwaters. The bodies provide a supply of nutrients for the salmon eggs and also for the young salmon when they hatch. The young are effectively made up of carbon from their parents.

CARBON AS A FOSSIL FUEL

Carbon is locked in the remains of living things that failed to completely decompose. During the Carboniferous period, 363–290 million years ago, plants died in shallow swamps, forming thick layers. Over millions of years, the heat of the Earth and the pressure of material building up above them turned this carbon into coal. In a similar way, vast deposits of tiny dead sea creatures became a liquid store of carbon – oil, which can be converted into gasoline. When these "fossil fuels" are burned, the carbon is finally released. About 50 times as much carbon is locked up in the Earth's coal and oil as there is in all living things. However, reserves of coal will only last about 250–300 years if they are used at the current rate. Oil reserves will probably only last 100 years.

The surface of the Earth

THE EARTH IS UNSTABLE. Over millions of years, its landscape has changed many times. The crust, or surface, of the Earth is made up of a number of pieces called tectonic plates. These plates move across the Earth's surface in response to forces and movements deep within the planet. The plate boundaries, where plates collide, rub shoulders, or move apart, are areas of intense geological activity. Most volcanoes and earthquakes occur at these boundaries. When two plates collide, one is forced beneath the other to form a subduction zone. The sinking plate partly melts and the light magma rises, feeding volcanoes just inside the plate boundary. The volcanoes take advantage of cracks in the plates, and molten rock bursts through to the surface.

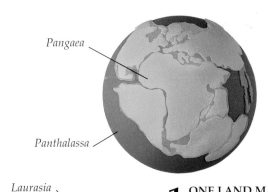

Pangaea

Panthalassa

1 ONE LAND MASS
220 million years ago there was only one land mass, Pangaea, in a vast ocean called Panthalassa

Laurasia

Tethys Sea

Gondwanaland

2 TWO CONTINENTS
200 million years ago the growing Tethys Sea split Pangaea into Gondwanaland and Laurasia

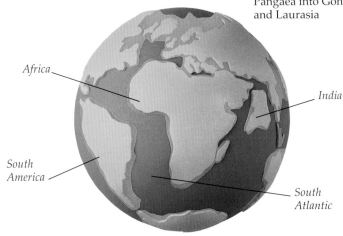

Africa

India

South America

South Atlantic

3 THE CONTINENTS DIVIDE
135 million years ago Gondwanaland split into Africa and South America as the south Atlantic opened up; India drifted toward Asia

FLASH POINT
Early volcano observers thought they saw flames or lightning flashes when a volcano erupted. This was probably the igniting of dangerous gases released by the volcano.

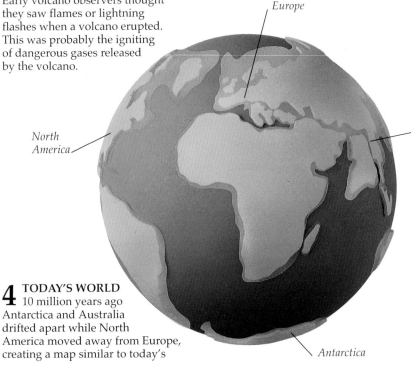

Europe

North America

Asia

4 TODAY'S WORLD
10 million years ago Antarctica and Australia drifted apart while North America moved away from Europe, creating a map similar to today's

Antarctica

TYPES OF VOLCANOES
There are different kinds of volcanoes. Most of the descriptions of volcanoes (right) refer to their shape. For example, during a large, ashy eruption, the empty magma chamber may not be able to support the weight of the volcano's slopes. These collapse inward, leaving a huge circular depression called a caldera. Some volcanoes, however, such as ash-cinder, are classified by their composition.

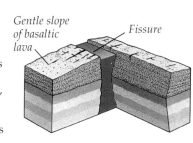

Gentle slope of basaltic lava

Fissure

Fissure volcano

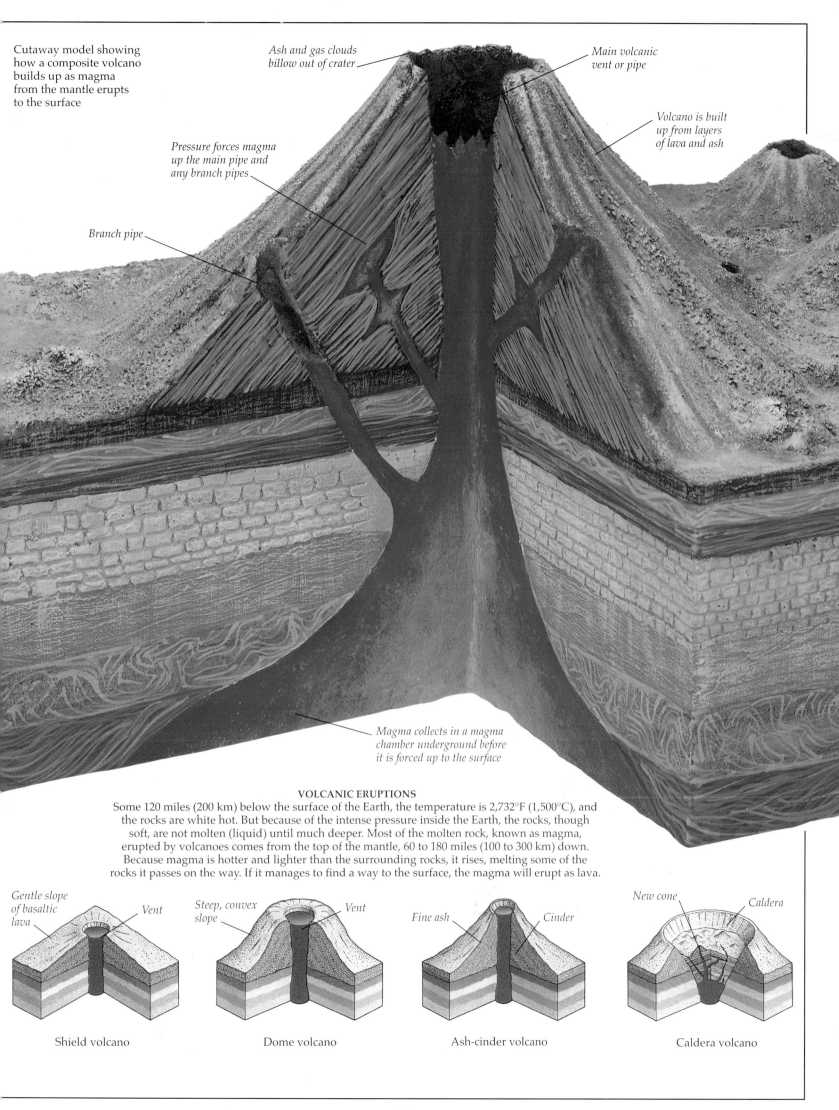

Cutaway model showing how a composite volcano builds up as magma from the mantle erupts to the surface

Ash and gas clouds billow out of crater

Main volcanic vent or pipe

Pressure forces magma up the main pipe and any branch pipes

Volcano is built up from layers of lava and ash

Branch pipe

Magma collects in a magma chamber underground before it is forced up to the surface

VOLCANIC ERUPTIONS

Some 120 miles (200 km) below the surface of the Earth, the temperature is 2,732°F (1,500°C), and the rocks are white hot. But because of the intense pressure inside the Earth, the rocks, though soft, are not molten (liquid) until much deeper. Most of the molten rock, known as magma, erupted by volcanoes comes from the top of the mantle, 60 to 180 miles (100 to 300 km) down. Because magma is hotter and lighter than the surrounding rocks, it rises, melting some of the rocks it passes on the way. If it manages to find a way to the surface, the magma will erupt as lava.

Gentle slope of basaltic lava

Vent

Shield volcano

Steep, convex slope

Vent

Dome volcano

Fine ash

Cinder

Ash-cinder volcano

New cone

Caldera

Caldera volcano

The changing Earth

FOR ALMOST ONE BILLION YEARS, nothing lived on Earth. Nothing wriggled or ran, flew or swam. But as the early planet steadily changed – as new rocks formed, as mountains grew, as oceans spread and earthquakes and volcanoes shook and rattled, as continents slowly shifted, and as climates changed – the chance was created for life to exist. Today, evidence of that early life is preserved as fossils found on the Earth's rocky surface.

HOT ROCKS
Volcanoes occur at weak, thin points in the Earth's crust. Molten lava pours out of fissures and solidifies as it cools. Ash and hot gases are thrown into the air. The ash falls to form a volcanic cone. In the early stages of the Earth's formation, the world was a hot mass of molten rock.

Granite solidified deep underground

Sandstone is made of eroded grains of quartz

Metamorphic marble was once sedimentary limestone

Basalt is a common volcanic igneous rock

BUILDING BLOCKS
Igneous rocks form from molten rock material deep in the Earth. Sedimentary rocks are formed by rock particles, eroded by wind and water, that settle in layers in rivers, seas, and lakes. Changes in temperature and pressure can transform both igneous and sedimentary rocks into metamorphic rocks.

WATERY GRAVES
Rivers build thick sedimentary layers of sand and mud on flood plains and deltas. When it reaches the sea, the sediment sinks to the seafloor. Quickly buried, animal and plant remains may be preserved as the sediment slowly turns to rock.

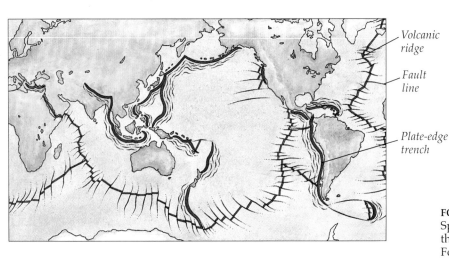

Volcanic ridge

Fault line

Plate-edge trench

MOVING PLATES
The Earth's surface is made of interlocking plates. Spreading out from volcanic ridges on the ocean floor, plate edges are constantly colliding. Some edges may sink, forming trenches where earthquakes and volcanoes often occur. Other collisions can produce huge mountain ranges, such as the Himalayas in Asia.

The "part" of a trilobite

FOSSIL EVIDENCE
Splitting apart a fossil rock reveals the positive "part" (above) of the fossil and the negative "counterpart" (right), the natural mold. Fossils are evidence of ancient animal and plant life. They may preserve an organism's detailed inner structure as well as its outer shape. Flowers, feathers, and even footprints can be fossilized. The conversion of buried organisms into stony replicas takes millions of years, as the organic material is destroyed and minerals in the rocks slowly fill the microscopic shapes. Sometimes the buried fossil is completely destroyed in the rock, leaving only a natural mold.

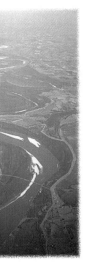

How a fossil is formed

A decaying *Procolophon* (1) was covered in silt sediments swept in by shallow streams (2). Burial must have been rapid since the skeleton was not broken up, although the flesh rotted. Over millions of years, the skeleton was buried deep underground (3). Under pressure, sand became stone and chemicals turned the bones into fossil. Erosion brought the fossil back to the surface (4).

1. Decaying and dead *Procolophon* carcass lies exposed on Earth's surface

2. Silt sediments from shallow streams quickly bury the reptile's body

3. Sediment turns to rock around the fossil over millions of years

4. Fossilized skeleton is exposed at the surface

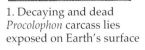

"Counterpart" of a trilobite, *Flexicalymene caractaci*

Procolophon trigoniceps South Africa

SMALL REPTILE
Procolophon was a small reptile that lived 245 million years ago. Its fossils, from the Karroo Basin in South Africa, are well known. Complete skeletons and skulls, perfectly preserved as white fossil bone, are buried in a red silty rock. This red color comes from the iron minerals that hold the quartz grains together, showing that the sediment was exposed to air and not continuously buried underwater.

HOT AND COLD
Rocks preserve clues about prehistoric climatic conditions that can help explain the shifting continents. Fossils of the large-leaved *Glossopteris* tree are found in abundance in Antarctic Permian rocks. During this period, Antarctica was part of a much larger continental mass and was not at the South Pole. Its climate was much warmer than it is today.

Fossil leaf

Glossopteris, Permian, New South Wales, Australia

MOLDED FROM LIFE
The natural mold left by a buried fossil fills with rock material and produces an accurate cast of the fossil's shape. This trilobite's overall shape has been preserved, but the hard fossil skeleton was destroyed over many years. Fossils are often flattened under the pressure of rock above and may be cracked and broken into many pieces.

OLD AGE
Evidence from meteorites and Moon rocks show that the Earth is about 4.5 billion years old. The oldest rocks on Earth, about 3.7 billion years old, are found in Greenland and are metamorphic. Originally sedimentary, some of these rocks were laid down at an even earlier date.

Turning to stone

Fossilization is a very risky process that takes place over millions of years. As soon as animals and plants die, they begin to decompose, or rot. Any hard parts, such as shells, bones, and teeth in animals, or wood in plants, last longer than soft tissue, but they are often scattered by animals, wind, or flowing water. In order for something to be fossilized it must be buried quickly, before it decomposes. This is most likely to be accomplished by sediment, such as sand or mud, washing over the fossil in water. Some fossils dissolve later; others may be changed chemically or be distorted by high temperatures and pressures. Only a tiny fraction will survive to be found.

LAND SHAPES
Over millions of years, rocks are eroded and shaped by wind and water, bringing ancient fossils to the surface.

2 DECAYING MUSSEL
When the mussel dies, the two chalky shells open out into a "butterfly" position. The soft parts of the mussel enclosed by the shells soon begin to rot or are eaten by scavenging animals.

Living mussel

Living mussels attach themselves to rocks by byssal threads

1 LIVING MUSSEL
The soft parts of the mussel are enclosed by two chalky shells. Each individual may spend its entire life in one place, and dense masses form mussel beds. If a mussel becomes detached it may die, especially if it is swept into a different environment.

FROM PRESERVATION TO DISCOVERY

These four drawings show how animals can be preserved and their remains discovered millions of years later. It is a very slow process and the climate and shape of the land will probably change as much as the animal and plant life.

1. Dead animals sink to the seabed and their remains are buried by layers of sediment.

2. The lower layers of sediment turn to rock and the remains harden to form fossils.

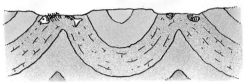

3. The rock is gradually folded and eroded.

4. The fossils are exposed on the surface.

Soft parts have rotted away

3 **HARD PARTS REMAIN** When the soft parts of the mussel have rotted away, the hard parts, the shells, remain.

Separated shell

4 **TOWARD FOSSILIZATION** The shells of dead mussels are often carried along by currents in the water and dropped together in one area where they mix with pebbles and sand to form "mussel beaches." Some of the individuals shown here still have their two shells held together by a tough bit of tissue called a ligament. Constant battering by the sea may break some shells into small pieces. All these may then be buried and slowly fossilized.

Tough ligament holding shells together

Fossil mussel shell

5 **FOSSILIZED MUSSELS** Many small mussels become firmly embedded in rock. Here, a natural mineral-cement binds the sediment grains and fossil shells together, making it difficult for a collector to take the shells out.

FOSSILS WITH COLOR The shells of living mussels are deep blue. Some of the blue color is still visible in these fossil mussels, which are an incredible two million years old.

LOST COLOR The color in shells is usually lost during the process of fossilization. The brown color in these fossils is from the rock in which they were fossilized.

Life in the ancient seas

THE EARTH, WITH ITS VAST EXPANSES of ocean, has not always looked the way it does today. Over millions of years the land masses have drifted across the face of the Earth as new oceans have opened up and old oceans disappeared. Today's oceans only started to take shape in the last 200 million years of the Earth's 4.5-billion-year existence. Simple organisms first appeared in the oceans 3.3 billion years ago and were followed by more and more complex life forms. As the oceans changed, so too did life in the waters. Soft-bodied creatures evolved into animals with hard shells and trilobites flexed their external skeletons with internal muscles alongside gigantic marine reptiles such as plesiosaurs. Some forms of life eventually became extinct, while others still survive in the oceans today, more or less unchanged.

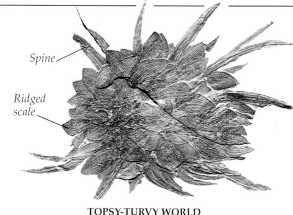

Spine

Ridged scale

TOPSY-TURVY WORLD
Wiwaxia lived on the seafloor 530 million years ago, yet this fossil was found high above sea level in the Rocky Mountains. This shows just how much the Earth's surface has changed, and how land originally formed under a sea has been forced upward to form mountain chains.

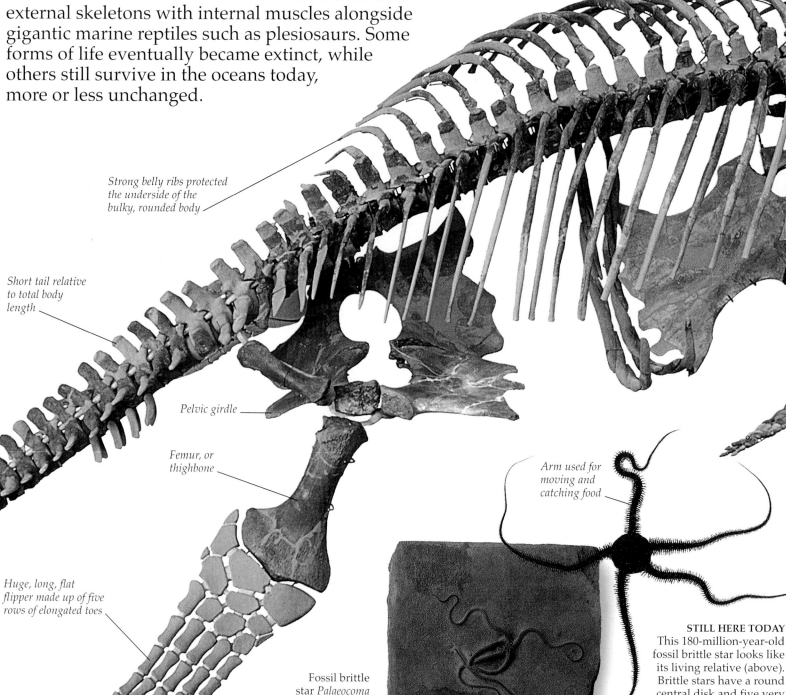

Strong belly ribs protected the underside of the bulky, rounded body

Short tail relative to total body length

Pelvic girdle

Femur, or thighbone

Huge, long, flat flipper made up of five rows of elongated toes

Fossil brittle star Palaeocoma

Arm used for moving and catching food

STILL HERE TODAY
This 180-million-year-old fossil brittle star looks like its living relative (above). Brittle stars have a round central disk and five very fragile, jointed arms. Today, as in the past, large numbers of brittle stars are often found together on sandy or muddy seabeds.

ANCIENT CORAL
Compared to their soft-bodied relatives, anemones and jellyfish, corals such as this 400-million-year-old fossil have been preserved well in rocks because of their hard skeletons. Each coral animal formed a skeleton that joined that of its neighbor, creating a network of chains with large spaces between them.

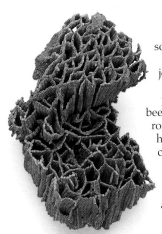

CHANGING OCEANS
One giant ocean, Panthalassa, surrounded the super-continent Pangaea (1) 290–240 mya (million years ago). At the end of this period, many kinds of marine life became extinct. Pangaea broke up, with part drifting north and part south, with the Tethys Sea between.

CONTINENTAL DRIFT
The northern part split to form the North Atlantic Ocean 208–146 mya (2). The South Atlantic and Indian Oceans began to form 146–65 mya (3). The continents continued to drift 1.64 mya (4). Today the oceans are still changing shape – the Atlantic Ocean gets wider by an inch or two each year.

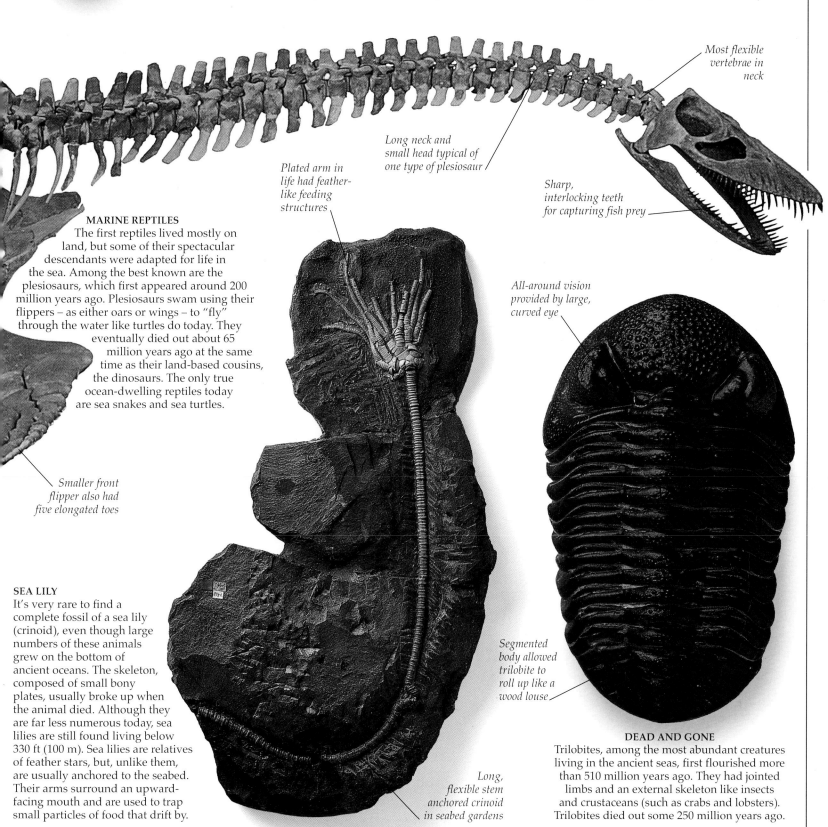

Most flexible vertebrae in neck

Long neck and small head typical of one type of plesiosaur

Plated arm in life had feather-like feeding structures

Sharp, interlocking teeth for capturing fish prey

MARINE REPTILES
The first reptiles lived mostly on land, but some of their spectacular descendants were adapted for life in the sea. Among the best known are the plesiosaurs, which first appeared around 200 million years ago. Plesiosaurs swam using their flippers – as either oars or wings – to "fly" through the water like turtles do today. They eventually died out about 65 million years ago at the same time as their land-based cousins, the dinosaurs. The only true ocean-dwelling reptiles today are sea snakes and sea turtles.

All-around vision provided by large, curved eye

Smaller front flipper also had five elongated toes

SEA LILY
It's very rare to find a complete fossil of a sea lily (crinoid), even though large numbers of these animals grew on the bottom of ancient oceans. The skeleton, composed of small bony plates, usually broke up when the animal died. Although they are far less numerous today, sea lilies are still found living below 330 ft (100 m). Sea lilies are relatives of feather stars, but, unlike them, are usually anchored to the seabed. Their arms surround an upward-facing mouth and are used to trap small particles of food that drift by.

Long, flexible stem anchored crinoid in seabed gardens

Segmented body allowed trilobite to roll up like a wood louse

DEAD AND GONE
Trilobites, among the most abundant creatures living in the ancient seas, first flourished more than 510 million years ago. They had jointed limbs and an external skeleton like insects and crustaceans (such as crabs and lobsters). Trilobites died out some 250 million years ago.

Fossil evidence

ABOUT 470 MILLION YEARS AGO, one group of animals – the
vertebrates – escaped the restrictions of living in shells
by developing internal, bony skeletons that anchored
muscles and supported internal organs. Bones, teeth, and
scales are tough and preserve well, so there is plenty of fossil
evidence. The first vertebrates were jawless fish. Some of them,
such as cephalaspids and placoderms, carried a heavy outer
armor. Many were restricted to living on seabeds. Later fish had
less of a bony covering on their heads and developed toothed,
gaping jaws. The success of advanced bony fish, the teleosts,
is obvious in the vast numbers of these mobile fish living
today in the world's rivers, lakes, and seas.

*Fossil of
Pterichthyodes milleri*

*Spiny pectoral
fin for scooting
along muddy
seafloor*

HEAVY ARMOR
One of the most armored
placoderm fish – the 370-
million-year-old, 5-in (13-cm)
long *Pterichthyodes* – had no inner
skeleton. Instead, it had a shell of
bony plates that completely covered
both its head and body. Even the
pectoral fins were enclosed in a bony
casing, which made them near-useless.

Large eye

*Fossil of
Cephalaspis
pagei*

SENSITIVE SUCKER
The first fish were jawless, sucking food and water through
their mouths. *Cephalaspis* had a bony shield covering its
jawless head, as well as a pair of pectoral fins protected by
swept-back spines. Two eyes and a single nostril perched
on the crest of the arched head shield, which had three
sensitive, scale-covered patches connected to the brain.
Cephalaspis was an ostracoderm – it had a "bony skin."

*Modern
African
lungfish*

*Symmetrical two-part
tail fin*

*Fossil of
Lepidotes elvensis*

*Dorsal fin supported
on ray of fine bones*

*Armored
head*

*Remains of
concretion*

EXPOSED WITH ACID
Unlike modern lungfish, which live in
freshwater, the prehistoric lungfish
Chirodipterus lived in shallow seas. It
was covered in thick, bony scales and
had an armored head. This specimen
from Australia was preserved in a hard
chalky mass called a concretion. The fossil
was exposed by being bathed in acid, which
dissolved the concretion, but not the fish inside.

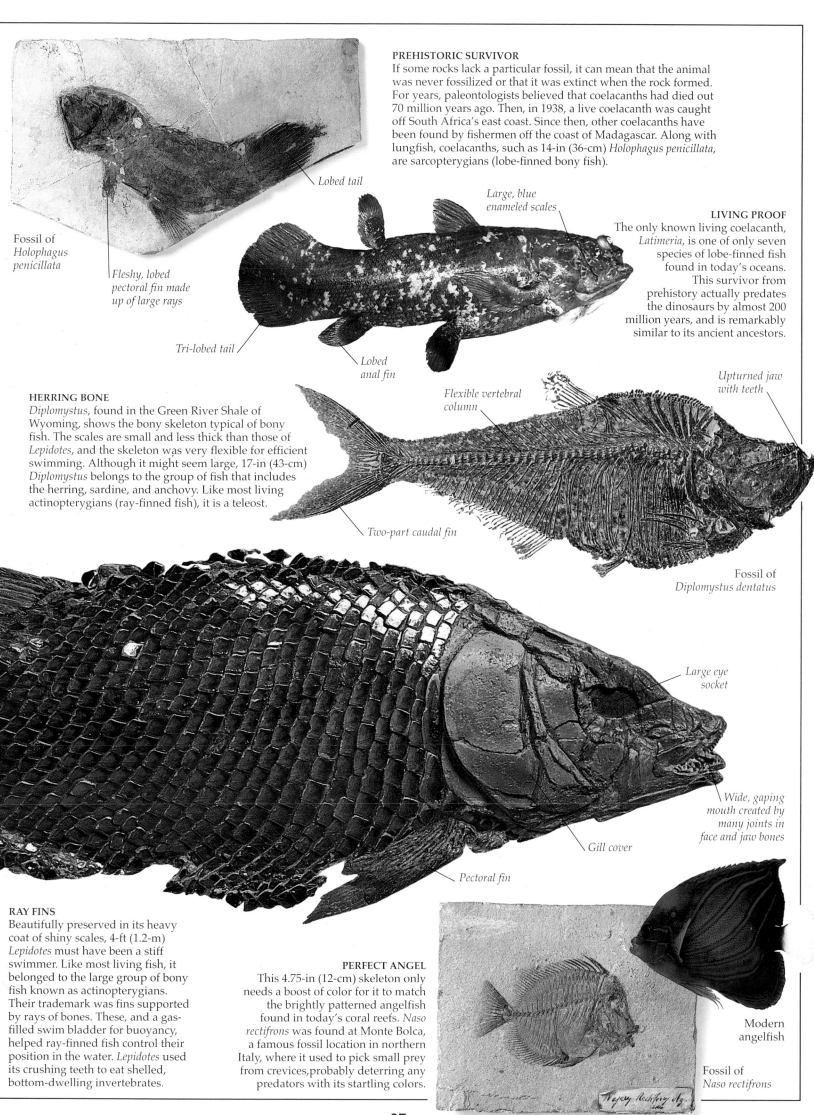

PREHISTORIC SURVIVOR
If some rocks lack a particular fossil, it can mean that the animal was never fossilized or that it was extinct when the rock formed. For years, paleontologists believed that coelacanths had died out 70 million years ago. Then, in 1938, a live coelacanth was caught off South Africa's east coast. Since then, other coelacanths have been found by fishermen off the coast of Madagascar. Along with lungfish, coelacanths, such as 14-in (36-cm) *Holophagus penicillata*, are sarcopterygians (lobe-finned bony fish).

Lobed tail

Fossil of
Holophagus penicillata

Fleshy, lobed pectoral fin made up of large rays

Large, blue enameled scales

LIVING PROOF
The only known living coelacanth, *Latimeria*, is one of only seven species of lobe-finned fish found in today's oceans. This survivor from prehistory actually predates the dinosaurs by almost 200 million years, and is remarkably similar to its ancient ancestors.

Tri-lobed tail

Lobed anal fin

HERRING BONE
Diplomystus, found in the Green River Shale of Wyoming, shows the bony skeleton typical of bony fish. The scales are small and less thick than those of *Lepidotes*, and the skeleton was very flexible for efficient swimming. Although it might seem large, 17-in (43-cm) *Diplomystus* belongs to the group of fish that includes the herring, sardine, and anchovy. Like most living actinopterygians (ray-finned fish), it is a teleost.

Flexible vertebral column

Upturned jaw with teeth

Two-part caudal fin

Fossil of
Diplomystus dentatus

Large eye socket

Wide, gaping mouth created by many joints in face and jaw bones

Gill cover

Pectoral fin

RAY FINS
Beautifully preserved in its heavy coat of shiny scales, 4-ft (1.2-m) *Lepidotes* must have been a stiff swimmer. Like most living fish, it belonged to the large group of bony fish known as actinopterygians. Their trademark was fins supported by rays of bones. These, and a gas-filled swim bladder for buoyancy, helped ray-finned fish control their position in the water. *Lepidotes* used its crushing teeth to eat shelled, bottom-dwelling invertebrates.

PERFECT ANGEL
This 4.75-in (12-cm) skeleton only needs a boost of color for it to match the brightly patterned angelfish found in today's coral reefs. *Naso rectifrons* was found at Monte Bolca, a famous fossil location in northern Italy, where it used to pick small prey from crevices, probably deterring any predators with its startling colors.

Modern angelfish

Fossil of
Naso rectifrons

Reptiles reign

THE FIRST REPTILES appeared 360–290 million years ago and probably did not look all that different from their amphibian ancestors. For 200 million years, they colonized the continents and dominated the Earth. Many reptiles evolved on land, like the dinosaurs. Others, such as the pterosaurs, took to the air, and some, such as the mesosaurs, lived in the sea. Many reptiles were amniotes: they produced an egg that enclosed the developing embryo in its own wet world, protecting it with a tough, waterproof shell. Reptiles were the first amniotes, followed by birds and mammals.

HOT STUFF
Reptiles were many different shapes. *Dimetrodon*, a carnivorous pelycosaur, was 10 ft (3 m) long and carried a huge fan of skin along its back, which it used as a giant radiator and heat absorber.

SETTING SAIL
The herbivorous *Edaphosaurus* had a skin sail supported on long, vertebral spines with cross pieces. It was a pelycosaur – a lizard with a basin-shaped pelvis.

Pelvis, legs, and five-toed feet separated from body

Individual spine in backbone

Neural spine of backbone helped form skin-covered sail of *Edaphosaurus*

Flattened skull

Backbone with ribs attached

REPTILE FIRST
Sandwiched between fine rock layers, this 338-million-year-old *Westlothiana lizziae* fossil is the oldest reptile and amniote ever found. Discovered in a small quarry in central Scotland, this distorted 8-in (20-cm) long fossil skeleton is nicknamed "Lizzie."

Dry, scaly skin

Very long body

Model of *Westlothiana lizziae* (viewed from above), based on scientific research and artist's rendering

UNDERSTANDING THE EVIDENCE
Westlothiana was discovered in ancient rocks formed in a lake once fed by hot, volcanic spring water. Four-legged, as well as legless, snakelike amphibian skeletons were also found, along with spiders, scorpions, and millipedes. Tree-sized seed ferns grew nearby. *Westlothiana* was about 1 ft (30 cm) long, its long body balanced on short legs. Some, but not all, features of the skull and limb bones match those found in later reptiles. It is not surprising that *Westlothiana*, so like its amphibian ancestors, is not easily distinguished from them.

Long, lizard-like tail

Tail made up a large part of the whole body length

Scales on its skin helped keep Westlothiana *waterproof*

Model of first known reptile, *Westlothiana lizziae*

Each foot had five toes

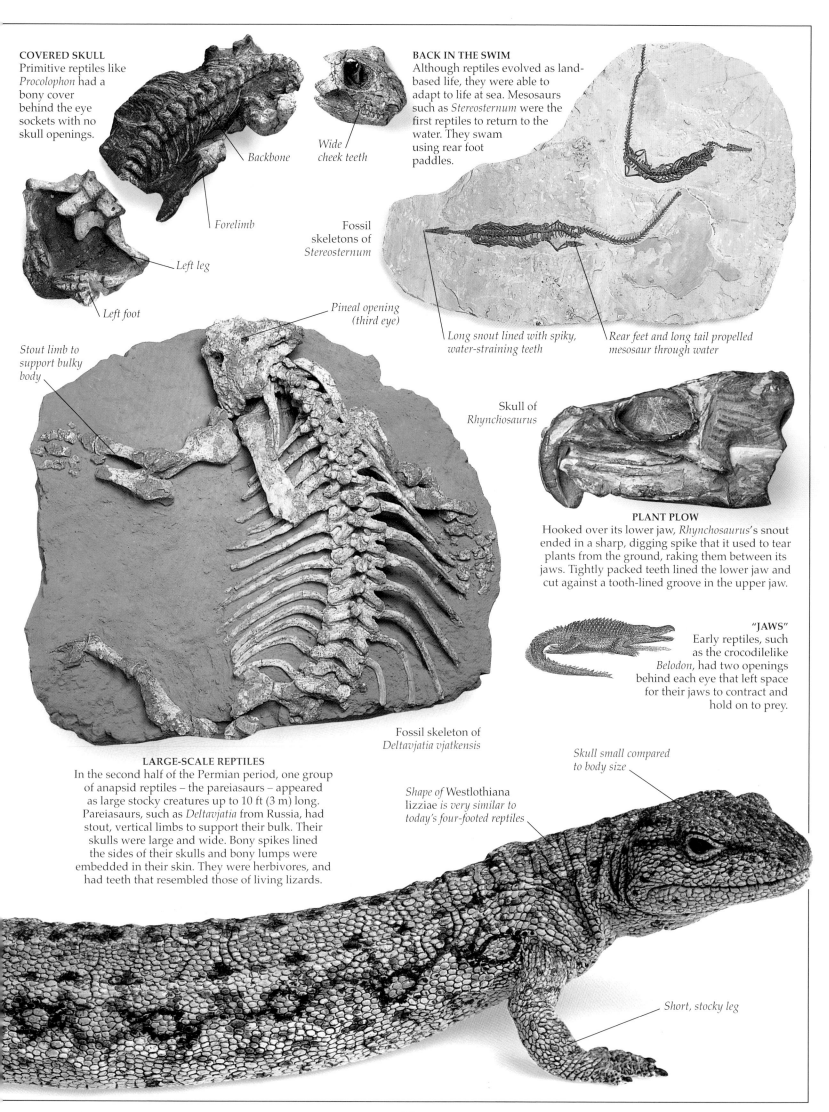

COVERED SKULL
Primitive reptiles like *Procolophon* had a bony cover behind the eye sockets with no skull openings.

Backbone

Forelimb

Left leg

Left foot

Wide cheek teeth

BACK IN THE SWIM
Although reptiles evolved as land-based life, they were able to adapt to life at sea. Mesosaurs such as *Stereosternum* were the first reptiles to return to the water. They swam using rear foot paddles.

Fossil skeletons of *Stereosternum*

Long snout lined with spiky, water-straining teeth

Rear feet and long tail propelled mesosaur through water

Pineal opening (third eye)

Stout limb to support bulky body

Skull of *Rhynchosaurus*

PLANT PLOW
Hooked over its lower jaw, *Rhynchosaurus*'s snout ended in a sharp, digging spike that it used to tear plants from the ground, raking them between its jaws. Tightly packed teeth lined the lower jaw and cut against a tooth-lined groove in the upper jaw.

"JAWS"
Early reptiles, such as the crocodilelike *Belodon*, had two openings behind each eye that left space for their jaws to contract and hold on to prey.

Fossil skeleton of *Deltavjatia vjatkensis*

LARGE-SCALE REPTILES
In the second half of the Permian period, one group of anapsid reptiles – the pareiasaurs – appeared as large stocky creatures up to 10 ft (3 m) long. Pareiasaurs, such as *Deltavjatia* from Russia, had stout, vertical limbs to support their bulk. Their skulls were large and wide. Bony spikes lined the sides of their skulls and bony lumps were embedded in their skin. They were herbivores, and had teeth that resembled those of living lizards.

Shape of *Westlothiana lizziae* is very similar to today's four-footed reptiles

Skull small compared to body size

Short, stocky leg

Birth of the dinosaurs

GIANT PREDATORS, lumbering plant processors, agile browsers, and pack hunters – dinosaurs occupy an impressive place in our knowledge of prehistoric life. All dinosaurs lived on land and walked on two or four upright legs held directly beneath their bodies. But based on their leg and hip structure, these amazing reptiles are split into two groups. The saurischians, or reptile-hipped dinosaurs, had the two lower bones of the pelvis (the pubis and the ischium) pointing in opposite directions below the pelvic upper bone, or ilium. The ornithischians, or bird-hipped dinosaurs, had pelvic bones with both the pubis and ischium pointing down and back. Dinosaurs appeared about 230 million years ago and quickly dominated life on land. Their ability to stand upright and move efficiently made them versatile and adaptable, but it did not save them from extinction 65 million years ago.

Bony crest

Cheek pouch

Toothless beak

CORYTHOSAURUS
This ornithischian dinosaur belonged to a group called the hadrosaurs that lived 97–65 million years ago in what is now North America, Asia, and Europe. Hadrosaurs had toothless beaks similar to ducks today. However, they had cheek teeth, sometimes more than 300 in each jaw, which they used for grinding tough vegetation. Hadrosaurs probably lived in herds, and their bony crests may have been displayed to attract mates.

Bony frill

Long brow horn

Model of *Triceratops*

Short nose horn

NESTING SITES
The most exciting discoveries of nesting sites have been made in Montana. The hadrosaur *Maiasaura* ("good mother lizard") laid its eggs in a raised and scooped-out hollow in sand, then covered them in vegetation to keep them warm. The 14-in (35.5-cm) long young would have stayed in the nest for a while after hatching and been fed by their parents. *Maiasaura* returned to their nesting colonies each season.

Parrotlike beak

TRICERATOPS
This ornithischian dinosaur lived 100 million years ago. It was 6–30 ft (1.8–9.1 m) long and weighed up to 6 tons (5.4 tonnes). All ornithischian dinosaurs were herbivores, feeding on leaves, fruits, seeds, and even conifer needles. *Triceratops* had a large hooked beak, which it used for snipping and tearing at plants, while its teeth and powerful jaws sheared them. *Triceratops* lived in herds and used its large defensive horns to ward off threats as fierce as *Tyrannosaurus rex*. The bony frill around *Triceratops*'s head may have been used to scare predators, attract mates, or simply to protect the neck from attack.

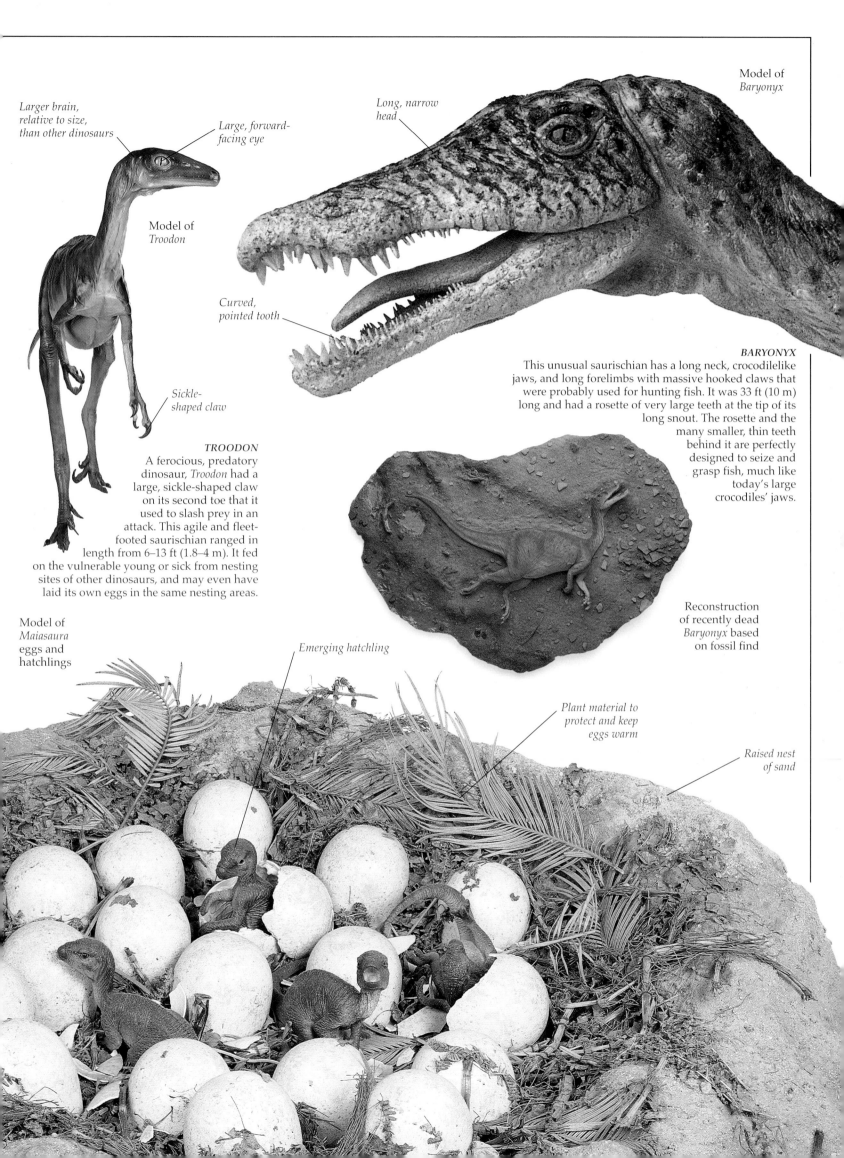

Larger brain,
relative to size,
than other dinosaurs

Large, forward-
facing eye

Model of
Troodon

Model of
Baryonyx

Long, narrow
head

Curved,
pointed tooth

Sickle-
shaped claw

BARYONYX
This unusual saurischian has a long neck, crocodilelike jaws, and long forelimbs with massive hooked claws that were probably used for hunting fish. It was 33 ft (10 m) long and had a rosette of very large teeth at the tip of its long snout. The rosette and the many smaller, thin teeth behind it are perfectly designed to seize and grasp fish, much like today's large crocodiles' jaws.

TROODON
A ferocious, predatory dinosaur, Troodon had a large, sickle-shaped claw on its second toe that it used to slash prey in an attack. This agile and fleet-footed saurischian ranged in length from 6–13 ft (1.8–4 m). It fed on the vulnerable young or sick from nesting sites of other dinosaurs, and may even have laid its own eggs in the same nesting areas.

Model of
Maiasaura
eggs and
hatchlings

Emerging hatchling

Reconstruction
of recently dead
Baryonyx based
on fossil find

Plant material to
protect and keep
eggs warm

Raised nest
of sand

Winged wonders

THE FIRST ANIMALS TO FLY were insects – fossil dragonflies more than 300 million years old have been found in rocks. Flying vertebrates (animals with backbones) appeared almost 100 million years later, and true flapping flight has since evolved in three vertebrate groups: the now-extinct pterosaurs, living bats, and birds. These animals are not closely related, and their ability to fly evolved independently. Pterosaurs ("flying lizards") were reptiles. They were related to dinosaurs and had an elongated fourth finger. This supported the fleshy membrane, a thin, skin-covered sheet of muscle and elastic fibers covered by skin, that was the wing. In birds, the feathered wing is supported by several fingers and the lower part of the forearm. Bats are flying mammals. Their wings are made of a fleshy membrane similar to the pterosaurs', but bat wings are supported by four fingers.

BIRDS OF FICTION
The discovery of fossil pterosaur remains fueled the imagination of many science fiction authors.

WELL BALANCED
Pteranodon was a pterosaur with a bony crest on its head that counterbalanced its long, toothless beak. It appears to have been a fish-eater that flew over the oceans like the albatross does today.

FURRY REPTILE
The sparrow-sized Jurassic pterosaur *Pterodactylus* had membranous wings, claws, a toothed beak, and a body covered by fine fur. Evidence of fur comes from Kazakhstan, where some pterosaurs were discovered with hairlike impressions around the body. This may indicate that pterosaurs were warm-blooded and used the fur as insulation. *Pterodactylus* had a short tail and a wingspan of only about 20 in (50 cm), but some pterosaurs had long tails, including *Rhamphorhynchus* with its 5-ft (1.5-m) wingspan.

Toothed beak

Greatly lengthened fourth finger

Membranous wing

Body covered by fine fur

Very short tail

Pterodactylus *had sharp claws for catching and tearing apart prey*

MISTAKEN IDENTITY
This small dinosaur belongs to a group that many scientists believe were ancestors of birds. In 1973, some museum paleontologists in Germany realized that one of their specimens, identified as *Compsognathus*, was really an *Archaeopteryx*!

FLYING MAMMAL
It is easy to see the similarity between this bat and the pterosaurs. Because bats often roost in caves, their fossilized bones can be found in large numbers in cave deposits.

Impression of birdlike feathers

Reptilian clawed fingers

Teeth, unlike a modern bird

Archaeopteryx *had a wingspan of about 20 in (50 cm)*

Fossil feather

Modern bird's feather

RARE FIND
Only birds sport feathers and they are very rarely fossilized. Very occasionally they are found in fine-grained sediments like this limestone.

THE FIRST BIRD
Archaeopteryx ("ancient wing") lived 150 million years ago. Specimens of it, all found in Germany, are generally regarded as the most precious fossils in the world. Only five more have been discovered since the first was found, in 1861. *Archaeopteryx* was intermediate between reptiles and birds. Some specimens show clear feather impressions.

Elephant bird egg

Reptilian bony tail

Claws

Ostrich egg

Ostrich
Struthio camelus

ELEPHANTINE EGG
The Madagascan elephant bird *Aepyornis maximus* stood over 6.5 ft (2 m) high. Its fossil eggs are the largest birds' eggs known, reaching 35 in (90 cm) in circumference. Here, one is compared with an egg from the largest modern bird, the ostrich, to show how enormous the eggs really are.

FINE SKULL
Fossilized remains of birds are rare. This finely preserved skull comes from the bird *Prophaethon*. Some scientists think that this was a close relative of the tropicbird of today.

Tropicbird
Phaethon lepturus

The elephant bird, like today's ostrich, was flightless

Elephant bird
Aepyornis maximus

The first mammals

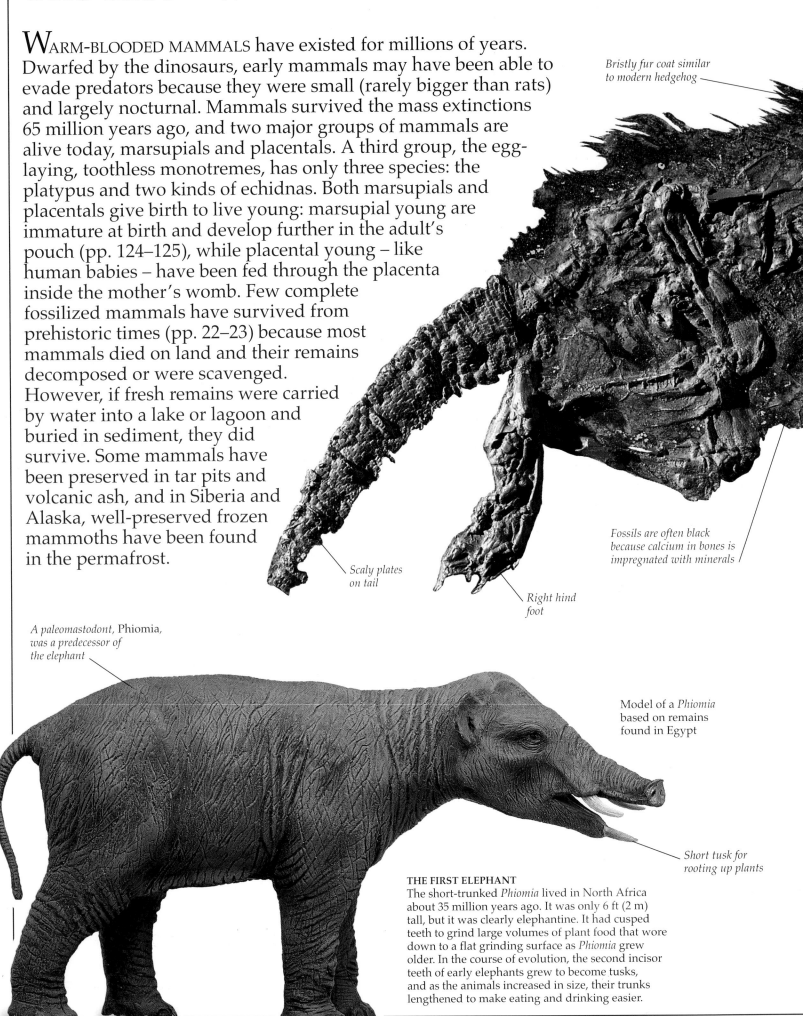

WARM-BLOODED MAMMALS have existed for millions of years. Dwarfed by the dinosaurs, early mammals may have been able to evade predators because they were small (rarely bigger than rats) and largely nocturnal. Mammals survived the mass extinctions 65 million years ago, and two major groups of mammals are alive today, marsupials and placentals. A third group, the egg-laying, toothless monotremes, has only three species: the platypus and two kinds of echidnas. Both marsupials and placentals give birth to live young: marsupial young are immature at birth and develop further in the adult's pouch (pp. 124–125), while placental young – like human babies – have been fed through the placenta inside the mother's womb. Few complete fossilized mammals have survived from prehistoric times (pp. 22–23) because most mammals died on land and their remains decomposed or were scavenged. However, if fresh remains were carried by water into a lake or lagoon and buried in sediment, they did survive. Some mammals have been preserved in tar pits and volcanic ash, and in Siberia and Alaska, well-preserved frozen mammoths have been found in the permafrost.

Bristly fur coat similar to modern hedgehog

Fossils are often black because calcium in bones is impregnated with minerals

Scaly plates on tail

Right hind foot

A paleomastodont, Phiomia, *was a predecessor of the elephant*

Model of a *Phiomia* based on remains found in Egypt

Short tusk for rooting up plants

THE FIRST ELEPHANT
The short-trunked *Phiomia* lived in North Africa about 35 million years ago. It was only 6 ft (2 m) tall, but it was clearly elephantine. It had cusped teeth to grind large volumes of plant food that wore down to a flat grinding surface as *Phiomia* grew older. In the course of evolution, the second incisor teeth of early elephants grew to become tusks, and as the animals increased in size, their trunks lengthened to make eating and drinking easier.

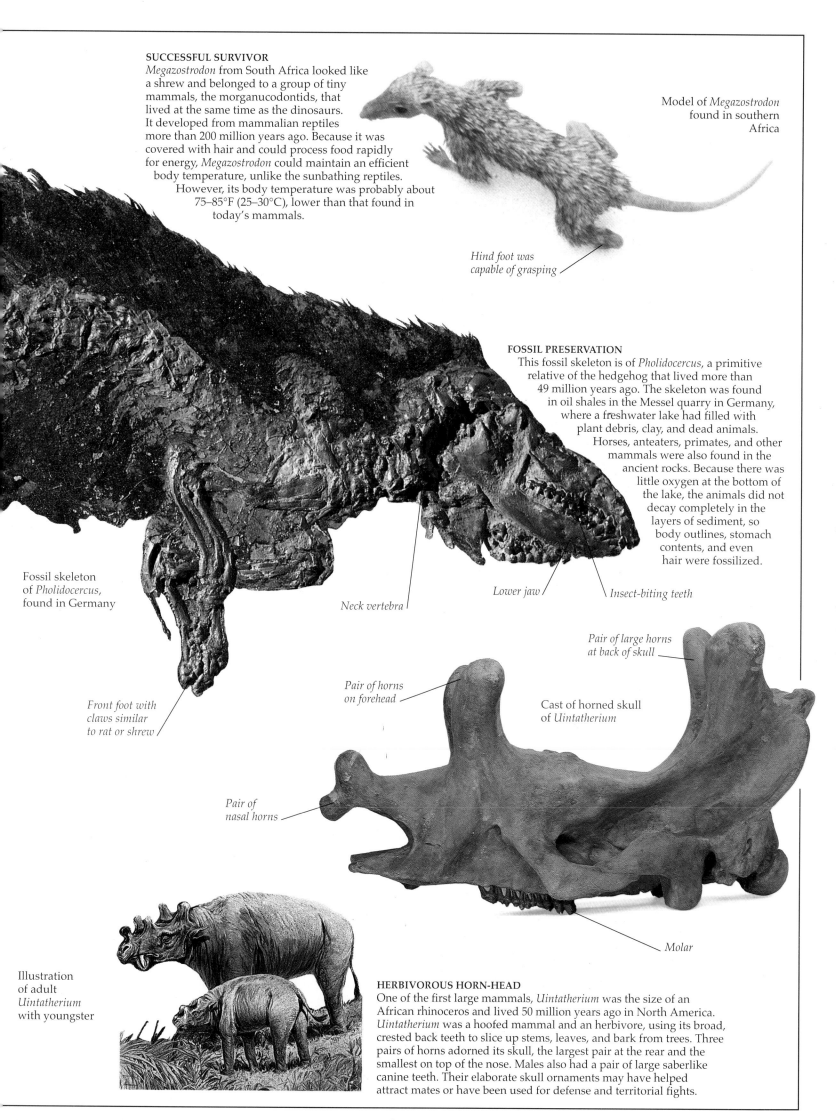

SUCCESSFUL SURVIVOR
Megazostrodon from South Africa looked like a shrew and belonged to a group of tiny mammals, the morganucodontids, that lived at the same time as the dinosaurs. It developed from mammalian reptiles more than 200 million years ago. Because it was covered with hair and and could process food rapidly for energy, *Megazostrodon* could maintain an efficient body temperature, unlike the sunbathing reptiles. However, its body temperature was probably about 75–85°F (25–30°C), lower than that found in today's mammals.

Model of *Megazostrodon* found in southern Africa

Hind foot was capable of grasping

FOSSIL PRESERVATION
This fossil skeleton is of *Pholidocercus*, a primitive relative of the hedgehog that lived more than 49 million years ago. The skeleton was found in oil shales in the Messel quarry in Germany, where a freshwater lake had filled with plant debris, clay, and dead animals. Horses, anteaters, primates, and other mammals were also found in the ancient rocks. Because there was little oxygen at the bottom of the lake, the animals did not decay completely in the layers of sediment, so body outlines, stomach contents, and even hair were fossilized.

Fossil skeleton of *Pholidocercus*, found in Germany

Neck vertebra

Lower jaw

Insect-biting teeth

Front foot with claws similar to rat or shrew

Pair of large horns at back of skull

Pair of horns on forehead

Cast of horned skull of *Uintatherium*

Pair of nasal horns

Molar

Illustration of adult *Uintatherium* with youngster

HERBIVOROUS HORN-HEAD
One of the first large mammals, *Uintatherium* was the size of an African rhinoceros and lived 50 million years ago in North America. *Uintatherium* was a hoofed mammal and an herbivore, using its broad, crested back teeth to slice up stems, leaves, and bark from trees. Three pairs of horns adorned its skull, the largest pair at the rear and the smallest on top of the nose. Males also had a pair of large saberlike canine teeth. Their elaborate skull ornaments may have helped attract mates or have been used for defense and territorial fights.

SUCCULENTS
No plant can survive entirely without water. Plants with fleshy leaves or stems for storing water are known as succulents and include the group of plants called cacti. There are three main kinds of succulents. Stem succulents store water in their stems, and are usually found in the driest climates. Leaf succulents store water in their leaves and grow in damper conditions. Root succulents have thickened roots that serve as water reservoirs.

CHAPTER 2
PLANT LIFE

Many living organisms depend on plants, either directly or indirectly, to survive. Plants grow in virtually every habitat on Earth, producing oxygen as a by-product and sustaining all animal life. They are an essential part of all food chains. After plants have grown and – many of them – burst into flower, they then ensure their own survival by spreading their seeds in an extraordinary and successful variety of ways.

GOLD DUST
The relationship between a plant and its pollinator (pp. 46–47) is often to their mutual benefit. A bumblebee helps carry the gold dust called pollen from one flower to another while it is feeding on the pollen and sugary nectar that the flowers produce. The bee combs the pollen from the hairs on its body and packs it into the pollen sacks on its back legs. It then carries the pollen back to its nest, where the young bees feed on the rich protein.

Parts of a plant

THE PART OF A FLOWERING PLANT that grows above the ground is the shoot, which stretches toward the light. It is supported by a complicated network of roots beneath the soil. These roots not only anchor the plant, they also absorb water and minerals from the soil, and are a vital part of a plant's supply system. Leaves are a plant's main sites of photosynthesis (pp. 40–41), and, via the plant stems, complete the supply system. The plant shoot eventually produces flowers, which make pollination and thus seed formation possible (pp. 46–47). Some plants also produce rhizomes, bulbs, corms, tubers, or other reproductive structures. Non-flowering plants, such as ferns and mosses, produce spores.

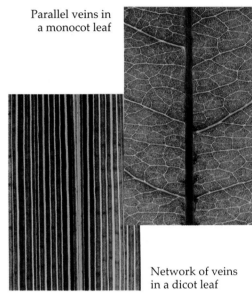

Parallel veins in a monocot leaf

Network of veins in a dicot leaf

LEAF VEINS
Flowering plants are either monocotyledons or dicotyledons. "Monocots" usually have parallel veins in their leaves. The leaves of "dicots" usually have a network of veins.

FUNGI
Fungi seem to grow like plants, but they have no roots or leaves and produce no seeds. Today they are classified separately by scientists, but are often described as plants. There are about 100,000 species of fungi in the world.

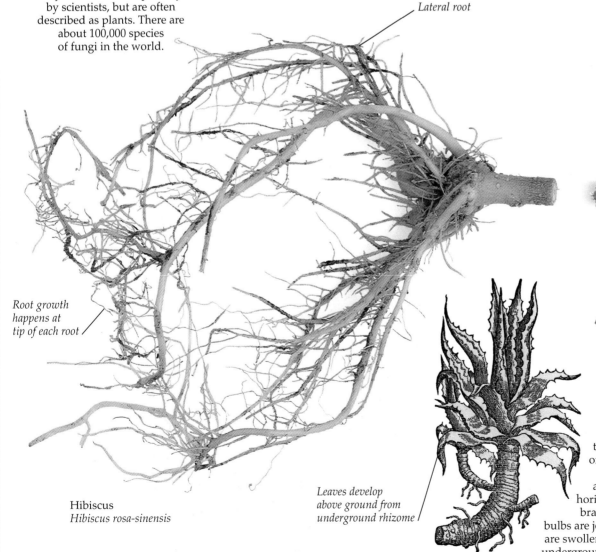

Lateral root

Midrib

Vein

Root growth happens at tip of each root

Hibiscus
Hibiscus rosa-sinensis

Leaves develop above ground from underground rhizome

STORAGE BINS
Rhizomes, bulbs, corms, and tubers are underground storage organs that various plants use to survive in adverse conditions and to reproduce. Rhizomes are horizontal underground stems that branch out to produce new plants; bulbs are joined swollen leaf bases; corms are swollen stems; and tubers are swollen underground stems. Gardeners are able to use these structures to propagate new plants.

Brightly colored tepal attracts insect pollinator

THE SUPPLY SYSTEM
Water, minerals, and sugars are carried up and down a plant in bundles of tubelike cells. One system, called the xylem, carries water and minerals upward. Another, called the phloem, can carry sugars either upward or downward to the parts of the plant that need them.

Large, colorful petals

Stigma

Anther

Filament

FLOWERS
Insects are drawn to a flower by the brightly colored petals. Once the flower has been pollinated, the petals fall off. The female part of the flower then grows larger to form a fruit containing seeds. The seeds are shed when the fully grown fruit opens.

Sepals are smaller and green

Branch

Stem

Node

Lateral bud

Pedicel (flower stalk)

Petiole (leaf stalk)

Bract (leaf-like structure)

Flower bud

Blade of leaf

A FLOWERING PLANT
The hibiscus is a dicotyledon. Its seedlings have two seed leaves, or cotyledons, and its leaves are broad with a central midrib and branched veins. Most species of hibiscus in the wild are pollinated by hummingbirds. A hummingbird hovers in front of the flower and inserts its long beak deep inside to reach the nectar. As it feeds, the anthers brush pollen on its head, while the stigma, also brushing its head, collects pollen from another flower.

39

A light diet

UNLIKE ANIMALS, plants do not need to find food – they can make it for themselves. The key is a green pigment called chlorophyll, which gives plants their characteristic green color. Chlorophyll allows plants to convert energy from sunlight into chemical energy, which can then be stored, usually as a carbohydrate, or starch. The stored energy is used to fuel the growth and development of the plant. In a process known as photosynthesis, the plant converts carbon dioxide and water into an energy-rich compound called glucose, which is then transported through a network of veins to the rest of the plant. Photosynthesis mainly takes place in the leaves of a plant. Many leaves have special adaptations, such as large, flat surfaces, to absorb more life-sustaining sunlight.

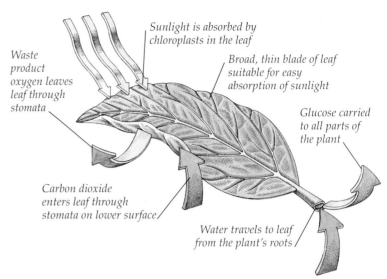

Waste product oxygen leaves leaf through stomata

Sunlight is absorbed by chloroplasts in the leaf

Broad, thin blade of leaf suitable for easy absorption of sunlight

Glucose carried to all parts of the plant

Carbon dioxide enters leaf through stomata on lower surface

Water travels to leaf from the plant's roots

THE PROCESS OF PHOTOSYNTHESIS
Photosynthesis takes place inside special structures called chloroplasts in the leaf cells. Chloroplasts contain the chlorophyll that traps energy from sunlight. Stomata (pores) in the lower surface of the leaves allow carbon dioxide and oxygen to pass into and out of the plant, while veins carry water into the leaves and transport glucose to the rest of the plant.

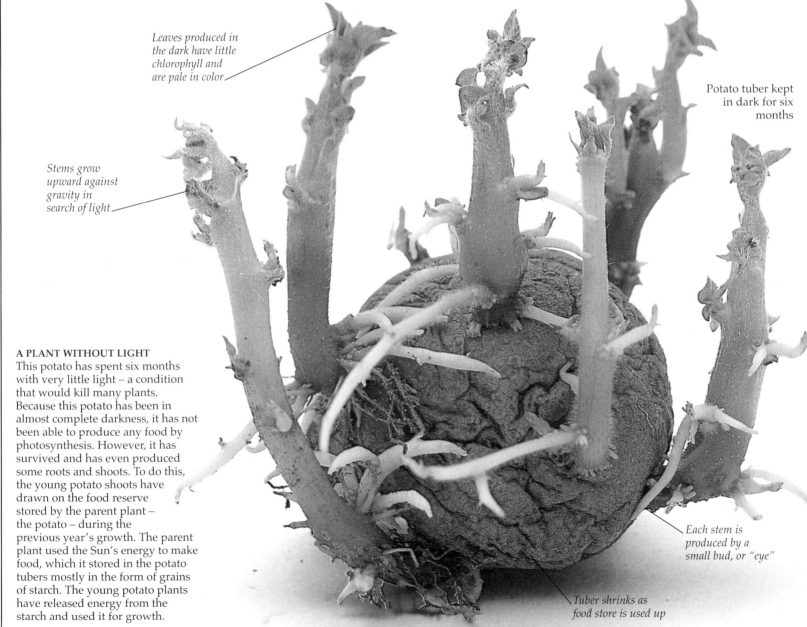

Leaves produced in the dark have little chlorophyll and are pale in color

Potato tuber kept in dark for six months

Stems grow upward against gravity in search of light

A PLANT WITHOUT LIGHT
This potato has spent six months with very little light – a condition that would kill many plants. Because this potato has been in almost complete darkness, it has not been able to produce any food by photosynthesis. However, it has survived and has even produced some roots and shoots. To do this, the young potato shoots have drawn on the food reserve stored by the parent plant – the potato – during the previous year's growth. The parent plant used the Sun's energy to make food, which it stored in the potato tubers mostly in the form of grains of starch. The young potato plants have released energy from the starch and used it for growth.

Each stem is produced by a small bud, or "eye"

Tuber shrinks as food store is used up

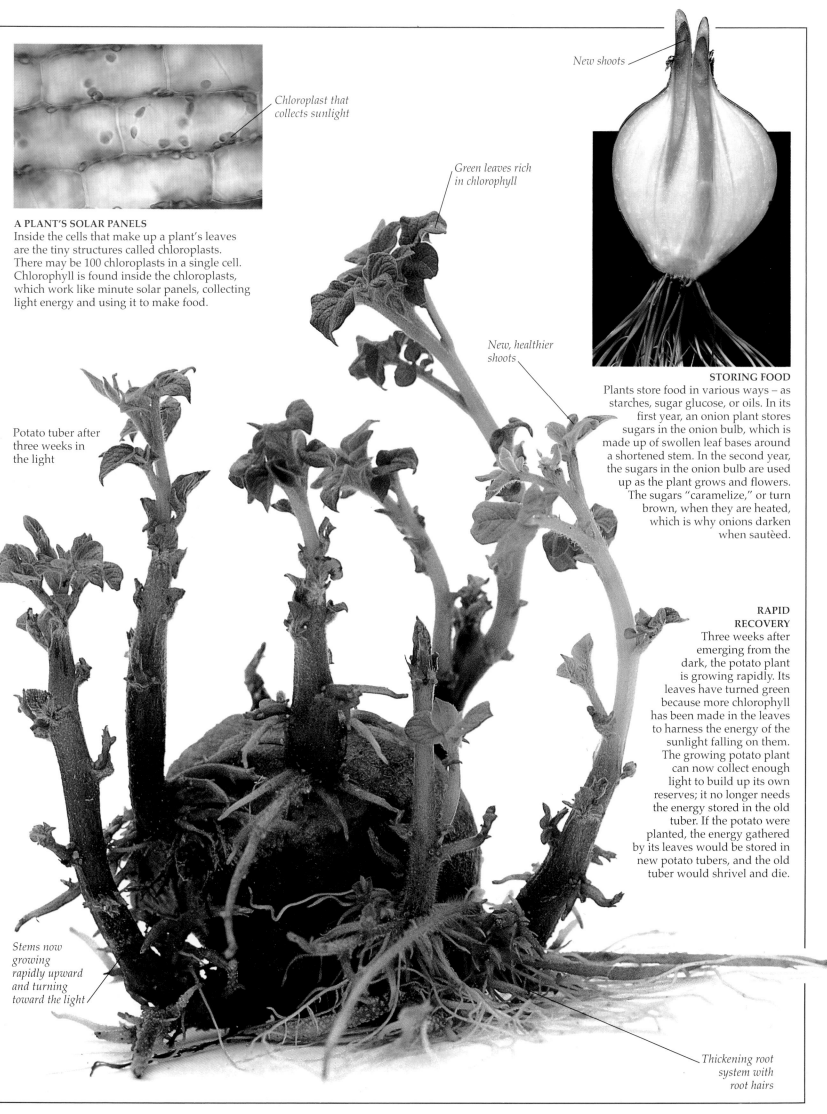

A PLANT'S SOLAR PANELS
Inside the cells that make up a plant's leaves are the tiny structures called chloroplasts. There may be 100 chloroplasts in a single cell. Chlorophyll is found inside the chloroplasts, which work like minute solar panels, collecting light energy and using it to make food.

Chloroplast that collects sunlight

Green leaves rich in chlorophyll

New, healthier shoots

New shoots

STORING FOOD
Plants store food in various ways – as starches, sugar glucose, or oils. In its first year, an onion plant stores sugars in the onion bulb, which is made up of swollen leaf bases around a shortened stem. In the second year, the sugars in the onion bulb are used up as the plant grows and flowers. The sugars "caramelize," or turn brown, when they are heated, which is why onions darken when sautèed.

Potato tuber after three weeks in the light

RAPID RECOVERY
Three weeks after emerging from the dark, the potato plant is growing rapidly. Its leaves have turned green because more chlorophyll has been made in the leaves to harness the energy of the sunlight falling on them. The growing potato plant can now collect enough light to build up its own reserves; it no longer needs the energy stored in the old tuber. If the potato were planted, the energy gathered by its leaves would be stored in new potato tubers, and the old tuber would shrivel and die.

Stems now growing rapidly upward and turning toward the light

Thickening root system with root hairs

A variety of leaves

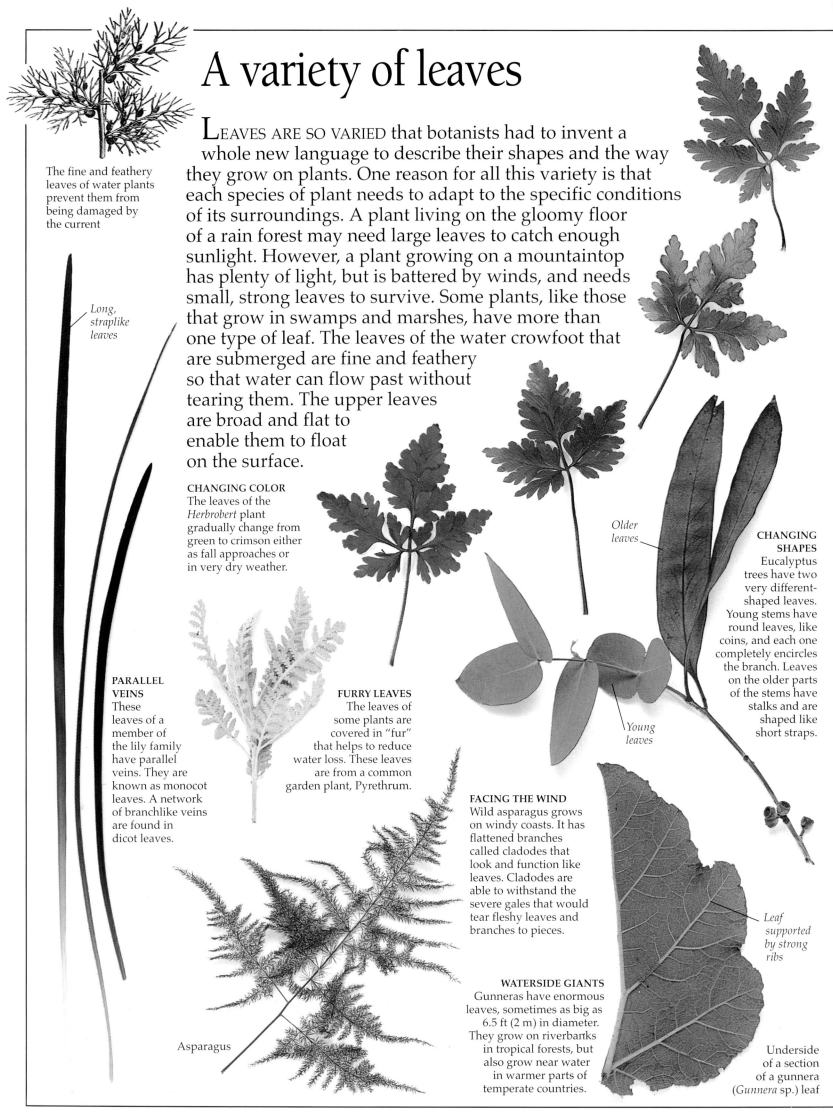

The fine and feathery leaves of water plants prevent them from being damaged by the current

L EAVES ARE SO VARIED that botanists had to invent a whole new language to describe their shapes and the way they grow on plants. One reason for all this variety is that each species of plant needs to adapt to the specific conditions of its surroundings. A plant living on the gloomy floor of a rain forest may need large leaves to catch enough sunlight. However, a plant growing on a mountaintop has plenty of light, but is battered by winds, and needs small, strong leaves to survive. Some plants, like those that grow in swamps and marshes, have more than one type of leaf. The leaves of the water crowfoot that are submerged are fine and feathery so that water can flow past without tearing them. The upper leaves are broad and flat to enable them to float on the surface.

Long, straplike leaves

CHANGING COLOR
The leaves of the *Herbrobert* plant gradually change from green to crimson either as fall approaches or in very dry weather.

PARALLEL VEINS
These leaves of a member of the lily family have parallel veins. They are known as monocot leaves. A network of branchlike veins are found in dicot leaves.

FURRY LEAVES
The leaves of some plants are covered in "fur" that helps to reduce water loss. These leaves are from a common garden plant, Pyrethrum.

Older leaves

CHANGING SHAPES
Eucalyptus trees have two very different-shaped leaves. Young stems have round leaves, like coins, and each one completely encircles the branch. Leaves on the older parts of the stems have stalks and are shaped like short straps.

Young leaves

FACING THE WIND
Wild asparagus grows on windy coasts. It has flattened branches called cladodes that look and function like leaves. Cladodes are able to withstand the severe gales that would tear fleshy leaves and branches to pieces.

Leaf supported by strong ribs

Asparagus

WATERSIDE GIANTS
Gunneras have enormous leaves, sometimes as big as 6.5 ft (2 m) in diameter. They grow on riverbanks in tropical forests, but also grow near water in warmer parts of temperate countries.

Underside of a section of a gunnera (*Gunnera* sp.) leaf

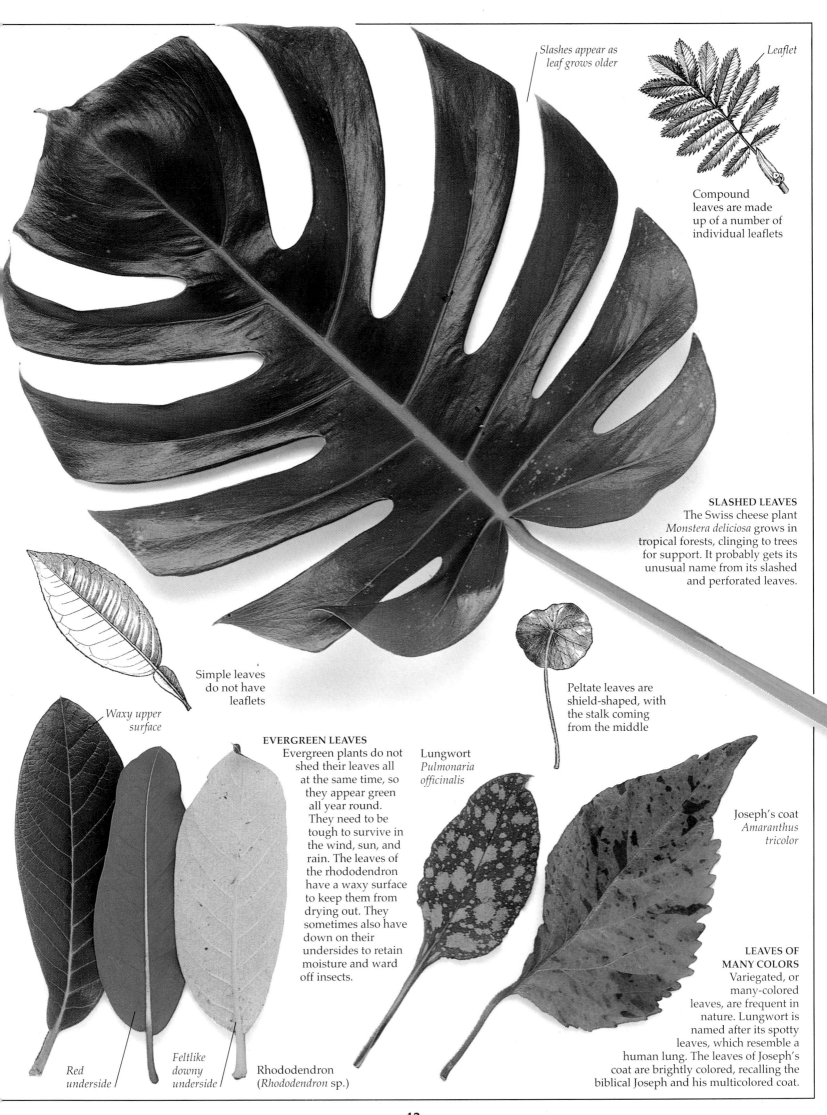

*Slashes appear as
leaf grows older*

Leaflet

Compound
leaves are made
up of a number of
individual leaflets

SLASHED LEAVES
The Swiss cheese plant
Monstera deliciosa grows in
tropical forests, clinging to trees
for support. It probably gets its
unusual name from its slashed
and perforated leaves.

Simple leaves
do not have
leaflets

*Waxy upper
surface*

Peltate leaves are
shield-shaped, with
the stalk coming
from the middle

EVERGREEN LEAVES
Evergreen plants do not
shed their leaves all
at the same time, so
they appear green
all year round.
They need to be
tough to survive in
the wind, sun, and
rain. The leaves of
the rhododendron
have a waxy surface
to keep them from
drying out. They
sometimes also have
down on their
undersides to retain
moisture and ward
off insects.

Lungwort
*Pulmonaria
officinalis*

Joseph's coat
*Amaranthus
tricolor*

**LEAVES OF
MANY COLORS**
Variegated, or
many-colored
leaves, are frequent in
nature. Lungwort is
named after its spotty
leaves, which resemble a
human lung. The leaves of Joseph's
coat are brightly colored, recalling the
biblical Joseph and his multicolored coat.

*Red
underside*

*Feltlike
downy
underside*

Rhododendron
(*Rhododendron* sp.)

Flowers

A PROFUSION OF DIFFERENT SHAPES and colors of flowers has been produced in the course of evolution. To add to this, people have bred flowers that are even more brilliant – or bizarre – than those found in the wild. Behind this dazzling array of shapes and colors, however, there is a common pattern. All flowers use the same underlying structure for seed production. The male parts, the stamens, produce pollen. The female parts, the carpels, produce ovules, which eventually become seeds. Around both the male and the female parts are sepals and petals that attract pollinators like insects, birds, or bats (pp. 46–47). In the flowers of the lily or clematis, the sepals and petals look the same. Then they are known as tepals.

Honeysuckle
Lonicera

SCENTED TUBES
Honeysuckle is a vine with arching branches that uses trees and other surfaces to climb toward the light. The flowers of this plant have sweet-smelling petals that are fused to form long tubes, a further extension of the plant and one that is very visible and attractive to pollinators.

ROUND AND ROUND
The florets (small flowers) of this sunflower are grouped together to resemble a single, large flower. The outer, yellow ring is made up of ray florets, and surrounds the inner ring of disk florets. Toward the center of the whorl are the inner, immature disk florets, which appear darker in color.

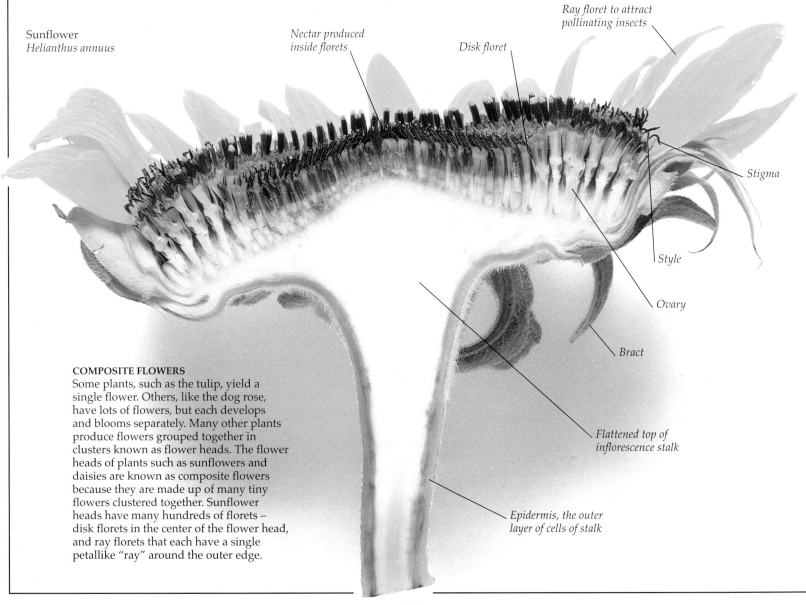

Sunflower
Helianthus annuus

Nectar produced inside florets

Disk floret

Ray floret to attract pollinating insects

Stigma

Style

Ovary

Bract

Flattened top of inflorescence stalk

Epidermis, the outer layer of cells of stalk

COMPOSITE FLOWERS
Some plants, such as the tulip, yield a single flower. Others, like the dog rose, have lots of flowers, but each develops and blooms separately. Many other plants produce flowers grouped together in clusters known as flower heads. The flower heads of plants such as sunflowers and daisies are known as composite flowers because they are made up of many tiny flowers clustered together. Sunflower heads have many hundreds of florets – disk florets in the center of the flower head, and ray florets that each have a single petallike "ray" around the outer edge.

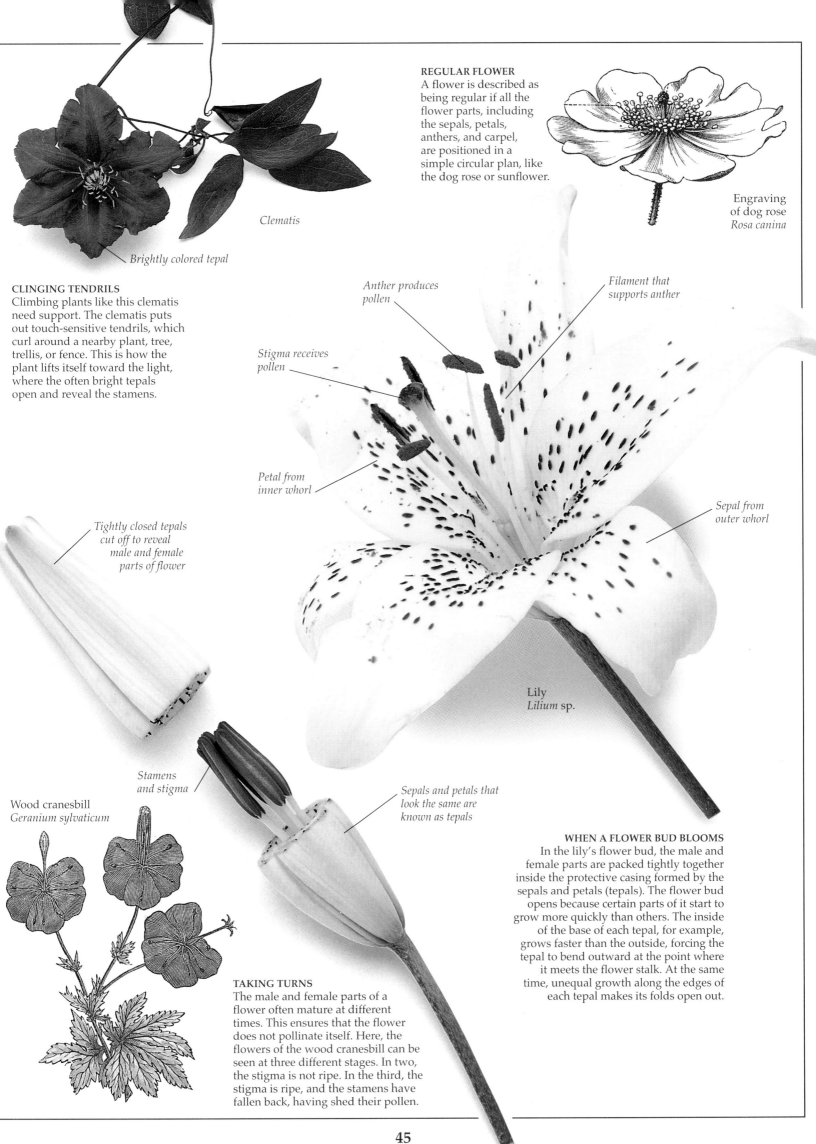

Clematis

CLINGING TENDRILS
Climbing plants like this clematis need support. The clematis puts out touch-sensitive tendrils, which curl around a nearby plant, tree, trellis, or fence. This is how the plant lifts itself toward the light, where the often bright tepals open and reveal the stamens.

Brightly colored tepal

REGULAR FLOWER
A flower is described as being regular if all the flower parts, including the sepals, petals, anthers, and carpel, are positioned in a simple circular plan, like the dog rose or sunflower.

Engraving of dog rose
Rosa canina

Anther produces pollen

Stigma receives pollen

Filament that supports anther

Petal from inner whorl

Sepal from outer whorl

Tightly closed tepals cut off to reveal male and female parts of flower

Lily
Lilium sp.

Stamens and stigma

Wood cranesbill
Geranium sylvaticum

Sepals and petals that look the same are known as tepals

WHEN A FLOWER BUD BLOOMS
In the lily's flower bud, the male and female parts are packed tightly together inside the protective casing formed by the sepals and petals (tepals). The flower bud opens because certain parts of it start to grow more quickly than others. The inside of the base of each tepal, for example, grows faster than the outside, forcing the tepal to bend outward at the point where it meets the flower stalk. At the same time, unequal growth along the edges of each tepal makes its folds open out.

TAKING TURNS
The male and female parts of a flower often mature at different times. This ensures that the flower does not pollinate itself. Here, the flowers of the wood cranesbill can be seen at three different stages. In two, the stigma is not ripe. In the third, the stigma is ripe, and the stamens have fallen back, having shed their pollen.

Pollination

THE EXTRAORDINARY SHAPES and brilliant colors of many flowers have evolved over millions of years to ensure that tiny grains of pollen are carried from one plant to another. Pollen grains must travel from the male stamens to the female carpels (pp. 44–45) for fertilization to occur. Some plants are able to pollinate themselves (self-pollination), but most rely on receiving pollen from another plant of the same species (cross-pollination). Pollen may be dispersed by wind or by water, but insects are the most important pollinators. Plants attract insects with bright colors and with food in the form of nectar. While the visiting insect eats, pollen from the anthers at the tops of the stamens presses onto the insect's body, often on its back or head. The stigma of the carpel, which receives the pollen, is in just the right position to collect it as the insect arrives. Some flowers are pollinated by a wide range of insects, such as honeybees, bumblebees, moths, and butterflies. Others rely on one particular pollinator.

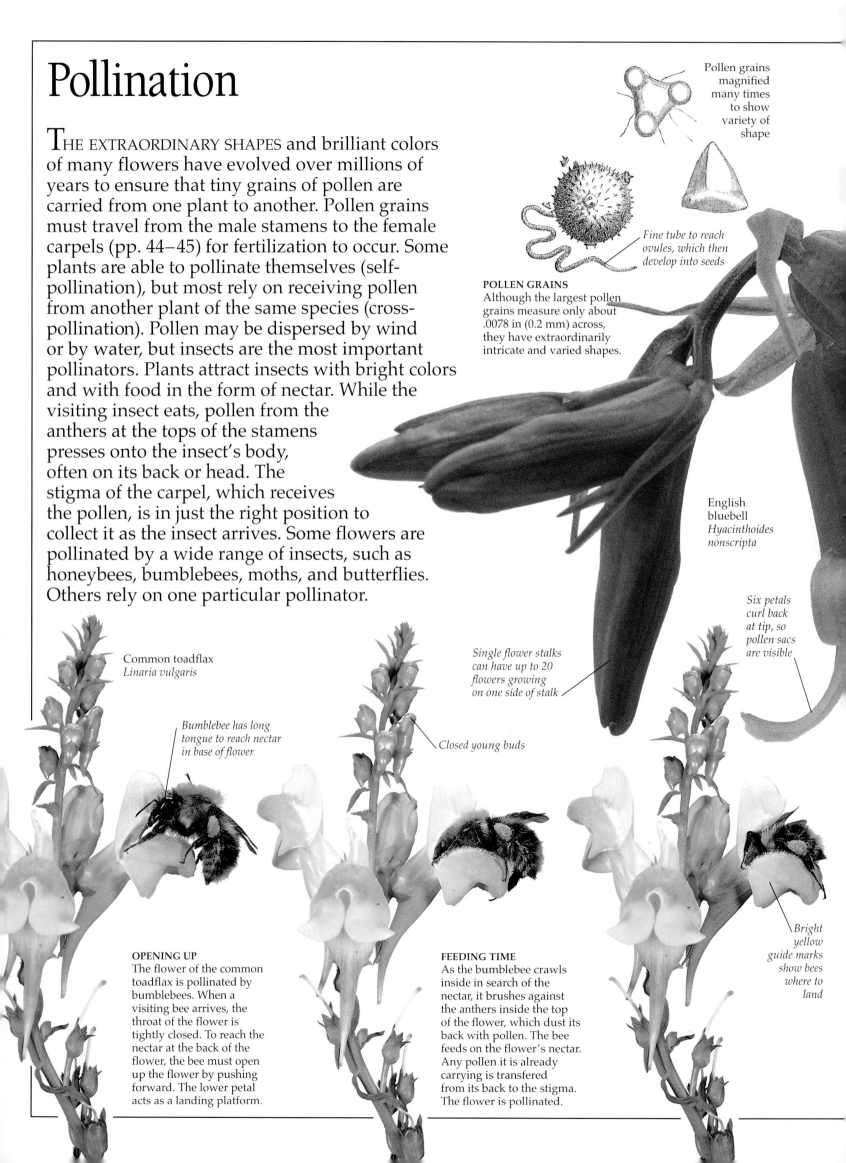

Pollen grains magnified many times to show variety of shape

Fine tube to reach ovules, which then develop into seeds

POLLEN GRAINS
Although the largest pollen grains measure only about .0078 in (0.2 mm) across, they have extraordinarily intricate and varied shapes.

English bluebell
Hyacinthoides nonscripta

Six petals curl back at tip, so pollen sacs are visible

Common toadflax
Linaria vulgaris

Single flower stalks can have up to 20 flowers growing on one side of stalk

Bumblebee has long tongue to reach nectar in base of flower

Closed young buds

Bright yellow guide marks show bees where to land

OPENING UP
The flower of the common toadflax is pollinated by bumblebees. When a visiting bee arrives, the throat of the flower is tightly closed. To reach the nectar at the back of the flower, the bee must open up the flower by pushing forward. The lower petal acts as a landing platform.

FEEDING TIME
As the bumblebee crawls inside in search of the nectar, it brushes against the anthers inside the top of the flower, which dust its back with pollen. The bee feeds on the flower's nectar. Any pollen it is already carrying is transfered from its back to the stigma. The flower is pollinated.

English bluebells are usually violet-blue, but can be white or pink

Pollen sacs, or anther

ATTRACTING INSECTS
Insect-pollinated flowers are brightly colored, scented, and produce nectar. In addition, these flowers usually have patterns on them that are not visible to the human eye. The patterns can be seen in ultraviolet light (below) and guide insect pollinators, since insects see ultraviolet light.

St. John's Wort, *Hypericum*, under normal light

Dark, central area with nectaries, anthers, and stigmas

Honey guide

St. John's Wort under ultraviolet light

INVISIBLE MESSAGES
Insects are attracted to the darkest, central part of the flower, visible in such dark colors here only because it is lit by ultraviolet light. The lines on the petals are honey guides that guide the insect to the central part of the flower where it will find pollen and nectar.

Green-veined white butterfly *Pieris napi*

BUTTERFLY POLLINATION
Butterflies and moths are also important pollinators but, unlike bees, they don't actively collect or eat pollen. When they land on a flower to feed on the nectar, pollen from the stamens sticks to their bodies, ready to be carried to the next flower. Because butterflies and moths have a highly developed sense of smell, flowers pollinated by these insects are often scented. Many bloom in the late summer, when butterflies and moths are most abundant. Butterflies and moths suck up nectar through their proboscis, which is hollow like a drinking straw. The proboscis may vary in length from a fraction of an inch to 1 foot (30 cm). It is coiled up under the butterfly's head when it's not in use.

Green color around veins gives this butterfly its name

Also known as wild hyacinths, English bluebells have single, thick, supporting stalks

Borne on the wind

Dandelion's tiny
fruits float away
on the breeze

ACCORDING TO TRADITION, if you blow on a dandelion's seed head, the number of puffs needed to blow away all the seeds will tell you the time of day. Whether or not it's true, the custom certainly helps the plant spread. The seeds of the dandelion are encased in tiny fruits and have their own special feathery parachutes to help them float through the air. The dandelion's flower is a composite flower head, composed of many tiny flowers, or florets, clustered together. Each of the tiny florets produces a single fruit. Like the dandelion, many other composite plants, such as hawkweeds, ragworts, and thistles, rely on the wind to disperse their seeds. The fruits of some of these have parachutes; others have fine hairs that stick out in all directions to form a feathery ball. Many of these plants are troublesome weeds because they quickly colonize bare soil in gardens and on farmland.

1 OPENING TIME
The dandelion's flower opens in the morning and closes in the afternoon or when it rains. The plant's name comes from the French *dent de lion*, meaning "lion's tooth," which describes the jagged edges of the leaves.

*Flower closes
before seeds form*

2 THE SEEDS START TO FORM
After opening and closing for a number of days, during which time it can be pollinated, the flower finally closes, and seed formation begins. Gradually the yellow petals wither away, and the "pappus," which is the name given to the small circle of hairs attached to the top of each fruit, starts to grow longer. This is the beginning of the parachute.

*Bracts protect
developing seed head*

*Seed head opens
when parachutes
are formed*

*Bracts
fold back*

3 OPENING OUT
The seed head begins to open
only in dry weather. At first, the
parachutes are squashed together,
but as the bracts around the edge
of the seed head fold back, the
parachutes can expand.

4 READY TO GO
In windless weather,
the fruits may spend
several days attached
to the seed head. This is
dangerous because seed-
eating birds like goldfinches are
likely to peck them off and eat them.

*Fully
opened
seed head*

*Parachutes
attached to
tiny fruits*

5 LIFT OFF
A slight breeze is all that is needed
to lift the parachutes into the air. They
may fall close by, but with enough
updraft they can travel long distances –
more than 6 miles (10 km) is an average
journey for a dandelion seed. When a
fruit lands, it no longer needs the
parachute that has carried it on its
journey, and this breaks off. Over the
winter months, the seeds inside the fruit
sink into the soil until the spring, when
they begin to germinate (pp. 52–53).

Scattering the seed

A PATCH OF BARE GROUND never stays bare for long. Within days, seedlings start to spring up, and, if the conditions are right, they eventually cover the ground. Even if the earth is sterilized by heat, so that all the seeds are killed, more somehow arrive and germinate (pp. 52–53). Plants have evolved very effective ways of spreading their seeds, often relying on transportation by wind, animals, and water. The fruit wall is part of a plant's dispersal method. In certain plants, exploding seed pods fling the seeds into the air. Some fruits are winged or cottony to help the seeds become airborne, and some air-filled seeds float on water. Animals also play their part. Many plants have fruits with hooks or burs that stick to fur, and the seeds some species develop inside tasty berries that are eaten by animals and birds. The seeds pass through these creatures unharmed and fall to the ground, where they germinate.

Seed heads of lotus
Nymphaea nucifera

Seed held in cup

Dried lotus head from above

Seed protected by fruit wall

Flat edge of seed coat

SPLITTING OPEN
The hard fruit walls of dry fruits such as money plant split open to release their seeds, which are then dispersed in the wind. The edges of the seed coats are flattened to make the seeds more aerodynamic.

Dry fruit wall

Money plant
Lunaria annua

Lotuses growing in ancient Egypt

WASHED AWAY
The lotus is a water plant that produces its seeds in a flattened head. When the seeds are ripe, they fall to the water's surface and float away. Lotus seeds can be extraordinarily long-lived. Some have been known to germinate more than 200 years after they were shed.

Long tail for climbing

Ring-tailed lemur
Lemur catta

FRUIT EATER
This ring-tailed lemur lives in tall trees near rivers in southern Madagascar. Fruit is the most important part of its diet, although it also eats insects and leaves. The seeds of the fruit are spread when the lemur spits them out, lets them fall, or passes them in its droppings.

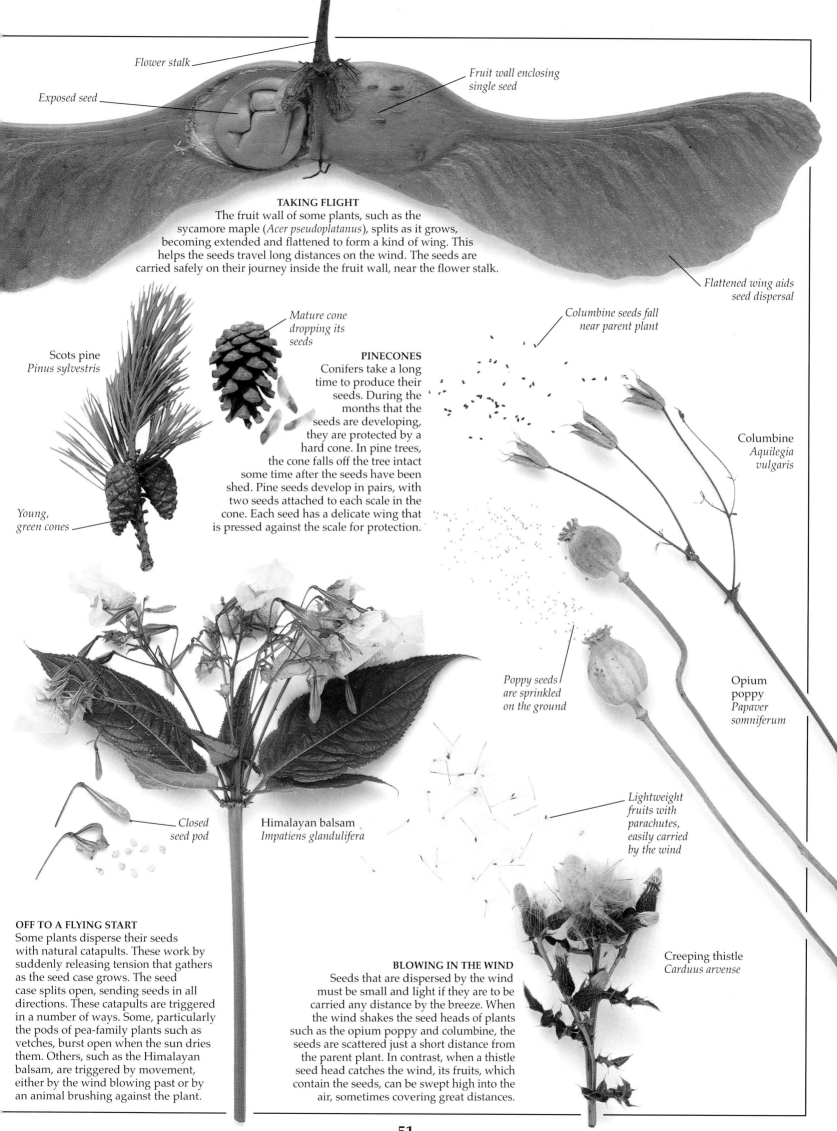

Flower stalk

Exposed seed

Fruit wall enclosing
single seed

Flattened wing aids
seed dispersal

TAKING FLIGHT
The fruit wall of some plants, such as the
sycamore maple (*Acer pseudoplatanus*), splits as it grows,
becoming extended and flattened to form a kind of wing. This
helps the seeds travel long distances on the wind. The seeds are
carried safely on their journey inside the fruit wall, near the flower stalk.

Scots pine
Pinus sylvestris

Mature cone
dropping its
seeds

Columbine seeds fall
near parent plant

PINECONES
Conifers take a long
time to produce their
seeds. During the
months that the
seeds are developing,
they are protected by a
hard cone. In pine trees,
the cone falls off the tree intact
some time after the seeds have been
shed. Pine seeds develop in pairs, with
two seeds attached to each scale in the
cone. Each seed has a delicate wing that
is pressed against the scale for protection.

Columbine
*Aquilegia
vulgaris*

Young,
green cones

Poppy seeds
are sprinkled
on the ground

Opium
poppy
*Papaver
somniferum*

Closed
seed pod

Himalayan balsam
Impatiens glandulifera

Lightweight
fruits with
parachutes,
easily carried
by the wind

OFF TO A FLYING START
Some plants disperse their seeds
with natural catapults. These work by
suddenly releasing tension that gathers
as the seed case grows. The seed
case splits open, sending seeds in all
directions. These catapults are triggered
in a number of ways. Some, particularly
the pods of pea-family plants such as
vetches, burst open when the sun dries
them. Others, such as the Himalayan
balsam, are triggered by movement,
either by the wind blowing past or by
an animal brushing against the plant.

BLOWING IN THE WIND
Seeds that are dispersed by the wind
must be small and light if they are to be
carried any distance by the breeze. When
the wind shakes the seed heads of plants
such as the opium poppy and columbine, the
seeds are scattered just a short distance from
the parent plant. In contrast, when a thistle
seed head catches the wind, its fruits, which
contain the seeds, can be swept high into the
air, sometimes covering great distances.

Creeping thistle
Carduus arvense

Seeds of life

A SEED IS A TINY LIFE-SUPPORT package. Inside it is an embryo, which consists of the basic parts from which a seedling will develop, or germinate. Food is needed to keep the embryo alive and fuel the process of germination. It is either packed around the embryo in an endosperm, or stored in special seed leaves known as cotyledons. For weeks, months, or even years, the seed may remain inactive. But then, when the conditions are right, it suddenly comes alive and begins to grow. During germination, the seed absorbs water, the cells of the embryo start to divide, and eventually the seed coat, or testa, breaks open.

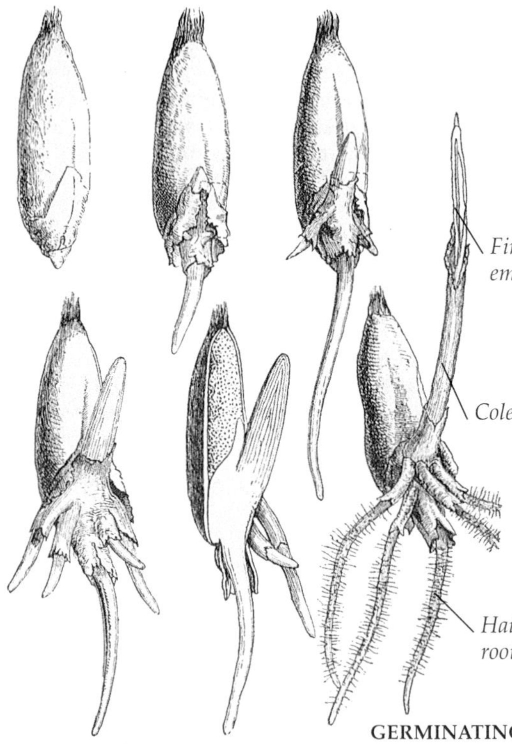

First leaves emerge

Coleoptile

Hairy roots

GERMINATING GRAIN
Wheat is a monocot – it has just one seed leaf. The young shoot grows upward through the soil, protected by a tube called a coleoptile. The growing point of a wheat plant remains at ground level and can continue to produce new shoots even if the leaves are removed.

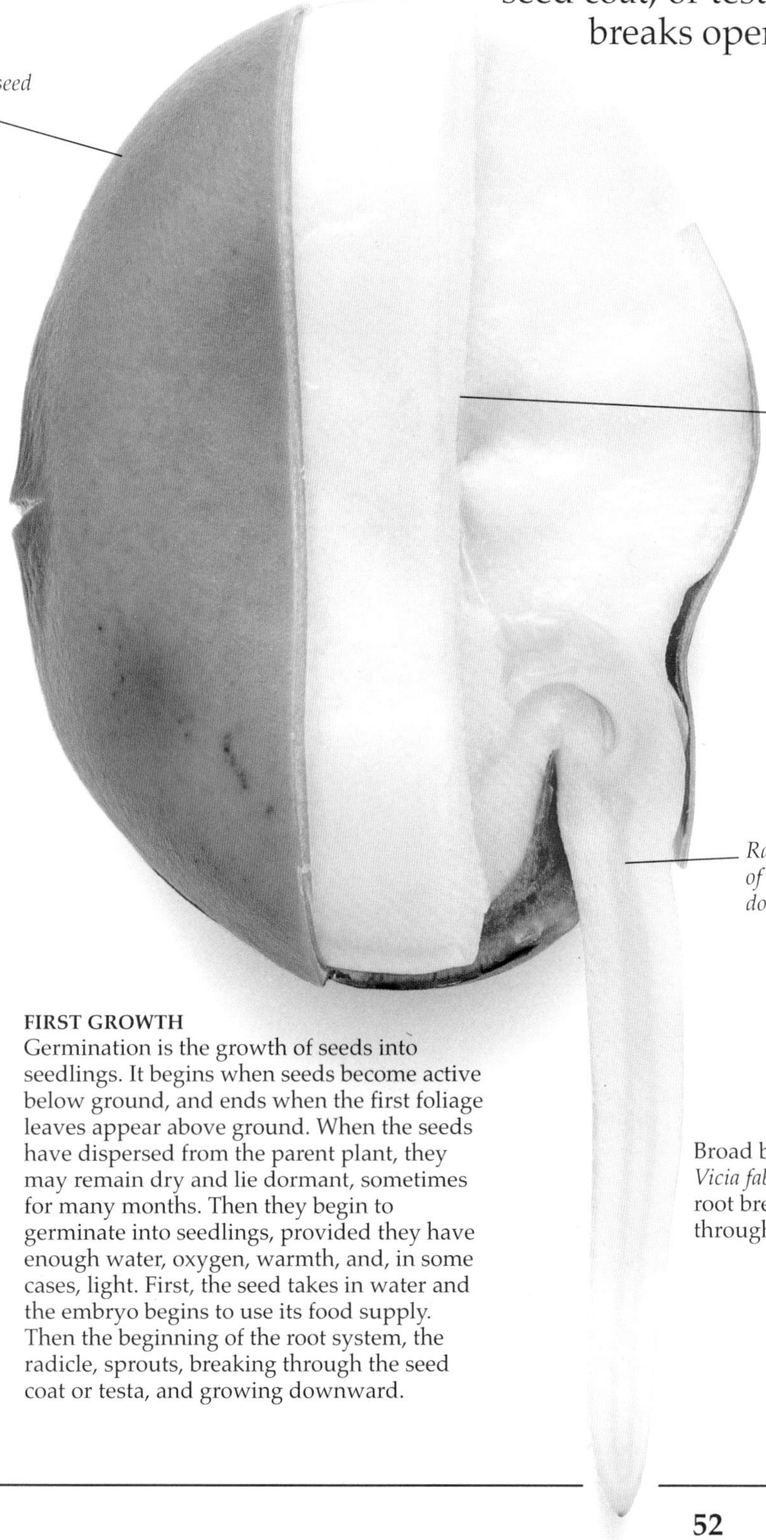

Testa (seed coat)

Cotyledon (seed leaf), where food is stored

Radicle breaking out of testa and growing downward

First true leaves emerging

Plumule (shoot) straightening toward light

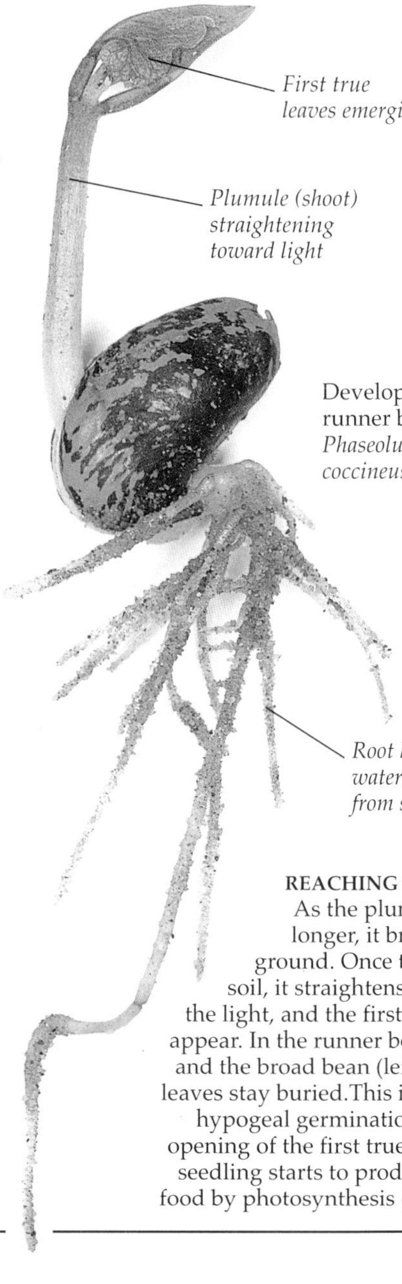

Developing runner bean
Phaseolus coccineus

Root hairs absorb water and salt from soil

FIRST GROWTH
Germination is the growth of seeds into seedlings. It begins when seeds become active below ground, and ends when the first foliage leaves appear above ground. When the seeds have dispersed from the parent plant, they may remain dry and lie dormant, sometimes for many months. Then they begin to germinate into seedlings, provided they have enough water, oxygen, warmth, and, in some cases, light. First, the seed takes in water and the embryo begins to use its food supply. Then the beginning of the root system, the radicle, sprouts, breaking through the seed coat or testa, and growing downward.

Broad bean
Vicia faba
root breaking through seed coat

REACHING THE LIGHT
As the plumule grows longer, it breaks above ground. Once through the soil, it straightens up toward the light, and the first true leaves appear. In the runner bean (above) and the broad bean (left), the seed leaves stay buried. This is known as hypogeal germination. With the opening of the first true leaves, the seedling starts to produce its own food by photosynthesis (pp. 40–41).

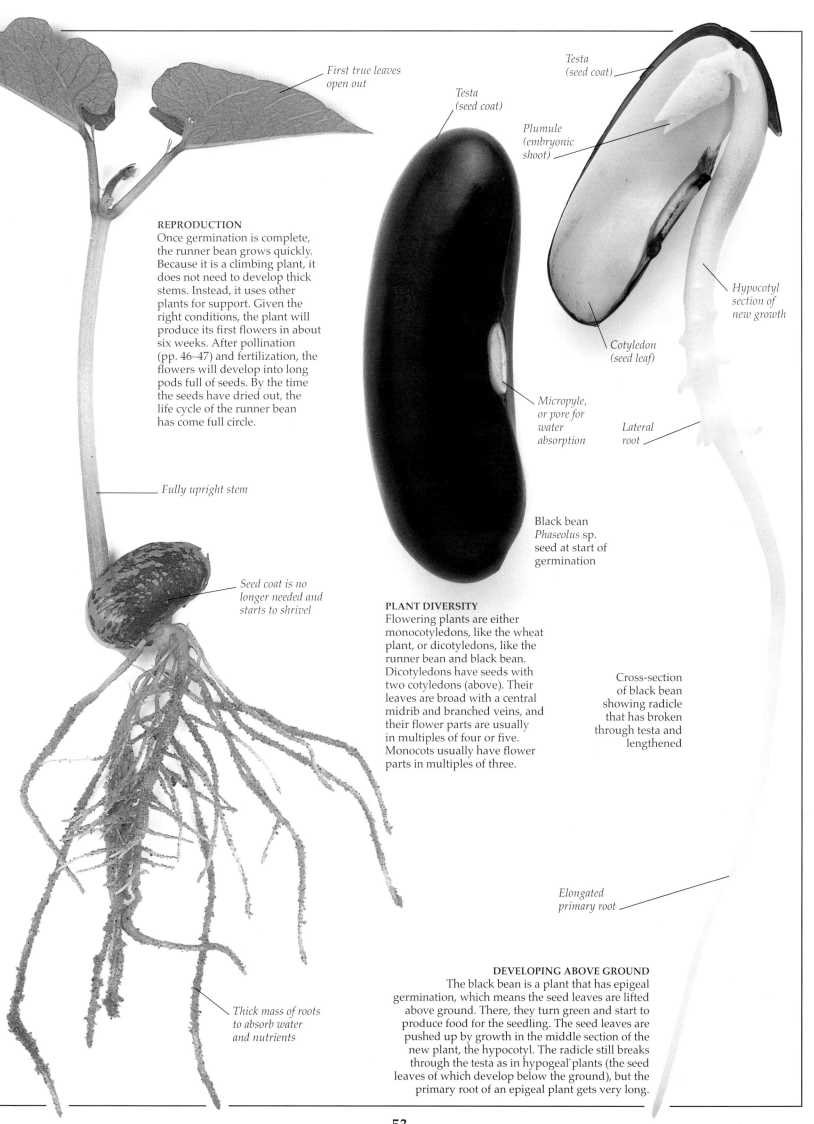

First true leaves
open out

Testa
(seed coat)

Testa
(seed coat)

Plumule
(embryonic
shoot)

REPRODUCTION
Once germination is complete,
the runner bean grows quickly.
Because it is a climbing plant, it
does not need to develop thick
stems. Instead, it uses other
plants for support. Given the
right conditions, the plant will
produce its first flowers in about
six weeks. After pollination
(pp. 46–47) and fertilization, the
flowers will develop into long
pods full of seeds. By the time
the seeds have dried out, the
life cycle of the runner bean
has come full circle.

Hypocotyl
section of
new growth

Cotyledon
(seed leaf)

Fully upright stem

Micropyle,
or pore for
water
absorption

Lateral
root

Black bean
Phaseolus sp.
seed at start of
germination

Seed coat is no
longer needed and
starts to shrivel

PLANT DIVERSITY
Flowering plants are either
monocotyledons, like the wheat
plant, or dicotyledons, like the
runner bean and black bean.
Dicotyledons have seeds with
two cotyledons (above). Their
leaves are broad with a central
midrib and branched veins, and
their flower parts are usually
in multiples of four or five.
Monocots usually have flower
parts in multiples of three.

Cross-section
of black bean
showing radicle
that has broken
through testa and
lengthened

Thick mass of roots
to absorb water
and nutrients

Elongated
primary root

DEVELOPING ABOVE GROUND
The black bean is a plant that has epigeal
germination, which means the seed leaves are lifted
above ground. There, they turn green and start to
produce food for the seedling. The seed leaves are
pushed up by growth in the middle section of the
new plant, the hypocotyl. The radicle still breaks
through the testa as in hypogeal plants (the seed
leaves of which develop below the ground), but the
primary root of an epigeal plant gets very long.

53

FIERCE FEEDER
In a typical food chain, the lion is the top predator. An adult male may eat 90 lb (40 kg) of meat in a sitting, although he may not feed again for several days. The lionesses in a group of lions, or pride, do most of the hunting. Often two or more will stalk and kill the antelope or zebras that are the pride's main food.

CHAPTER 3
ANIMAL LIFE

THERE IS AN INCREDIBLE VARIETY of animal life in the world, from brightly colored beetles and many-legged centipedes to waddling penguins, writhing snakes, scuttling brown rats, and fierce polar bears. The variety is reflected in the animals' lifestyles. They have all developed ingenious ways of protecting and feeding themselves and their young.

LAYING IN STORES
Female butterflies and moths lay batches of eggs on the plants that will provide food for the caterpillars when they hatch (pp. 60–61). Caterpillars are voracious and continuous feeders, eating and growing larger until they pupate. In the pupa, or chrysalis (pp. 58–59), a caterpillar develops further, eventually emerging as a fully grown butterfly.

Insect life

INSECTS ARE THE MOST ABUNDANT creatures on Earth – there are more than five million species. They first appeared 300 million years ago, and were the first animals to fly. All insects have six legs and a skeleton on the outside of their body. This outer skeleton, or exoskeleton, forms a soft, protective covering around the vulnerable internal organs. When a young insect, or larva, grows, it must shed its exoskeleton. As it grows too large, the skeleton splits, revealing a new one underneath. Most insects have two pairs of wings, each with a network of veins to give strength to their structure. Insects also have antennae, or feelers, which they use to investigate their surroundings. Some insects have very long antennae, used mainly for touch. Others have antennae that can sense airborne chemicals, even in minute quantities. These are often feathery, which provides a large surface area for collecting scent molecules from the air.

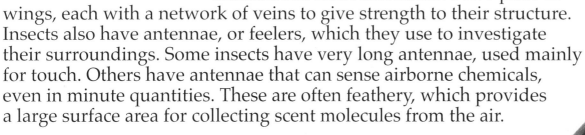

Back legs pulled in to push insect into air

JUMPING INSECTS
Grasshoppers, crickets, and locusts are all powerful jumpers. They bring the long, slender parts of their hind legs close under their bodies. The large muscles shorten, or contract, and the legs are suddenly straightened, throwing the insect into the air.

DANGER ON EIGHT LEGS
Although many people think they are, spiders are not insects. This red-kneed tarantula, *Brachypelma smithi*, stays in its silk-lined burrow during the day, emerging after dark to hunt for large insects or small invertebrates.

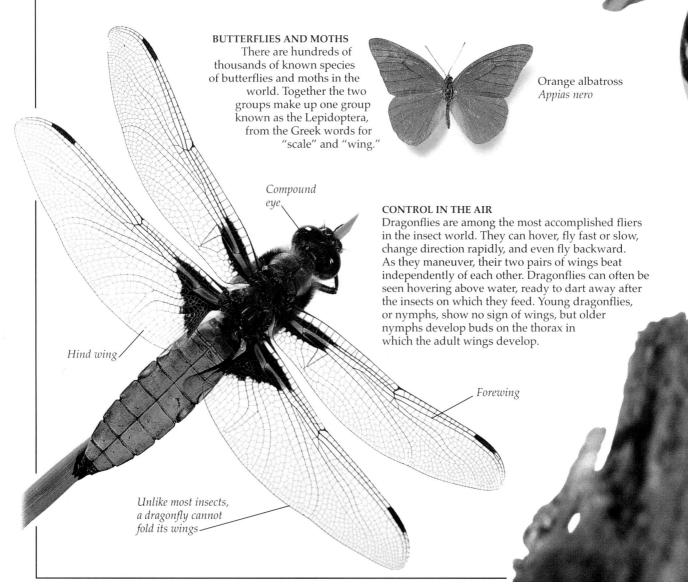

BUTTERFLIES AND MOTHS
There are hundreds of thousands of known species of butterflies and moths in the world. Together the two groups make up one group known as the Lepidoptera, from the Greek words for "scale" and "wing."

Orange albatross
Appias nero

Compound eye

CONTROL IN THE AIR
Dragonflies are among the most accomplished fliers in the insect world. They can hover, fly fast or slow, change direction rapidly, and even fly backward. As they maneuver, their two pairs of wings beat independently of each other. Dragonflies can often be seen hovering above water, ready to dart away after the insects on which they feed. Young dragonflies, or nymphs, show no sign of wings, but older nymphs develop buds on the thorax in which the adult wings develop.

Hind wing

Forewing

Unlike most insects, a dragonfly cannot fold its wings

LIVING FOOD

Many insects practice a form of parasitism that involves laying eggs on or in another insect, which then acts as a living food supply for the insect's grubs to feed on. This striped field digger wasp is paralyzing a fly that it will carry back to its nest for its grubs to eat. Insects that carry out this kind of parasitism, indirect predation, can be used by humans to keep down the population of pests that attack many economically important crops. It is a natural form of biological control, which is less harmful than the use of poisonous chemicals.

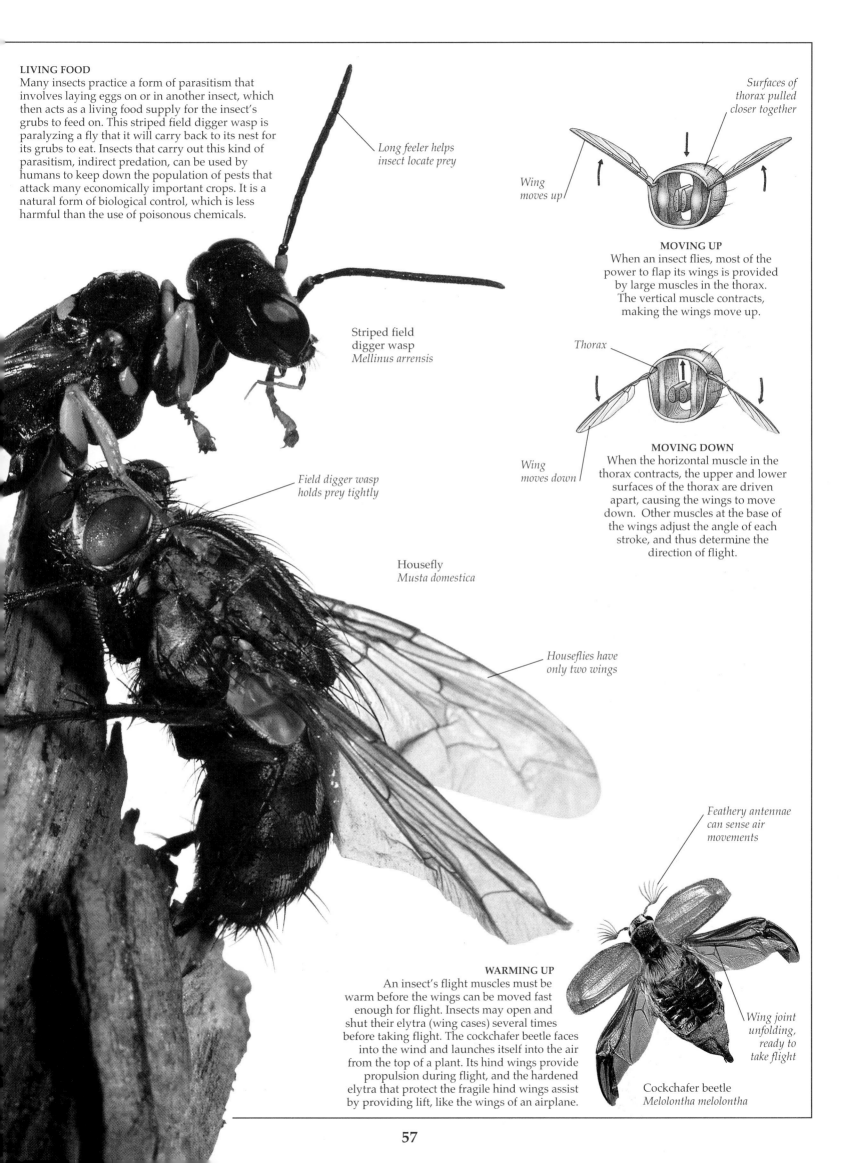

Long feeler helps insect locate prey

Striped field digger wasp
Mellinus arrensis

Field digger wasp holds prey tightly

Housefly
Musta domestica

Houseflies have only two wings

Surfaces of thorax pulled closer together

Wing moves up

MOVING UP

When an insect flies, most of the power to flap its wings is provided by large muscles in the thorax. The vertical muscle contracts, making the wings move up.

Thorax

Wing moves down

MOVING DOWN

When the horizontal muscle in the thorax contracts, the upper and lower surfaces of the thorax are driven apart, causing the wings to move down. Other muscles at the base of the wings adjust the angle of each stroke, and thus determine the direction of flight.

Feathery antennae can sense air movements

Wing joint unfolding, ready to take flight

WARMING UP

An insect's flight muscles must be warm before the wings can be moved fast enough for flight. Insects may open and shut their elytra (wing cases) several times before taking flight. The cockchafer beetle faces into the wind and launches itself into the air from the top of a plant. Its hind wings provide propulsion during flight, and the hardened elytra that protect the fragile hind wings assist by providing lift, like the wings of an airplane.

Cockchafer beetle
Melolontha melolontha

57

Insect transformation

METAMORPHOSIS MEANS "change of body form and appearance." The most advanced insects have a complex life cycle involving "complete" metamorphosis. The eggs hatch to produce larvae (caterpillars, grubs, or maggots) that are completely different from adult insects in both shape and appearance. The larvae grow and molt several times, producing a pupa, or chrysalis. Inside the pupa, the insect's whole body is reorganized, and a winged adult finally emerges. This life cycle enables larvae to specialize in feeding and adults to specialize in breeding and looking for new sites. Wasps, bees, ants, flies, beetles, butterflies and moths, caddis flies, fleas, lacewings, and scorpion flies all undergo complete metamorphosis. Grasshoppers, cockroaches, termites, mayflies, dragonflies, and many other bugs undergo "incomplete" metamorphosis. Like the original primitive insects, they transform gradually through a series of stages, the nymphs becoming more and more like the adults. There is no pupal stage.

MATING
Mexican bean beetles (*Epilachna varivestis*) are a species of plant-eating ladybug beetle. The adult males and females look very similar and mate frequently.

EGGS
Female Mexican bean beetles glue their eggs in groups of about 50 to the underside of leaves, where the eggs will be well protected. Each egg stands on its end and takes about seven days to hatch.

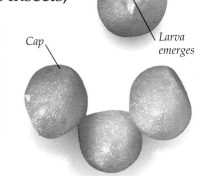

Cap

Larva emerges

1 EGG HATCHES
Even eggs have to breathe. Each egg has a ring of pores at the top, that allow air to reach the developing larva inside. About a week after the egg has been laid, the cap at the top is broken or chewed off and the larva emerges.

Old larval skin

New pupal skin

4 ABOUT TO CHANGE
When the larva has eaten enough food, it attaches itself to the underside of a damaged, netted leaf, ready to pupate. The larval skin is shed, and soft new pupal skin forms beneath it. This quickly hardens.

Larva feeding on plant shoot

DIET OF LEAVES
Mexican bean beetles feed on leaves both as larvae and adults. Because they only eat the fleshy parts between the veins, the leaf becomes netted and lacy.

Old larval skin with long spines

New pupal skin with short spines

Dead, lacy leaves that larvae have eaten

5 RESTING
A pupa is often called a "resting stage." But there is no rest for all the cells in the insect's body. The muscles, nerves, and other structures all dissolve, and new limbs, with new muscles and nerves, form. In this photo, the smooth yellow of the adult beetle's wing cases and the first segment of its thorax can be seen through the thin, spiny skin of the pupa.

Old larval skin

Larval skin splits

Head emerges first

6 READY TO FEED
The thin, spiny pupal skin splits along the underside, and the smooth, young adult slowly pulls itself free, headfirst. It takes about an hour from the splitting of the pupal skin for the young beetle to free itself.

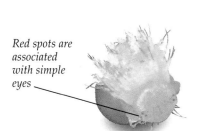

Eggs   Young larva

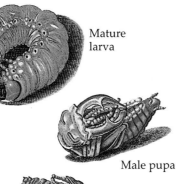

Mature larva

Male pupa

Female pupa

STAG BEETLE DEVELOPMENT
The larvae of stag beetles and other scarab beetles always take a C-shaped posture. The male pupa is easily distinguished from the female pupa by its large jaws.

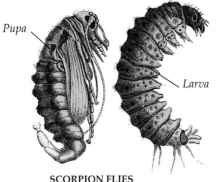

Pupa

Larva

SCORPION FLIES
Scorpion flies undergo a complete metamorphosis. This drawing shows a pupa with well-developed wing buds (left) and a larva (right).

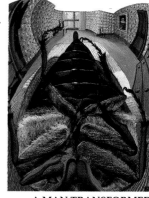

A MAN TRANSFORMED
This painting by Barbara Lofthouse depicts a scene from Kafka's *Metamorphosis*, in which a man is transformed into a cockroach.

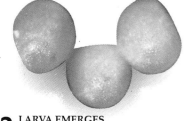

Red spots are associated with simple eyes

Soft spines harden quickly

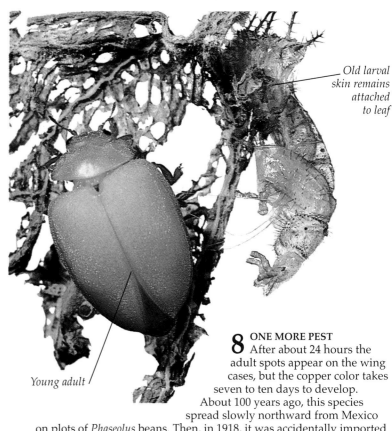

PROTECTION FROM PARASITES
The spines on the surface of the larvae are branched, with hard, pointed tips. Spines like this are found on the larvae of all plant-eating ladybugs, but not on any of the more common predatory species. The spines make the larvae unpleasant for bird predators and may deter parasites from laying eggs.

2 LARVA EMERGES
As the soft-spined larva crawls out of its egg, three red pigment spots are visible on either side of the insect's head. Unlike adult insects, larvae do not have compound eyes; the spots are associated with simple eyes.

3 A FIRST MEAL
In many insect species, as soon as a young larva is free from its egg, it eats the nutrient-rich shell. The soft spines on the surface of the larva quickly harden.

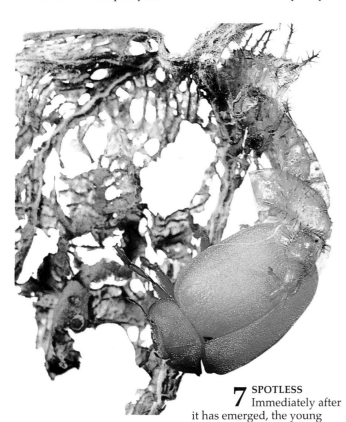

7 SPOTLESS
Immediately after it has emerged, the young beetle is yellow and has no spots, although its wing cases quickly harden. Before the beetle can fly away to safety, there is a crucial drying stage that can last two to three hours. The young beetle holds its wing cases up and expands the wings below to allow them to dry in the air.

Young adult

Old larval skin remains attached to leaf

8 ONE MORE PEST
After about 24 hours the adult spots appear on the wing cases, but the copper color takes seven to ten days to develop. About 100 years ago, this species spread slowly northward from Mexico on plots of *Phaseolus* beans. Then, in 1918, it was accidentally imported to the eastern United States and spread rapidly toward Canada. Today, it is a serious pest in bean crops in North and Central America, although it does not survive the harsher winters in central areas.

An emerging caterpillar

BUTTERFLIES AND MOTHS usually lay large numbers of eggs. The amount laid at one time varies greatly; some females lay more than 1,000, although only a few eggs will survive to become adults. Eggs also vary from one species to another in color and in surface texture, which can be smooth or intricately sculptured. The two main types are a flattened oval shape, usually with a smooth surface, and a more upright shape, which often has a heavily ribbed surface. In many cases, the eggs are laid on a leaf or stem, but species that feed on a wide variety of plants often scatter their eggs in flight. Both methods are designed to place the caterpillar as near as possible to the plant that is its food source. On these two pages, the caterpillar of a South American Owl butterfly (*Caligo idomeneus*) hatches from its egg.

Pattern of ridges can be useful aid to identification of eggs

Darker color shows egg will soon be ready to hatch

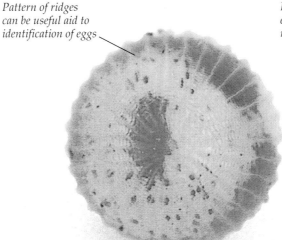

THE EGGS IN POSITION
The South American Owl butterfly lays its eggs in groups. The color of the individual eggs can vary in this species. The eggs get darker (top right) as the time of hatching approaches.

1 RESTING
Many butterflies and moths in temperate regions lay their eggs in fall. Once laid, the eggs enter a resting stage called "diapause" to survive the winter months. This state is disrupted by warm or fluctuating temperatures.

2 WARMING UP
Diapause ends when the environment is warm enough for the caterpillar to stand a chance of survival after the winter months. The egg darkens in color as the tiny caterpillar gets ready to emerge.

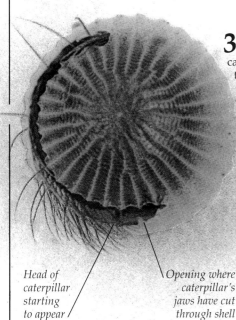

3 CUTTING A CIRCLE
In order to hatch, the caterpillar must bite its way through the shell of its egg. This is not a hard, brittle shell like a bird's egg, but it is still a tough task for the tiny caterpillar. Its jaws have to cut a circle big enough for the head to emerge, so it has enormous mouthparts.

4 EMERGING HEADFIRST
The caterpillar seems to have a disproportionately large head and jaws, but it can be difficult for the caterpillar to extract itself from the egg headfirst. The dark spots on each side of the head are simple eyes, or ocelli. The caterpillar also gets sensory information from its tiny antennae, which it uses for touch and smell.

Head of caterpillar starting to appear

Opening where caterpillar's jaws have cut through shell

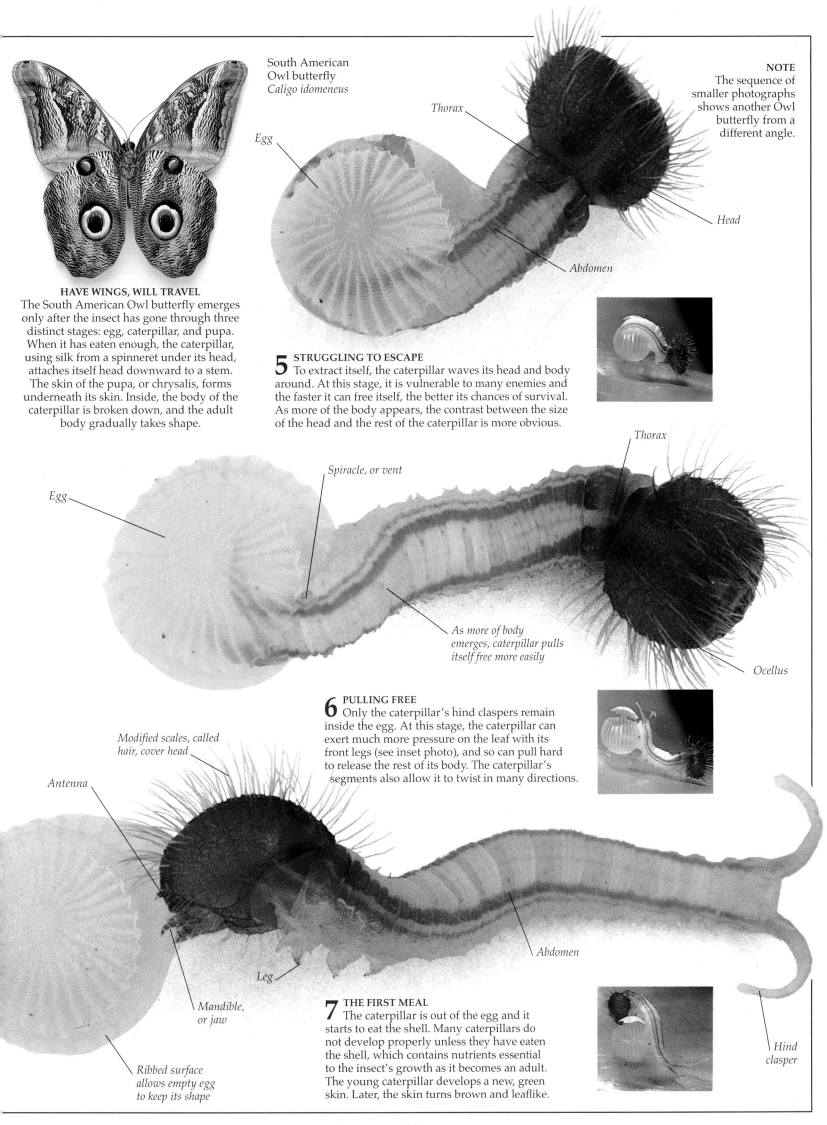

South American
Owl butterfly
Caligo idomeneus

NOTE
The sequence of smaller photographs shows another Owl butterfly from a different angle.

HAVE WINGS, WILL TRAVEL
The South American Owl butterfly emerges only after the insect has gone through three distinct stages: egg, caterpillar, and pupa. When it has eaten enough, the caterpillar, using silk from a spinneret under its head, attaches itself head downward to a stem. The skin of the pupa, or chrysalis, forms underneath its skin. Inside, the body of the caterpillar is broken down, and the adult body gradually takes shape.

Egg

Thorax

Head

Abdomen

5 STRUGGLING TO ESCAPE
To extract itself, the caterpillar waves its head and body around. At this stage, it is vulnerable to many enemies and the faster it can free itself, the better its chances of survival. As more of the body appears, the contrast between the size of the head and the rest of the caterpillar is more obvious.

Egg

Spiracle, or vent

Thorax

As more of body emerges, caterpillar pulls itself free more easily

Ocellus

6 PULLING FREE
Only the caterpillar's hind claspers remain inside the egg. At this stage, the caterpillar can exert much more pressure on the leaf with its front legs (see inset photo), and so can pull hard to release the rest of its body. The caterpillar's segments also allow it to twist in many directions.

Modified scales, called hair, cover head

Antenna

Abdomen

Leg

Mandible, or jaw

7 THE FIRST MEAL
The caterpillar is out of the egg and it starts to eat the shell. Many caterpillars do not develop properly unless they have eaten the shell, which contains nutrients essential to the insect's growth as it becomes an adult. The young caterpillar develops a new, green skin. Later, the skin turns brown and leaflike.

Ribbed surface allows empty egg to keep its shape

Hind clasper

Anatomy of a butterfly

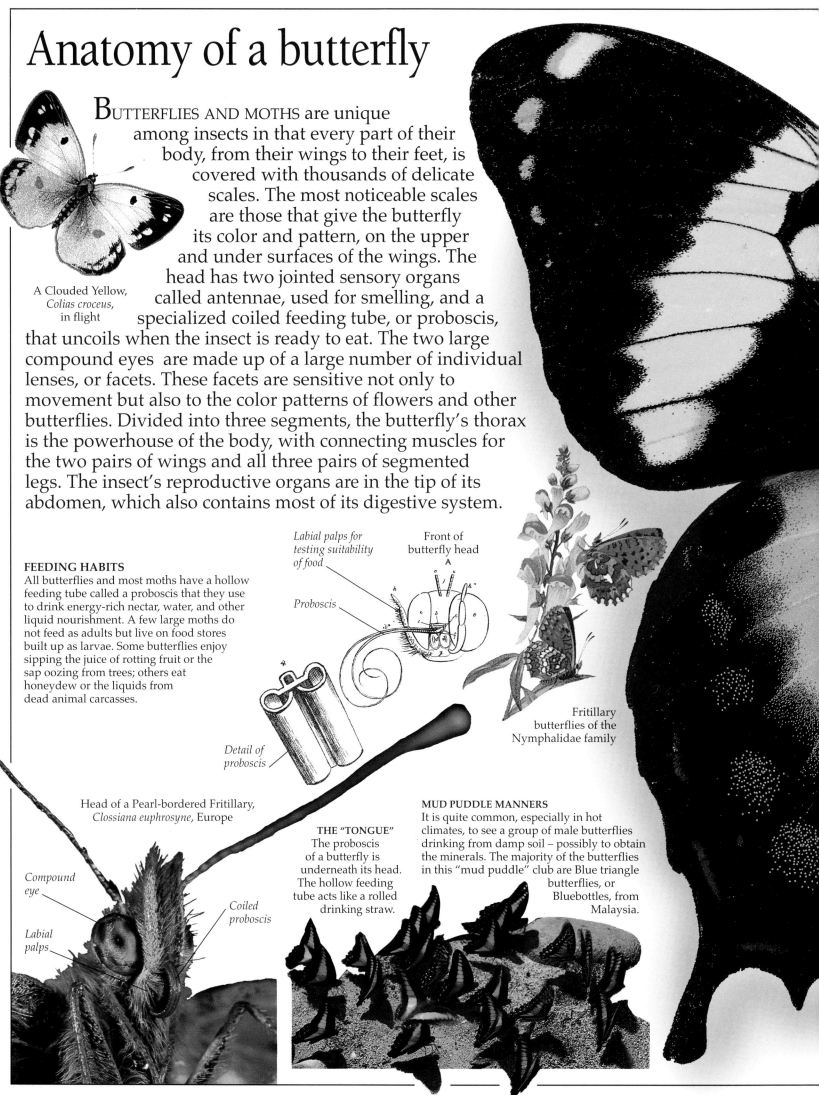

BUTTERFLIES AND MOTHS are unique among insects in that every part of their body, from their wings to their feet, is covered with thousands of delicate scales. The most noticeable scales are those that give the butterfly its color and pattern, on the upper and under surfaces of the wings. The head has two jointed sensory organs called antennae, used for smelling, and a specialized coiled feeding tube, or proboscis, that uncoils when the insect is ready to eat. The two large compound eyes are made up of a large number of individual lenses, or facets. These facets are sensitive not only to movement but also to the color patterns of flowers and other butterflies. Divided into three segments, the butterfly's thorax is the powerhouse of the body, with connecting muscles for the two pairs of wings and all three pairs of segmented legs. The insect's reproductive organs are in the tip of its abdomen, which also contains most of its digestive system.

A Clouded Yellow,
Colias croceus,
in flight

FEEDING HABITS

All butterflies and most moths have a hollow feeding tube called a proboscis that they use to drink energy-rich nectar, water, and other liquid nourishment. A few large moths do not feed as adults but live on food stores built up as larvae. Some butterflies enjoy sipping the juice of rotting fruit or the sap oozing from trees; others eat honeydew or the liquids from dead animal carcasses.

Labial palps for testing suitability of food

Front of butterfly head

Proboscis

Detail of proboscis

Fritillary butterflies of the Nymphalidae family

Head of a Pearl-bordered Fritillary,
Clossiana euphrosyne, Europe

THE "TONGUE"
The proboscis of a butterfly is underneath its head. The hollow feeding tube acts like a rolled drinking straw.

MUD PUDDLE MANNERS
It is quite common, especially in hot climates, to see a group of male butterflies drinking from damp soil – possibly to obtain the minerals. The majority of the butterflies in this "mud puddle" club are Blue triangle butterflies, or Bluebottles, from Malaysia.

Compound eye

Labial palps

Coiled proboscis

Scarce swallowtail,
Iphiclides podalirius

Forewing

Hind wing

AT REST
This engraving shows a
Scarce swallowtail resting
in a typical swallowtail
position, with its wings
folded up above its body.

Thorax

Abdomen

Antenna

*Rows of scales
form the patterns
and colors*

Homerus swallowtail,
Papilio homerus

WHICH FAMILY?
The veins in the wings of
butterflies and moths help
keep the wing in the correct
flight position. The way the
veins are arranged also helps
scientists and butterfly
fanciers identify the family
to which a species
belongs.

A LARGE FAMILY
The Homerus swallowtail, found only in Jamaica
and an endangered species because of its
popularity with collectors, is one of 500 species
belonging to a large family of butterflies, the
Papilionidae, that contains some of the most
beautiful butterflies in the world. Most of the
species are found in the tropics and are strong
fliers. They have large wings and three fully
developed pairs of legs. Swallowtails get their
name from the tapered shape of their hind wings.

COMING IN FOR A LANDING
With its wings slightly curved,
this Peacock butterfly is about to
land on a buddleia. Butterflies
have enormous control over
their flight movements
and can easily manage
sudden landings.

Spinning silk

Illustrations from *Vermis sericus*, a popular 17th-century book on silk moths

Sɪʟᴋ ɪs ᴘʀᴏᴅᴜᴄᴇᴅ by the caterpillars of most moths, but the finest silk is made by species of moths in the families Saturniidae and Bombycidae. In particular it is made by the caterpillars of the large white moth *Bombyx mori*, more commonly known as the Chinese silkworm. Today, this silkworm is so thoroughly domesticated that it no longer occurs in the wild. According to Chinese legend, silk fiber was first discovered as early as 2700 BC. However, the methods used to produce silk commercially were kept closely guarded for centuries and the export of silkworms or their eggs out of China was a crime punishable by death. Despite this, silkworm eggs, and the seeds of the mulberry trees on which the caterpillars feed, were eventually smuggled out of China, possibly hidden in a walking stick. In Europe, silk had been a highly valued material for making luxurious clothing for a long time. Even after Arabs introduced silkworms into Spain, and silk-weaving centers had been set up in Italy, silk continued to command high prices.

REELING OF THE COCOONS
The production of silk originated in China. This 19th-century engraving shows the thread being transferred to smaller bobbins as it becomes finer. The bobbins of silk were then dyed before being used to weave rich cloth. Today, silk-making is more mechanized, but the basic process remains the same.

UNWINDING THE THREAD
In 17th-century Europe, the methods used to produce silk changed little. Before they could hatch, the insects inside the cocoons were killed in boiling water to prevent them breaking the thread of silk and also to dissolve the gumlike substance that held the strands together. The threads from several cocoons were then caught up and twisted together.

Thread was wound onto a reel or frame

3 BUILDING UP THE WALLS
As the caterpillar works backward and forward between the leaves, the cocoon is made thicker. A fine thread of silk is forced out through the spinneret.

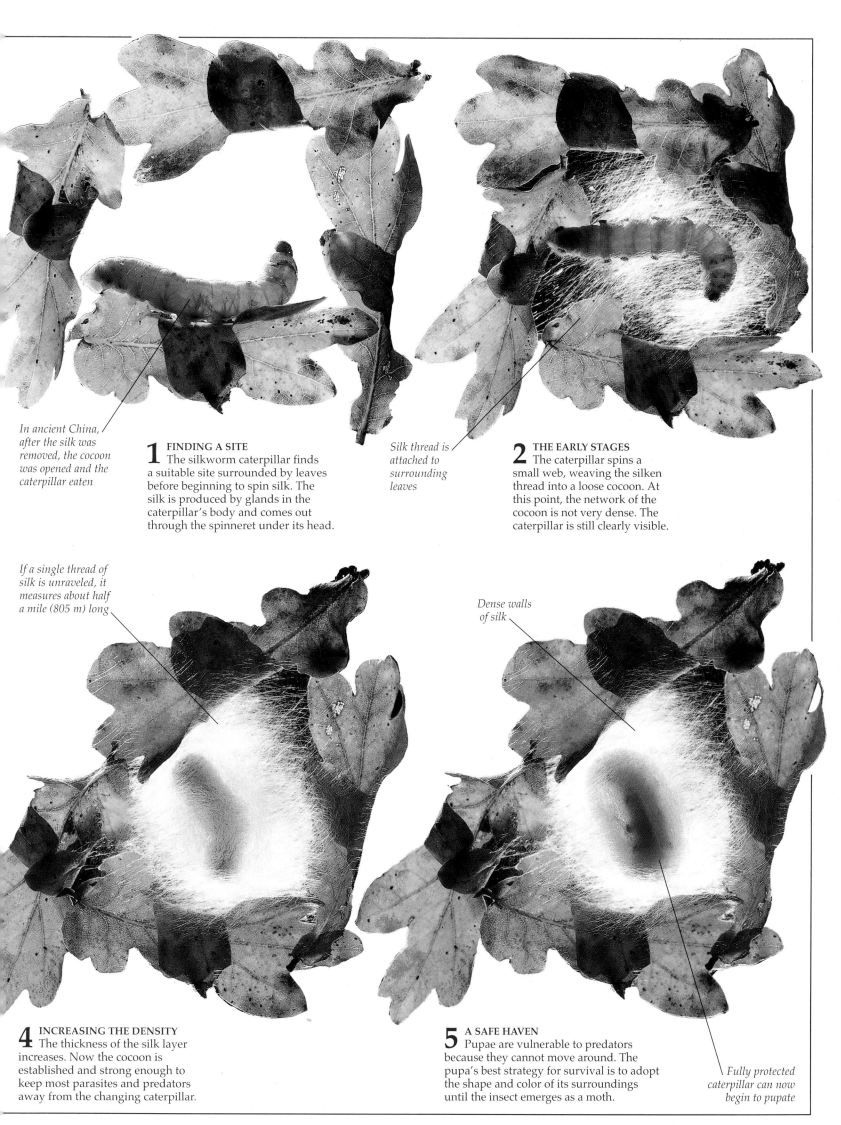

In ancient China, after the silk was removed, the cocoon was opened and the caterpillar eaten

1 FINDING A SITE
The silkworm caterpillar finds a suitable site surrounded by leaves before beginning to spin silk. The silk is produced by glands in the caterpillar's body and comes out through the spinneret under its head.

Silk thread is attached to surrounding leaves

2 THE EARLY STAGES
The caterpillar spins a small web, weaving the silken thread into a loose cocoon. At this point, the network of the cocoon is not very dense. The caterpillar is still clearly visible.

If a single thread of silk is unraveled, it measures about half a mile (805 m) long

Dense walls of silk

4 INCREASING THE DENSITY
The thickness of the silk layer increases. Now the cocoon is established and strong enough to keep most parasites and predators away from the changing caterpillar.

5 A SAFE HAVEN
Pupae are vulnerable to predators because they cannot move around. The pupa's best strategy for survival is to adopt the shape and color of its surroundings until the insect emerges as a moth.

Fully protected caterpillar can now begin to pupate

Moths

THERE ARE AT LEAST 170,000 DIFFERENT SPECIES of butterflies and moths, but the vast majority – more than 150,000 – are moths. The German word for moths, *nachtschmetterlinge* ("night-butterflies"), reflects what most people think of their behavior. Most moths are active at dusk or during the night, but a large number fly during daytime, too. Although many species of moths, such as the silkworm (pp. 64–65), are useful to people, a few species are harmful. These include the moths that destroy crops, fruit, or trees; the moths that nibble holes in wool; and moths that spread diseases in cattle by feeding on the moisture around their eyes. Most moths are harmless, pollinating flowers and forming a vital part of the complex web of life.

Old engraving showing main parts of a moth; the darker lines represent part of the wing pattern

Darwin's hawkmoth, *Xanthopan morganii*

THE LONGEST TONGUE?
This amazing proboscis belongs to Darwin's hawkmoth, from Madagascar. The celebrated 19th-century English naturalist Charles Darwin (1809–82) knew of a Madagascan orchid that had its nectar at the base of a 12-in (30-cm) corolla. Because the orchid obviously needed to be pollinated to survive, Darwin reasoned that there must be a moth with a proboscis that measured 12 to 14 in (30 to 35 cm) in length. Years later, the discovery of the hawkmoth proved Darwin's theory correct.

Feeding

Like butterflies, most moths take nectar from flowers. Day-flying moths often hover in front of a flower as they eat. Many large moths, however, don't eat at all as adults. During its short adult life, the Indian moon moth (right and below) lives entirely off food stored in its body during the caterpillar stage.

FINDING NECTAR
The long proboscis of the hawkmoth is used to seek out and drink nectar. During probing, pollen is picked up and transferred from flower to flower.

Eye

Proboscis

Hawkmoths are powerful fliers, with a characteristic thick body and long forewings

MOTH HEAD
In a moth's head (right) the brain receives information about its environment from the eyes, antennae, and sense organs called palps.

Labial palp

FACE TO FACE WITH A MOTH
An almost frontal view of the Indian moon moth shows its antennae, as well as its front and middle legs. The antennae have minute sensory organs that probably detect not only scent but also subtle changes in air pressure.

Female uses its antennae to choose correct food plant on which to lay eggs

No proboscis – moth does not eat as an adult

Trailing tails help protect this moth

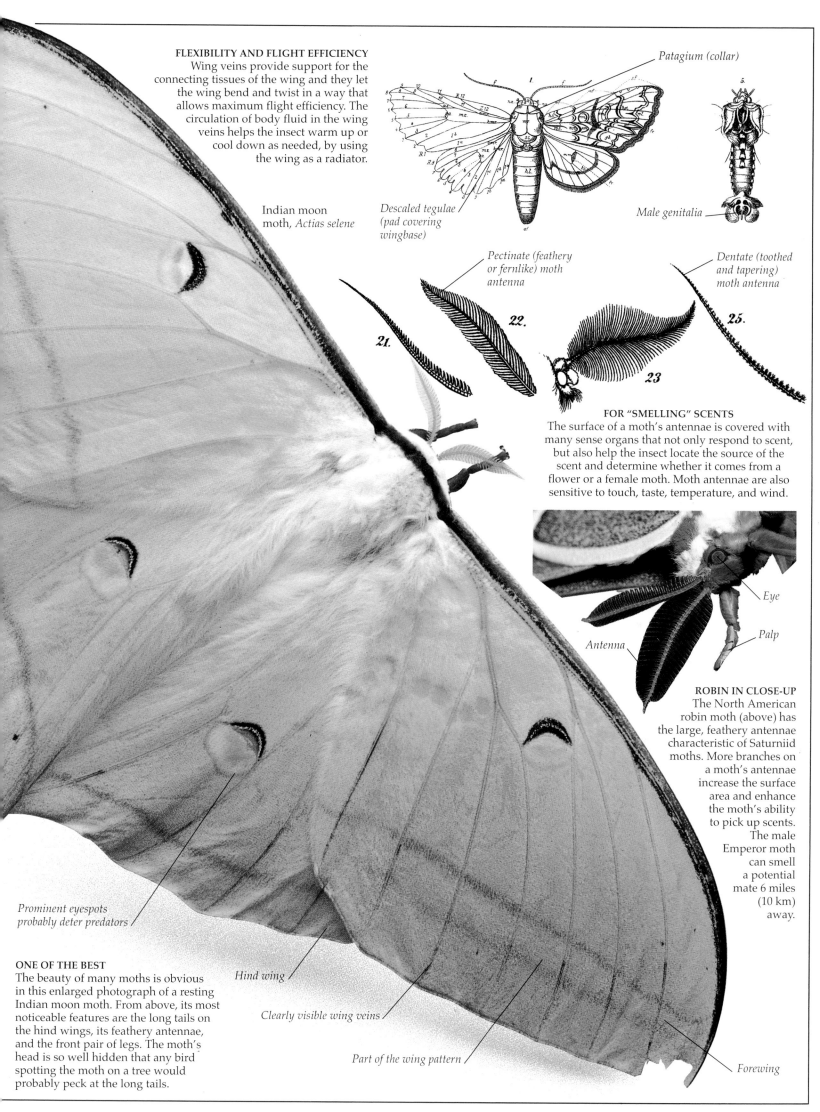

FLEXIBILITY AND FLIGHT EFFICIENCY
Wing veins provide support for the connecting tissues of the wing and they let the wing bend and twist in a way that allows maximum flight efficiency. The circulation of body fluid in the wing veins helps the insect warm up or cool down as needed, by using the wing as a radiator.

Indian moon moth, *Actias selene*

Patagium (collar)

Descaled tegulae (pad covering wingbase)

Male genitalia

Pectinate (feathery or fernlike) moth antenna

22.

21.

Dentate (toothed and tapering) moth antenna

25.

23.

FOR "SMELLING" SCENTS
The surface of a moth's antennae is covered with many sense organs that not only respond to scent, but also help the insect locate the source of the scent and determine whether it comes from a flower or a female moth. Moth antennae are also sensitive to touch, taste, temperature, and wind.

Eye

Palp

Antenna

ROBIN IN CLOSE-UP
The North American robin moth (above) has the large, feathery antennae characteristic of Saturniid moths. More branches on a moth's antennae increase the surface area and enhance the moth's ability to pick up scents. The male Emperor moth can smell a potential mate 6 miles (10 km) away.

Prominent eyespots probably deter predators

ONE OF THE BEST
The beauty of many moths is obvious in this enlarged photograph of a resting Indian moon moth. From above, its most noticeable features are the long tails on the hind wings, its feathery antennae, and the front pair of legs. The moth's head is so well hidden that any bird spotting the moth on a tree would probably peck at the long tails.

Hind wing

Clearly visible wing veins

Part of the wing pattern

Forewing

Homes with hinges

BIVALVES ARE AMONG THE BEST KNOWN of all marine creatures. They are mollusks, but their shells are divided into two parts, or valves, that completely enclose and protect the soft body of the mollusk inside. The valves are attached by a shell-like ridge or by teeth that form a hinge, and can be opened and closed with strong muscles and ligaments. Bivalves do not lead very active lives – unable to extend far out of their shells to crawl, many live buried in sand and mud or hidden in rock crevices, while others attach themselves to a hard surface. They eat by opening their valves and filtering water through their gills to catch tiny creatures in the water around them.

THE BIRTH OF VENUS
This detail from Botticelli's famous painting shows the birth of Venus from an enormous scallop shell.

Royal cloak scallop

SCURRYING SCALLOPS
Scallops are very common bivalve mollusks. Some unique scallops can open and close their valves to swim away rapidly when disturbed.

Spiky exterior

Pacific thorny oyster

SPINY SHELL
Spiny, or thorny, oysters are also known as chrysanthemum shells because their spines resemble that flower's spiky petals. Although not related to the true oyster, they are similar in that they remain attached to a solid base throughout their lives.

BUTTERFLY WINGS
Shiny, colorful tellin shells often wash ashore still in pairs, resembling butterfly wings.

Ligament

BEAN CLAMS
Generally tiny and wedge-shaped, these creatures live in large numbers on warm-water beaches. They are an abundant food source, and one often used in chowders and other soups.

Noble pen shell

THE GIANT PEN SHELL
The pinna, or pen shell,
spends its life in an upright
position with its tapered
end half-buried in soft
bases, usually among weeds.
The giant pen shell, which
lives in the Mediterranean
Sea, is one of the largest
bivalve mollusks, reaching
a length of 2 ft (60 cm).

GIANT BATH
The enormous
tridacna shell houses an
animal that can feed up to
20 people! Common in
the Molucca islands, the
shell can be used as a
child's bathtub.

OPEN-AND-SHUT CASE
Although bivalves live
mainly with their valves
slightly apart, they must
be able to close the
gap quickly and
securely to protect
themselves from predators.
For this purpose, the two
halves of a bivalve shell
match perfectly. When the
valves clamp shut, the
former opening is as
impenetrable as the
rest of the shell.

Cock's-comb
oyster

Baby noble
pen shell

Spiny oyster
and cockle

Fluted giant clam

MINIATURE PEOPLE-EATERS
There are many different types and
sizes of clams, but the giant clam is
the biggest of all shelled mollusks.
Its valves can measure 4 ft (1.2 m),
and it can outweigh most people,
reaching weights of 550 lb (250 kg). These
huge shells are put to many uses, including
bathtubs and feeding troughs, and the shell
is so strong that it can be made into ax-
heads. Living clams are rumored to have
killed pearl divers by trapping their
arms or legs between the two valves.

Unusual partnerships

THERE ARE MANY TYPES OF RELATIONSHIPS in the animal world. A very familiar example is when one animal hunts and eats another. This is the predator–prey relationship, yet nature is rarely so black and white. On the seashore, as in other habitats, different kinds of animals regularly coexist in the relationship called parasitism. One partner, the parasite, gains, but the other, the host, loses. Some shore crabs are host to *Sacculina*, a strange creature related to barnacles. *Sacculina* attaches itself to a young crab and then grows "tentacles" that eat into the crab's body, nourishing itself but disabling the crab. Another type of relationship, called mutualism, allows both partners to benefit. The hermit crab (*Pagurus bernhardus*) and the calliactis anemone (*Calliactis parasitica*) live in this way. The calliactis is sometimes called the parasitic anemone, but it does not seem to harm its hermit crab host. It feeds on particles that the crab drops, while the crab is protected by the anemone's stinging tentacles.

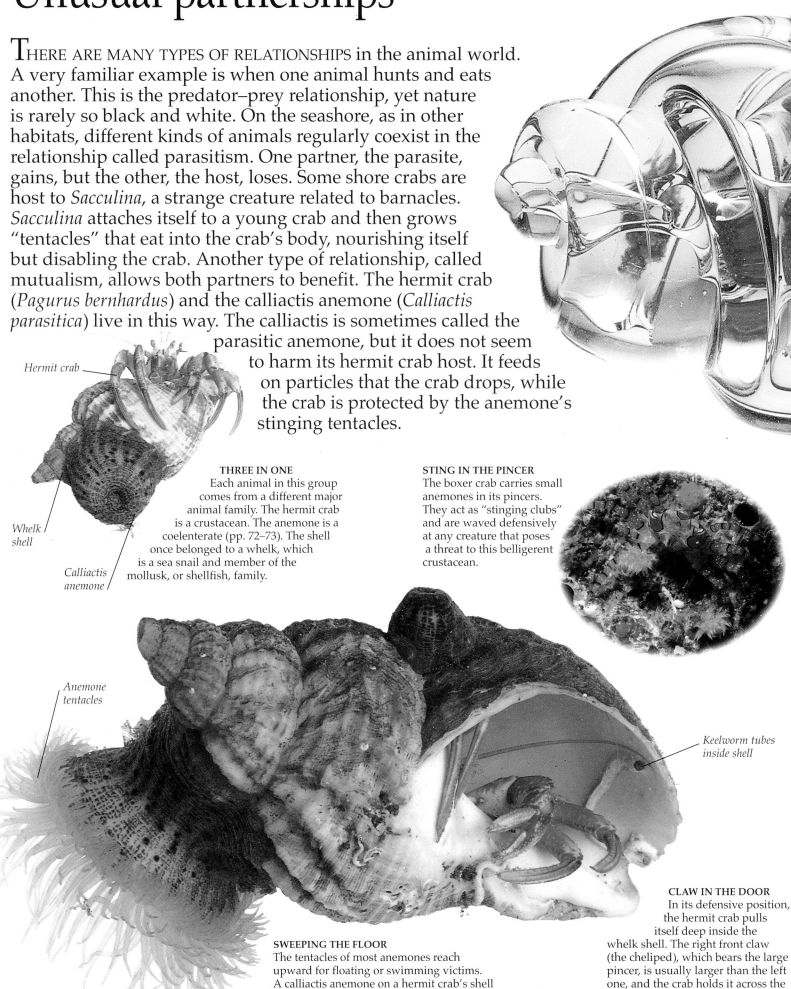

Hermit crab

Whelk shell

Calliactis anemone

Anemone tentacles

Keelworm tubes inside shell

THREE IN ONE
Each animal in this group comes from a different major animal family. The hermit crab is a crustacean. The anemone is a coelenterate (pp. 72–73). The shell once belonged to a whelk, which is a sea snail and member of the mollusk, or shellfish, family.

STING IN THE PINCER
The boxer crab carries small anemones in its pincers. They act as "stinging clubs" and are waved defensively at any creature that poses a threat to this belligerent crustacean.

SWEEPING THE FLOOR
The tentacles of most anemones reach upward for floating or swimming victims. A calliactis anemone on a hermit crab's shell tends to hang down and sweep the rocks for bits of food dropped by the hermit crab.

CLAW IN THE DOOR
In its defensive position, the hermit crab pulls itself deep inside the whelk shell. The right front claw (the cheliped), which bears the large pincer, is usually larger than the left one, and the crab holds it across the shell's entrance to make an effective barrier against predators.

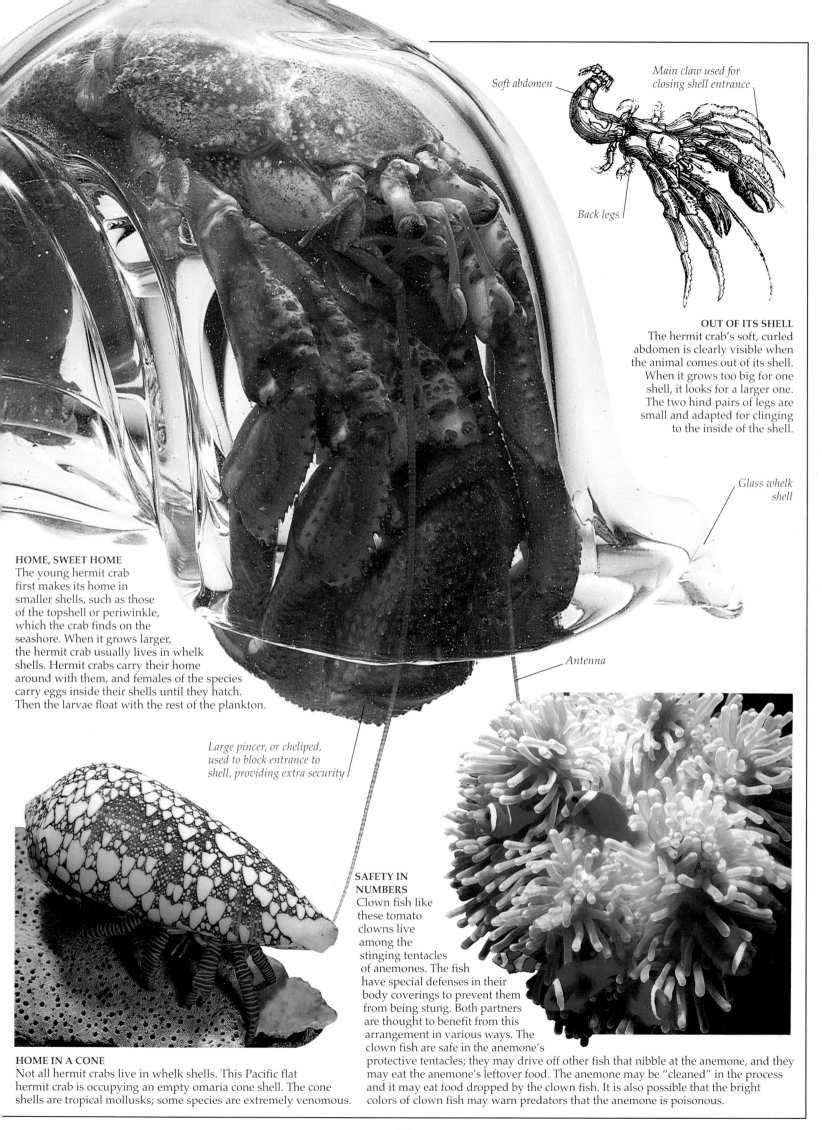

Soft abdomen

Main claw used for closing shell entrance

Back legs

OUT OF ITS SHELL
The hermit crab's soft, curled abdomen is clearly visible when the animal comes out of its shell. When it grows too big for one shell, it looks for a larger one. The two hind pairs of legs are small and adapted for clinging to the inside of the shell.

Glass whelk shell

HOME, SWEET HOME
The young hermit crab first makes its home in smaller shells, such as those of the topshell or periwinkle, which the crab finds on the seashore. When it grows larger, the hermit crab usually lives in whelk shells. Hermit crabs carry their home around with them, and females of the species carry eggs inside their shells until they hatch. Then the larvae float with the rest of the plankton.

Antenna

Large pincer, or cheliped, used to block entrance to shell, providing extra security

SAFETY IN NUMBERS
Clown fish like these tomato clowns live among the stinging tentacles of anemones. The fish have special defenses in their body coverings to prevent them from being stung. Both partners are thought to benefit from this arrangement in various ways. The clown fish are safe in the anemone's protective tentacles; they may drive off other fish that nibble at the anemone, and they may eat the anemone's leftover food. The anemone may be "cleaned" in the process and it may eat food dropped by the clown fish. It is also possible that the bright colors of clown fish may warn predators that the anemone is poisonous.

HOME IN A CONE
Not all hermit crabs live in whelk shells. This Pacific flat hermit crab is occupying an empty omaria cone shell. The cone shells are tropical mollusks; some species are extremely venomous.

Flowerlike animals

ANEMONES ARE THE SURPRISING "FLOWERS" of the shore – surprising because they are not flowers at all. They are hollow, jellylike animals belonging to the coelenterate group, also called the cnidarian group, which includes jellyfish and corals. Anemones are unable to move quickly, so they cannot pursue prey or escape from predators. Their best form of attack and defense lies in their "petals," which are really tentacles equipped with specialized stinging cells. Inside each cell is a capsule called a nematocyst that contains a long, coiled thread. In some species these are barbed, in others they contain venom. Stimulated by touch or by particular chemicals, the threads flick out and either hold on to prey with the barbs, or inject venom into it. The prey is then pulled through the mouth into a digestive cavity where it is absorbed. Any remains are excreted through the mouth.

Scallop shell

OPEN FOR DINNER
Anemones are beautiful but deadly. The waving tentacles of a colony are a forest of danger for any small sea creatures that float or swim near them.

Mouth in center of red beadlet anemone's body

TRAFFIC-LIGHT ANEMONES
Like flowers, anemones have evolved many beautiful colors even within the species. Beadlet anemones are found in various colors, including red, amber, and green. When the tide recedes, they fold in their tentacles and look like overgrown jujubes scattered on the rocks. When fully grown, beadlet anemones have about 200 tentacles.

SWEEPING THE SEA
Fan worms are sometimes mistaken for anemones, but they belong to a different group of animals – the annelids, which include earthworms. The tentacles of the "fan" filter tiny food particles from the water and withdraw into the tube if danger threatens.

"FLOWER" ON A "STALK"
A side view of a beadlet anemone shows that it has a stubby "stalk" (body) with an iridescent sheen around the base. Beadlets can survive out of water for some time, and can live very high up on the shoreline.

A grayish beadlet anemone

FEATHERY PLUMES
The plumose, or frilled, anemone is brown, reddish, or white, and may grow up to 1 ft (30 cm) tall. Its feathery tentacles catch very small bits of food and waft them down to the mouth by the beating action of tiny hairs called cilia.

*Snow-white tentacles
and brown body of a
beadlet anemone*

*Living cup coral
with tentacles
extended*

*Limy skeleton of
dead cup coral*

LIVING CORAL
Corals are similar to
anemones and members
of the same overall group,
the coelenterates. This cup
coral lives alone, unlike its (mostly)
tropical, reef-building cousins.

MEDUSA OF THE SEAS
Snakelock anemones range
from gray with delicate sheens of
pink or green to all-over deep green
in color. The tentacles, tipped in
deep pink, do not withdraw in this
species, even when it is out of water.

*The body "warts"
of this wartlet
anemone are
visible in this
closed-up
individual*

*Side view of dead
cup coral*

GIANT OF ITS KIND
The largest anemones may grow to
more than 3.3 ft (1 m) across. This is
a giant green anemone found in
tropical waters. It can move, if
only slowly, by sliding its
muscular base along the
rock surface.

TINY GHOSTS
There are many species
of these tiny, ghost-white
encrusting anemones, which
cover areas of rocky shore.
As the tide ebbs, most
anemones pull in their
tentacles and become
jellylike blobs to
avoid drying out.

*Encrusted remains
of barnacle shells*

*Coiled chalky
remains of
tube worm*

*Acontia (strings)
of stinging cells*

STINGING STRINGS
The colorful sagartia anemone
(this is the "rosea" variety) ejects
pale, stringy groups of stinging cells
through its mouth or through slits in its
body to defend itself or to catch a meal. The
"stings" are in fact parts of the animal's guts.

A fish in water

MOST FISH LIVE IN WATER, breathe by means of gills, swim and maneuver with fins, and are covered in an outer layer of transparent plates called scales. These scales vary in size and shape, but most are small and rounded, flexible, and single-layered. The skin underneath the scales produces a special mucus that makes the fish seem slimy and helps it glide easily through water. All fish are vertebrates – they have a backbone and an internal skeleton. They use color as a means of camouflage and defense, or to advertise a territory.

PEARLY SCALES
In the pearl-scaled butterfly fish, the yellow and orange colors, typical of butterfly fish, are limited to the tail end. The large pearly scales create a rainbow effect of color, and the fish's eye is camouflaged by a black stripe. The deep body but thin profile of the butterfly fish allow it to slip easily between plant stems.

Tall dorsal fins

Strong spines on back

Yellow dorsal fin of ribbon eel

Large, gaping mouth

Pectoral fin

Flat back because fish hangs just below surface, waiting for flies

Silver hatchetfish
Argyropelecus lychnus

FRESHWATER COUSIN
The silver hatchetfish, with its extraordinary deep belly, can leap from the water while beating its large pectoral fins and "fly" short distances, skimming the surface of the water. It is a freshwater fish found in South America; other hatchetfish live in the deep sea.

HUNGRY PREDATOR
The European John Dory has a deep body but is extremely thin. It creeps up on smaller fish and prawns, keeping head on to make itself look inconspicuous. Then its great jaws suddenly lever forward and engulf the prey. The John Dory is well protected by the sets of spines in front of its dorsal and anal fins.

European John Dory
Zeus faber

IN SHOALS
Young cod feed at the surface on small crustaceans. The adults feed in deeper water on small fish, crustaceans, and worms. They swim in shoals, making it hard for predators to target an individual.

74

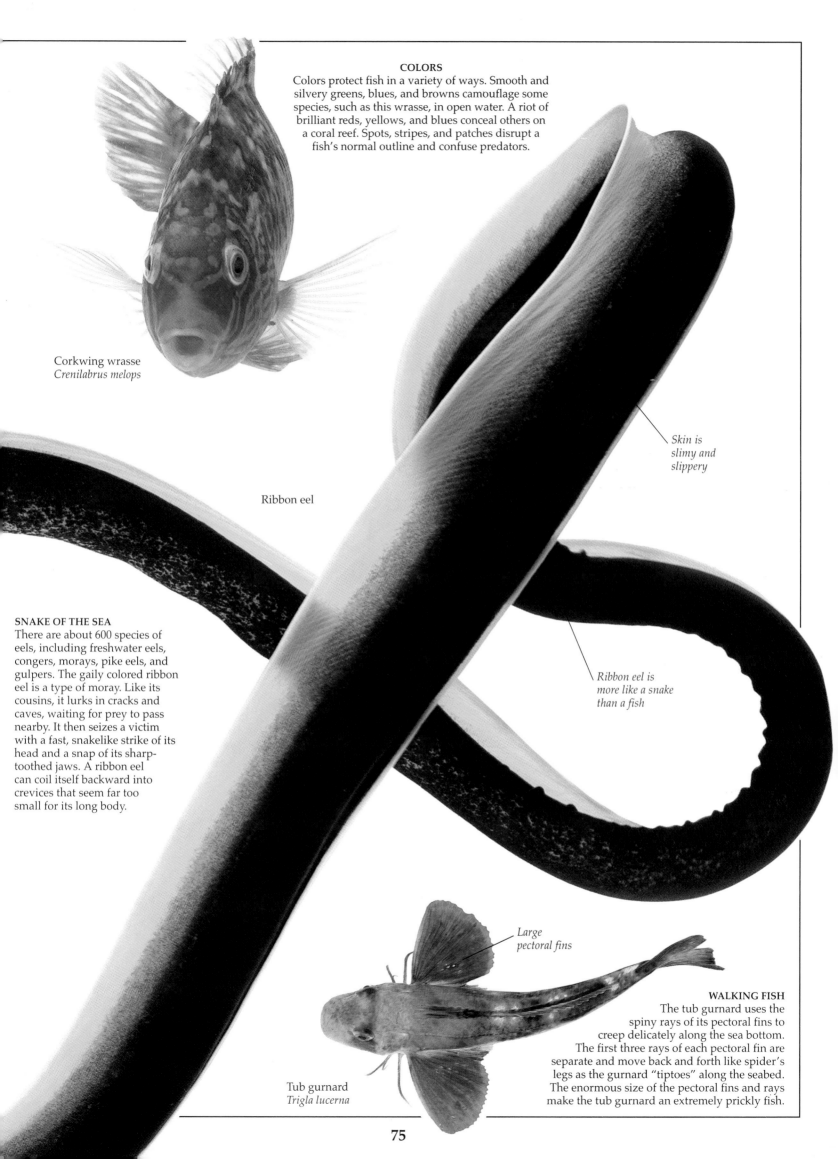

COLORS
Colors protect fish in a variety of ways. Smooth and silvery greens, blues, and browns camouflage some species, such as this wrasse, in open water. A riot of brilliant reds, yellows, and blues conceal others on a coral reef. Spots, stripes, and patches disrupt a fish's normal outline and confuse predators.

Corkwing wrasse
Crenilabrus melops

Ribbon eel

Skin is slimy and slippery

Ribbon eel is more like a snake than a fish

SNAKE OF THE SEA
There are about 600 species of eels, including freshwater eels, congers, morays, pike eels, and gulpers. The gaily colored ribbon eel is a type of moray. Like its cousins, it lurks in cracks and caves, waiting for prey to pass nearby. It then seizes a victim with a fast, snakelike strike of its head and a snap of its sharp-toothed jaws. A ribbon eel can coil itself backward into crevices that seem far too small for its long body.

Large pectoral fins

WALKING FISH
The tub gurnard uses the spiny rays of its pectoral fins to creep delicately along the sea bottom. The first three rays of each pectoral fin are separate and move back and forth like spider's legs as the gurnard "tiptoes" along the seabed. The enormous size of the pectoral fins and rays make the tub gurnard an extremely prickly fish.

Tub gurnard
Trigla lucerna

Moving along

FLYING FISH
Gathering speed underwater, flying fish leap clear of the surface to escape predators. They can then glide for more than 30 seconds by spreading out side fins.

EVERY SWIMMER KNOWS that moving through seawater is harder than moving through air. To be a fast, powerful swimmer like a dolphin, tuna, or sailfish, it also helps to have a streamlined shape to reduce drag (resistance to water). A smooth skin and few projections from the body allow an animal to move through the water more easily. The density of seawater has an advantage too, in that it helps support the weight of very heavy bodies, such as the heaviest animal to ever live on Earth, the blue whale, which weighs up to 165 tons (150 tonnes). Some heavy-shelled creatures, like the chambered nautilus, have gas-filled floats to buoy them. Some ocean animals, such as dolphins and flying fish, gather enough speed underwater to leap briefly into the air, but not all ocean animals are good swimmers. Many can only swim slowly, others drift along in the currents, crawl along the bottom, burrow in the sand, or simply stay put, anchored to the seabed.

AT SCHOOL
Fish often swim together in schools, like these blue-striped snappers. In schools, a single fish is less likely to be attacked by a predator than if it was swimming on its own. The moving mass of individuals may confuse the predator, and there are more pairs of eyes on the lookout for an attacker.

IN THE SWING
During the day, many electric rays prefer to stay hidden on the sandy bottom, relying on their electric organs for defense, but they do swim if disturbed and at night, when searching for prey. There are more than 30 kinds of electric rays, mostly living in warm waters. Most other rays have spindly tails (unlike the electric ray's broad tail) and move through water using their pectoral fins. Waves pass from the front to the back of the pectoral fins, that, in larger rays like mantas, become so exaggerated the fins actually beat up and down like watery wings.

Spiracle (a one-way valve) takes in water, which is pumped out through gill slits

Electric ray's smooth skin can be either dark green or brown

Electric rays can grow to 6 ft (1.8 m) and weigh as much as 110 lb (50 kg)

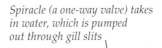

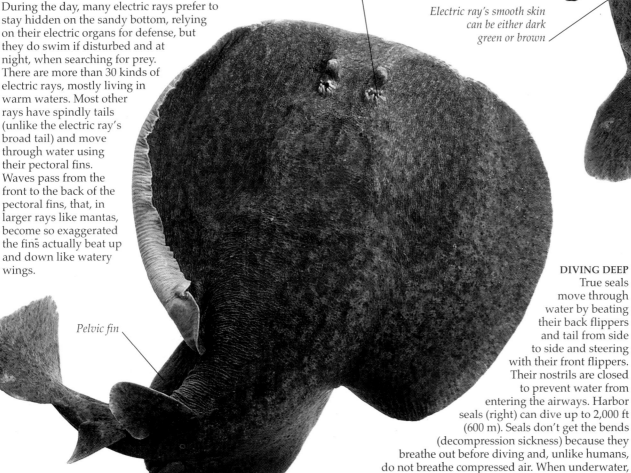

Pelvic fin

DIVING DEEP
True seals move through water by beating their back flippers and tail from side to side and steering with their front flippers. Their nostrils are closed to prevent water from entering the airways. Harbor seals (right) can dive up to 2,000 ft (600 m). Seals don't get the bends (decompression sickness) because they breathe out before diving and, unlike humans, do not breathe compressed air. When underwater, seals use oxygen that is stored in their blood.

Broad tail fin, swinging from side to side, helps propel ray along

Pectoral fin provides extra propulsion as waves pass along flexible edges of its rounded side

Smaller second dorsal fin

Clasper (male reproductive organ)

Swimming sequence of an electric ray
Torpedo nobiliana

Electric organ, at base of pectoral fin, helps catch fish by stunning them – some species can deliver more than 200 volts

Model of great white shark
Carcharodon carcharias

TAKING OFF
Dolphins leap out of the water for fun, to signal to other dolphins, and when feeding. They can also porpoise (skim over the water for short distances) when moving quickly. They do this because it is easier to move in air, which puts less friction on their bodies.

Tall dorsal fin

Pectoral fin

Pelvic fin

Tail propels shark forward in water

Starry smooth-hound
Mustelus asterias

Undulations (S-shaped waves) pass down body, ending at the tail, which produces forward thrust

LEAN MACHINE
Sharks propel themselves through the water by beating their tails from side to side. The pectoral fins are held out away from the body. As water flows over them, the fins act like airplane wings and keep the shark from sinking. When the fins are tilted, they also act as brakes, just like the raised flaps on the wings of an airplane during landing. Some sharks that live on the seabed, such as horn sharks and epaulette sharks, use their pectoral fins to crawl along the ocean floor.

Mobile mollusks

MOLLUSKS ARE A LARGE GROUP of animals that includes cephalopods (octopuses, squid, and cuttlefish), bivalves (scallops, mussels, and oysters), and gastropods (snails, limpets, and abalones). Cephalopods move by jet propulsion. They have a small shell or no shell, and a muscular body wall that can expel water. Bivalves have a shell that is in two halves, and some, such as scallops, also "swim" using jet propulsion. Most clams, however, can only bury themselves in the sand or are anchored to the seabed. Gastropods usually have a coiled external shell, although some, like slugs, have a small internal shell or no shell at all. They travel by moving the muscles of their single, flat foot.

MOVING LIKE A SNAIL
Great pond snails move slowly, on a single, large, flat foot, among water plants looking for food. The muscles of the foot move in and out in waves, and the snail moves forward as each wave passes along the foot. Special glands produce a slime that helps the foot glide smoothly along.

INK SCREEN
Cephalopods like this squid produce a cloud of ink when threatened. This confuses an enemy and allows the squid to escape. The ink is produced in a gland linked to the gut and is ejected in a blast of water from the tubelike funnel near the squid's head.

JET PROPULSION
Squid are very efficient at swimming by jet propulsion. Their torpedo-shaped bodies are naturally streamlined so that they can swim fast to escape predators. It may be no coincidence that they are among the most common animals in the ocean.

Squid
Loligo forbisi

Tentacle, also known as "leg" or "arm"

Two rows of suckers under each tentacle

Powerful suckers grip rocky surfaces so octopus can pull itself along or hold prey

Funnel, or siphon, through which octopus squeezes water when swimming

Eye with horizontal iris

Common octopus
Octopus vulgaris

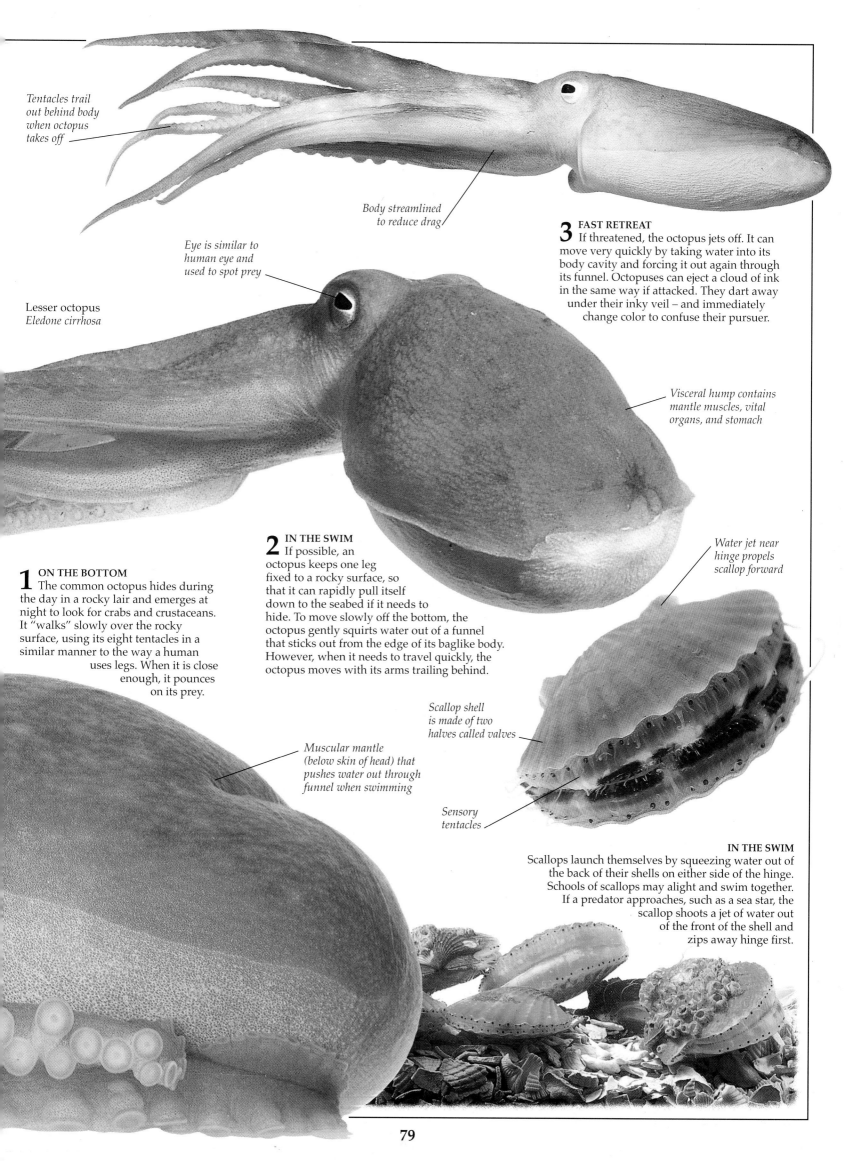

Tentacles trail
out behind body
when octopus
takes off

Body streamlined
to reduce drag

Eye is similar to
human eye and
used to spot prey

Lesser octopus
Eledone cirrhosa

3 FAST RETREAT
If threatened, the octopus jets off. It can
move very quickly by taking water into its
body cavity and forcing it out again through
its funnel. Octopuses can eject a cloud of ink
in the same way if attacked. They dart away
under their inky veil – and immediately
change color to confuse their pursuer.

Visceral hump contains
mantle muscles, vital
organs, and stomach

2 IN THE SWIM
If possible, an
octopus keeps one leg
fixed to a rocky surface, so
that it can rapidly pull itself
down to the seabed if it needs to
hide. To move slowly off the bottom, the
octopus gently squirts water out of a funnel
that sticks out from the edge of its baglike body.
However, when it needs to travel quickly, the
octopus moves with its arms trailing behind.

Water jet near
hinge propels
scallop forward

1 ON THE BOTTOM
The common octopus hides during
the day in a rocky lair and emerges at
night to look for crabs and crustaceans.
It "walks" slowly over the rocky
surface, using its eight tentacles in a
similar manner to the way a human
uses legs. When it is close
enough, it pounces
on its prey.

Scallop shell
is made of two
halves called valves

Muscular mantle
(below skin of head) that
pushes water out through
funnel when swimming

Sensory
tentacles

IN THE SWIM
Scallops launch themselves by squeezing water out of
the back of their shells on either side of the hinge.
Schools of scallops may alight and swim together.
If a predator approaches, such as a sea star, the
scallop shoots a jet of water out
of the front of the shell and
zips away hinge first.

The importance of water

WATER IS AN ESSENTIAL PART of an amphibian's double life. Amphibians need fresh water to keep their skin moist, and most amphibious species need a watery environment to reproduce – especially those that spend all, or part, of their lives as larvae in water. In aquatic or watery habitats, water passes rapidly through the skin and has to be eliminated via the kidneys. In dry areas, amphibians risk losing more water than they can absorb. Frogs can reduce water loss by having a less porous skin, by seeking out damp, shady places, by burrowing, and by absorbing water from damp or wet surfaces. Some toads obtain almost three-quarters of the water they need through a baggy patch, or "seat," on their pelvis that they press against moist surfaces. Amphibians rarely drink water, although a little water may be consumed as part of their food. They have adapted their behavior and skin-surface structure to a surprising variety of habitats, from ponds and trees to high in the forest canopy where the only free-standing water collects in pockets formed by leaves. They have also adapted to life in the desert by burrowing and forming heat-sparing and water-conserving cocoons.

FLOWER POWER
Amphibians are popular subjects for stories. *Thumbelina* is a children's story about a flower fairy stolen by a toad who wants her to marry his ugly son. The toad imprisons Thumbelina on a lily pad in the middle of a river, but she escapes (with the help of fish) and eventually marries the Prince of the Flower People.

Female crested newt
Triturus cristatus

Young tiger salamander
Ambystoma tigrinum
with gills

BREATHING UNDERWATER
The larva of the tiger salamander uses its three pairs of large, feathery gills to breathe underwater. The deep red gills are rich in blood vessels, which absorb the dissolved air from the water.

WET AND DRY
Great crested newts spend most of the year on land, returning to the water to breed in spring. Once in the water they shed their dry, warty skin to reveal a new, smoother one.

One of three pairs of gills

Sequence of Australian
water-holding frog
Cyclorana platycephalus
burrowing

A CAVE SALAMANDER
The cave-dwelling olm lives in cold, underground streams along the Adriatic coast of Italy and Croatia. It is a sexually mature larva like the axolotl (see below), but unlike the axolotl, it will not grow to adulthood if iodine is added to the water, or if it is given hormones.

1 BURROWING
Like many other amphibians, the Australian water-holding frog burrows deep into the ground to avoid drying out. In an underground chamber, the frog survives long droughts in desert conditions.

Olm ranges in length
from 8–12 in (20–30 cm)

LIFE AND ART
Frogs are often used in ornaments and designs, like this frog-shaped flagon made in China during the 16th century.

2 STAYING UNDERGROUND
In the underground chamber, the moisture level is higher and the surrounding temperature is lower than outside. The frog also stores water in its bladder.

3 COMING UP FOR AIR
The frog sheds the outer layers of its skin to form a cocoon, drastically reducing water loss. The frog emerges to eat and breed when the rainy season comes.

*Flagon used
to hold water*

*Adult lives on dry land in
leaf litter or small burrows*

California newt
Taricha torosa
ranges in length
from 5–8 in
(13–20 cm)

*Powerful
back leg*

*Full
webbing
on foot*

AN UNDERWATER LIFE
The African clawed toad spends most of its life in water, only coming on to land to migrate to nearby ponds or lakes where it spawns. Its flattened head and body, powerful back legs, and webbed feet make this toad an excellent swimmer.

CALIFORNIA NEWT
This newt lays a round clump of 12–24 eggs on underwater plants in late winter or early spring. The young newts leave the water the next fall or early spring.

*Feathery
red gills*

WATER BABY
In some species of newts and salamanders, larvae never develop into adults. Instead they remain in the water and become sexually mature in the larval state. This is known as "neoteny." Neoteny may be caused by something in the environment, such as low water temperature, or a low level of iodine in the water. The axolotl (left) is the best-known example of a neotenous larva.

*Flat
body*

Young
albino
African
clawed toad
Xenopus larvis

Axolotl
Ambystoma mexicanus

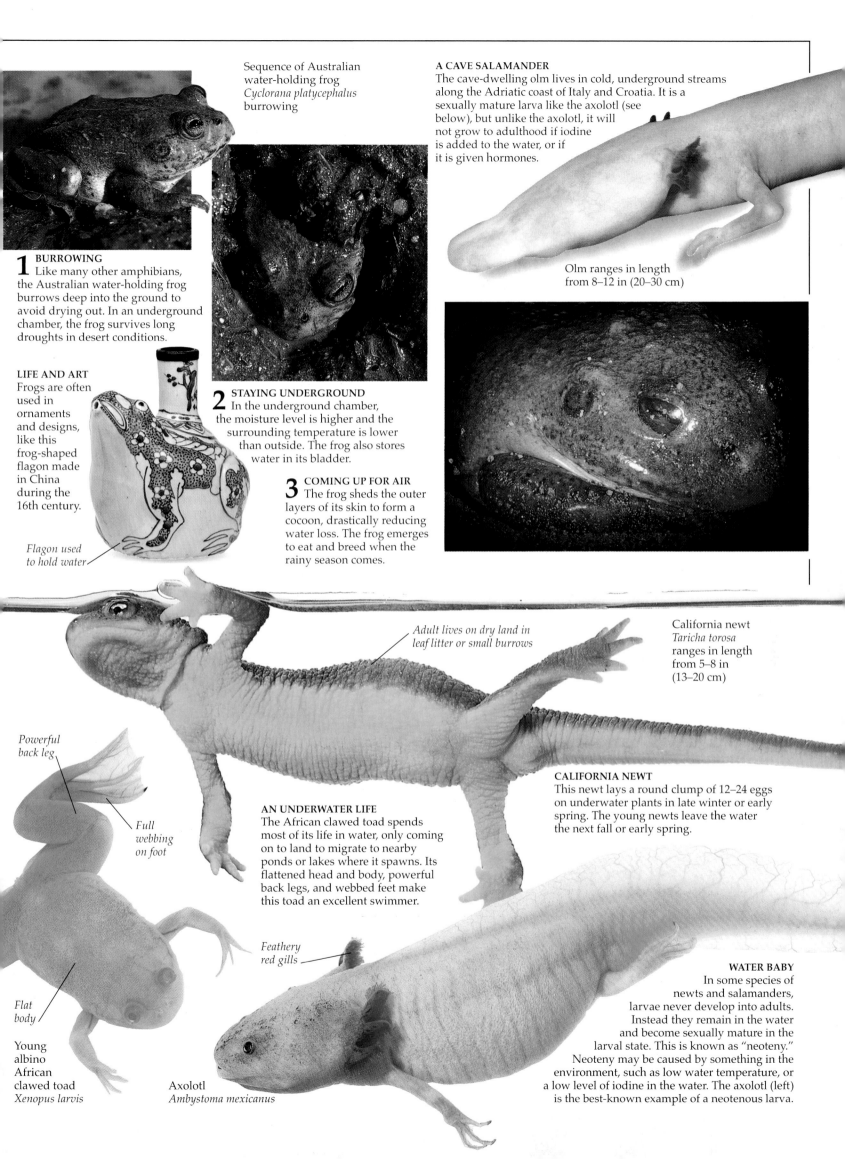

On all fours

NEWTS AND SALAMANDERS usually move very slowly. They walk or crawl – on land, underground, in the trees, or on pond bottoms – but they can move quickly to escape danger. Some salamanders that live in grasses, on low bushes, and even high up in the trees have stubby, webbed feet for gripping leaves. Certain species can also burrow or swim: mole and tiger salamanders burrow with their hands and feet, and the male aquatic newt performs a swimming courtship display in front of the female. In this, they are like another relatively unknown group of amphibians – the wormlike, legless caecilians. Most of the 170 species of caecilians are burrowers, but one group actually lives in water.

SWIMMING NEWT
Swimming involves many different leg, body, and tail movements. Newts float with their legs outstretched and bodies slightly inflated with air. Slow, lazy, swimming movements use the legs like oars in a two-person rowboat. To move faster, newts paddle with their front legs alone, with their hind legs, or sometimes with both together.

Japanese fire-bellied newt

Foot in forward position ready for next step

Tail is straight

Foot presses against ground, pushing body forward

Foot pushes body forward

Tail curves to right, helping salamander balance

Foot in forward position ready to press against ground and push forward

Foot moves forward

Front foot pushes body forward

1 ONWARD AND UPWARD
The European fire salamander walks slowly, like most salamanders. The legs move in an alternate and opposite pattern: the salamander lifts and moves the front foot of one side forward at the same time as the hind foot on the other side of its body. The other two feet remain on the ground, pushing the body forward, ready for the next step.

Foot ready to lift
for next step

Foot about
to push body
forward

Foot
ready to
push body
forward

Foot about to
lift and move
forward

3 FORWARD MARCH
The third step completes the
sequence, with the left front and
right hind feet together and the
other two feet stationary. In addition
to pushing the salamander forward,
this alternate and opposite pattern
pushes the middle of its body from side
to side. The swaying motion increases with
walking speed and looks like a crawling baby.

Foot ready to lift
and move forward

UNDULATING CAECILIANS
Most caecilians live in soft earth or in the leaf litter of the rain
forest floor. About 20 species have moved back into the water
and swim using undulating, wavelike movements. All caecilians
can burrow by pushing their head into the soil and opening up
a hole with movements of the neck. Then they either "swim"
forward through the soil with undulating movements that pass
back along the body, or use a special, wormlike concertina
movement, in which the spine folds inside the body.

Foot in
forward
position

2 NEXT STEP
With the next step, the front right and left
hind feet of the salamander move together, while
the other two feet stay in the same position on the
ground, getting ready to push the body forward.

Foot pressing on
surface, ready to
push body forward

Foot about
to lift

Foot ready to
lift and move
body forward

Foot
pressing down

NEWT WALK
When moving at slow speed on land, newts and salamanders walk
in similar ways. This view from beneath shows which foot is actively
pressing against the surface, pushing the newt forward, and which is
being lifted off the surface before being set down again. In water, the
newt is lighter and more buoyant (just as a person is in a swimming
pool) and often uses just the tips of its fingers and
toes to walk over the muddy
bottom of its pond.

View from below of a
newt walking

Foot
ready
to lift
and move
body forward

A tight squeeze

ALL SNAKES EAT MEAT, but they have had to develop many different ways of killing their food. Some kill their prey with venom, but boas and pythons feed mainly on mammals, which they kill by constriction. Constrictors do not crush their victims, as you might think. The snake coils its body around its struggling victim, making it harder and harder for the prey to breathe, until it finally suffocates. The snake applies just enough pressure to match the breathing movements of the prey. Any mammal from a mouse to a deer could be that prey, depending on the size of the snake. Giant snakes can swallow surprisingly large animals: an anaconda more than 26 ft (8 m) long can eat a caiman nearly 6.5 ft (2 m) long – it can take more than a week to digest its meal!

TO THE RESCUE!
Only a few Asian and African records exist of humans who have been killed and eaten by some of the larger species of pythons. In one of the famous Tintin books, Zorrino the guide makes a lucky escape (contrary to appearances), saved just in the nick of time by his friend, the redoubtable Tintin.

DANGEROUS ACT
Sideshow and circus performers who dance with constrictors do so at great risk. This dancer was nearly suffocated by a python, and was rescued only seconds before certain death.

2 DEADLY EMBRACE
The constricting snake reacts to every tiny movement of the rat, always tightening its grip. It responds to even the smallest vibrations produced by the rat's beating heart; the snake will not release its hold until the beating finally stops. Death is fairly quick and bones are rarely broken. The snake then shifts the rat so that it can be swallowed headfirst.

3 BIG MOUTH
The snake's mouth is very flexible. The jaws move easily together from side to side, while the backward-pointing teeth grip tightly. As the powerful jaws move over the rat's head, it looks like the snake is "walking over" its food.

4 SAFETY FIRST
A small animal can disappear completely in only one or two gulps, but it takes an hour or more for some of the larger victims. The swallowing action of the snake is mainly automatic, and the prey is drawn in by the trunk muscles of the snake. If the snake is frightened or disturbed while it is eating, it can regurgitate its meal in order to escape.

5 TIGHT FIT
Most of the rat has disappeared. A flexible ligament, an elastic muscle that connects both halves of the snake's lower jaw, allows the snake to open its mouth very wide. As the lower jaws are forced apart, the muscle between them stretches to accomodate the shape of the prey.

Body can expand to allow for large prey

Dinnertime

If a meal walks by that might put up a fight, a snake can usually afford to ignore it. After an enormous feast, when a constrictor might work its way through an entire leopard, the snake may not eat again for as much as a year.

1 FANGS OF DEATH

When a boa constrictor attacks prey, it has to find somewhere it can start swallowing, usually at the head. If the victim is wriggly, like this rat, the snake strikes with its long, front teeth. With the rat secure in its jaws, the boa starts to coil around it.

Prey is swallowed headfirst so that it cannot attack the snake

Special hinged bone

Jaw closed

Jaw open

OPEN WIDE

The jaws of a snake are very flexible so that prey can be swallowed headfirst and whole, even when the victim's body is wider than the snake's. A special bone, linking the lower jaw to the skull, works like a double-jointed hinge. The lower jaw can stretch sideways because the two halves are connected at the chin by a flexible ligament that works like an elastic muscle.

SNAKE EATS SNAKE

When a California king snake meets a rattlesnake, it grips the rattler with its jaws just behind the head. Then the king snake loops its body around the victim, squeezing until the rattler suffocates.

WILD CAT STRIKE

In Kenya, a Thompson's gazelle falls victim to a cheetah. The massive jaws of the cat clamp on to the throat of the struggling prey, probably causing it to suffocate in the same way a boa suffocates its prey. It is probably finished off by the sharp teeth and claws of the cheetah.

Rat's tail

6 END OF THE ROAD

At this point the snake could be faced with breathing problems, but it overcomes them by pushing its windpipe forward toward the front of its mouth, using its windpipe as a built-in "snorkel."

Lizards

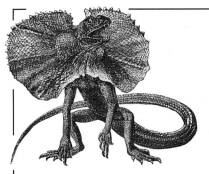

FIERCE FRILLS
The frilled lizard of the Australian desert spreads out the frill around its neck to make itself look larger to scare away enemies. The frill is supported by rods (like an umbrella's) that are attached to a bone at the base of the tongue.

THERE ARE MORE THAN 3,000 species of lizards. They form the most successful of all the reptilian groups, having evolved many different lifestyles. Although most of them live on the ground, many live in trees, some are burrowers, and some are aquatic. Some lizards have no limbs and are snakelike; others can parachute or fly. The lizards on these two pages all live in desert regions, where they are more numerous than snakes. They like to bask in the sun in the early morning to warm up their muscles after a cold desert night. In the heat of the day, they retreat into the shade of rocks or plants or into cool burrows. Most desert lizards can change color to blend into their backgrounds and avoid being spotted by predators. When threatened, some lizards put on intimidating displays. If this does not work, then some lizards will bite, but most simply run away.

Fringe of scales on toe

FRINGE TOES
This fast-moving lizard can run across the sand dunes in the Sahara, where it lives. It has a fringe of scales on its feet that acts like a snowshoe to spread its weight and prevent it from sinking into the sand. To stay cooler on hot sand, it holds its head and body high above the surface of the ground.

Tail and opposing toes grip plants as chameleon climbs

CHAMELEON
A chameleon sits on the stem of a welwitschia plant growing in the Namib Desert. Chameleons and other lizards are attracted to the plant because insects like to shelter under the shade of its leaves. They catch the insects by shooting out their long, sticky-tipped tongues.

GILA MONSTER
The Gila monster is one of only two lizards with a venomous bite, although it is seldom fatal to humans. Gila monsters live in desert scrub and are mainly active at night, feeding on small mammals, snakes, and other lizards.

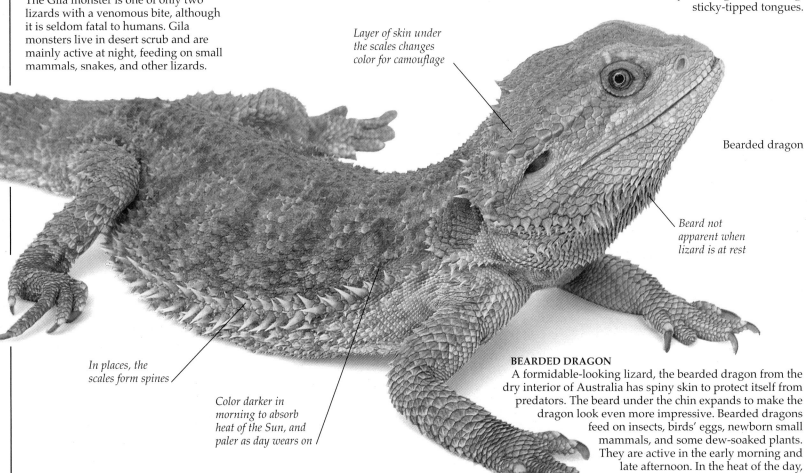

Layer of skin under the scales changes color for camouflage

Bearded dragon

Beard not apparent when lizard is at rest

In places, the scales form spines

Color darker in morning to absorb heat of the Sun, and paler as day wears on

BEARDED DRAGON
A formidable-looking lizard, the bearded dragon from the dry interior of Australia has spiny skin to protect itself from predators. The beard under the chin expands to make the dragon look even more impressive. Bearded dragons feed on insects, birds' eggs, newborn small mammals, and some dew-soaked plants. They are active in the early morning and late afternoon. In the heat of the day, they climb into shrubs, where it is cooler.

*Sturdy tail
serves as a
fat reserve*

LIZARD EGGS
These eggs belong to the eyed lizard
from northern Africa. It lays up to
20 eggs in sandy soil, which
hatch out two to three months
later. Eyed lizards grow more
than 2 ft (60 cm) long. These
large lizards feed on insects,
small mammals, and
other reptiles.

SPINY-TAILED, OR DAB, LIZARD
One of the hardiest desert lizards in the
Sahara, the African spiny-tailed lizard
tolerates high temperatures and
survives on small amounts of water
obtained from dew and the plants and few
insects that it eats. This lizard is active in
the day, but avoids the midday heat
by staying deep in its burrow.

THORNY DEVIL
A spiny body helps
protect this lizard
from being attacked. It lives in the
deserts in Australia and has a similar
ant-eating lifestyle to horned toads.
Thorny devils collect rain or dew on
their backs, which finds its way
down tiny channels into their
mouths. These lizards are
also known as molochs.

*Keen sense of smell
helps lizard hunt*

*Wide gape to
deter predators*

Collared lizard
Crotophytus collaris

*The collared lizard can
inflict a nasty bite
with its sharp teeth*

COLLARED LIZARD
In a defensive pose, the collared lizard opens
its mouth in a wide gape. If attacked, the lizard will
bite, but it would rather leap away over the rocks where
it lives in the deserts of the southwestern United States.
The collared lizard is an active predator. It hunts
during the day for insects, smaller lizards, and
small snakes and mice. Highly agile, it can
even leap into the air to catch flying insects.

*Sharp claws
for gripping
rocks*

Birds of a feather

THERE ARE MORE THAN 9,000 species of birds in the world – flying and flightless, brightly colored and dull-hued, huge like the ostrich, or tiny like the hummingbird. Birds are the only creatures to have feathers, and these are lightweight, strong, and flexible. Birds also have two wings, a strong bill, no teeth, scaly legs and feet, and three or four toes with claws on the ends. Like mammals, birds breathe air, have a skeleton, and are warm-blooded. Unlike most mammals, they lay eggs. Bird colors help individuals of the same species identify each other, and they also help birds attract mates, threaten rivals, or camouflage themselves.

WADER
The black crake of East Africa has long, widely spaced toes to stop it from sinking into mud and to help it walk over floating water plants. The short, thick bill is used to peck small invertebrates and seeds off the surface of the water.

FLIGHTLESS
The brown kiwi, *Apteryx Australis*, is a medium-sized flightless bird that lives in New Zealand. It is nocturnal and eats worms, beetles, grubs, and berries, which it finds by smelling with the nostrils at the end of its long bill.

Zebra finch
Taeniopygia guttata

Short, seed-eating bill

Distinctive stripes around bill

SEED EATER
The colorful zebra finch lives on the dry grasslands of Australia, where it is one of the most common birds. Pairs of these gregarious birds mate for life, living in flocks of between 10 to 100 birds, and breeding within the group. In drier areas, they lay eggs whenever it is warm enough and there is enough rain to sustain their young. Zebra finches are perching birds as well as strong fliers. They feed on grass seeds and insects and are well known as songbirds.

Mandarin duck
Aix galericulata

Female

Short legs set well back on body

Male

Powerful grip for perching

WATERBIRD
Mandarin ducks live near ponds and lakes surrounded by woods, where they nest in tree holes. Like many other bird species, the male is more colorful than the female. However, once a year the mandarin molts his feathers, and at this time the female is the one who receives attention. Ducks have webbed feet and broad, flat bills.

DIVING BIRD
Great white pelicans live in swamps and marshes, and usually fish in groups, making a circle and herding the fish together so they can scoop them up. A pelican's bill can hold more food than its stomach, and the bird has a daily intake of more than 2 lb (1 kg). Pelicans can hold prey in their throat pouches in order to transport it back to their nests.

Great white pelican
Pelecanus onocrotabus

Powerful hooked bill used to tear prey into bite-sized pieces

Golden eagle
Aquila chrysaetos

Large, webbed feet

BIRD OF PREY
Like all other birds of prey, the golden eagle uses its talons to catch and carry prey and its sharp, hooked bill to pull apart the animals it kills. It hunts for medium-sized mammals and birds, and will scavenge on carcasses as well. It is a very good flier, and the most numerous large eagle in the northern hemisphere. It makes its nest, called an eyrie, out of branches on high crags and rocky places. The eagle is named after the golden feathers on the top of its head and the back of its neck.

Broad, rounded wings

Golden eagles can be 39 in (79 cm) tall

Sharp talons to hold prey

Primary flight feathers, used for power and steering

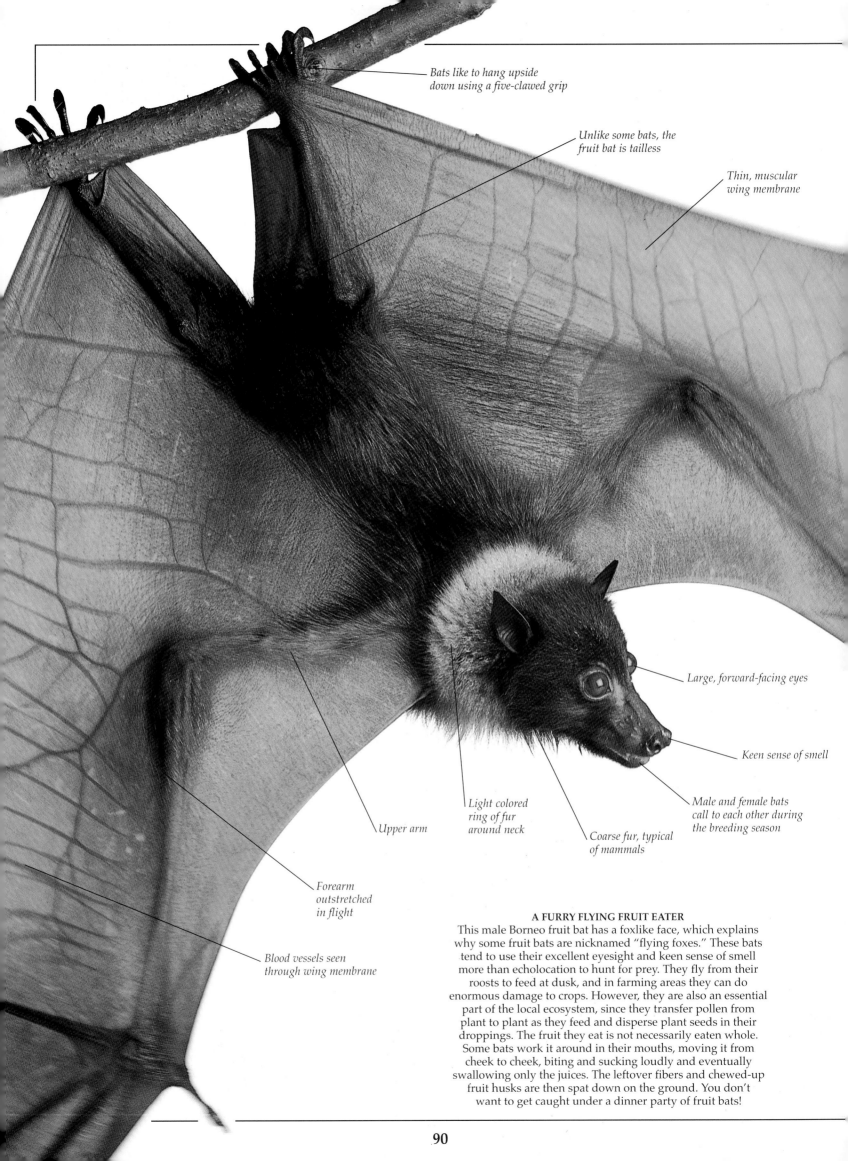

Bats like to hang upside
down using a five-clawed grip

Unlike some bats, the
fruit bat is tailless

Thin, muscular
wing membrane

Large, forward-facing eyes

Keen sense of smell

Male and female bats
call to each other during
the breeding season

Light colored
ring of fur
around neck

Coarse fur, typical
of mammals

Upper arm

Forearm
outstretched
in flight

Blood vessels seen
through wing membrane

A FURRY FLYING FRUIT EATER
This male Borneo fruit bat has a foxlike face, which explains
why some fruit bats are nicknamed "flying foxes." These bats
tend to use their excellent eyesight and keen sense of smell
more than echolocation to hunt for prey. They fly from their
roosts to feed at dusk, and in farming areas they can do
enormous damage to crops. However, they are also an essential
part of the local ecosystem, since they transfer pollen from
plant to plant as they feed and disperse plant seeds in their
droppings. The fruit they eat is not necessarily eaten whole.
Some bats work it around in their mouths, moving it from
cheek to cheek, biting and sucking loudly and eventually
swallowing only the juices. The leftover fibers and chewed-up
fruit husks are then spat down on the ground. You don't
want to get caught under a dinner party of fruit bats!

Fliers in the night

BATS ARE UNIQUE in that they are the only mammals that can truly fly. They are second only to rodents as the most numerous mammal species – there are about 950 different kinds. Bats vary enormously in size, ranging from the tiny hog-nosed bat, which measures just 5 in (13 cm) with its wings outstetched, to the large flying fox, which is the size of a small dog and has a wingspan of 6.5 ft (2 m). Bats' wings are made of thin, skin-covered sheets of muscle and elastic fibers. The bones of the arm and the second to fifth fingers support the wing. The first finger, or "thumb," sticks out like a claw and can be used to crawl, groom, fight, or hold food. Some bats can fly faster than 30 mph (50 km/h). Their wings are powered by the same muscles we use to "flap" our arms, but the bat's muscles are much stronger in proportion to the size of its body. Bats are some of the most sociable mammals. They roost together by the thousands in caves or trees, and some species help each other in the nightly hunt for food.

PEGASUS
People have always been fascinated by the possibility of flight. Observation of animals such as bats has led to the invention of many fanciful creatures, including the mythical flying horse Pegasus.

5th finger
4th finger
3rd finger
2nd finger
1st finger

OTHER FLIERS
Although bats are the only mammals capable of winged flight, other mammals – flying squirrels, opossums and flying lemurs – glide on the air. They use a membrane that acts as a kind of parachute.

MOTHER AND CHILD
A baby bat clings to its mother's furry abdomen and drinks milk, just like any other mammal.

FROM MOTHS TO BUDS TO BLOOD
Most bats are insectivores, eating moths, midges, flies, and other nocturnal insects. This fruit bat feeds on buds and the soft parts of plants. Vampire bats bite mammals and birds to drink their blood, but do not usually attack humans.

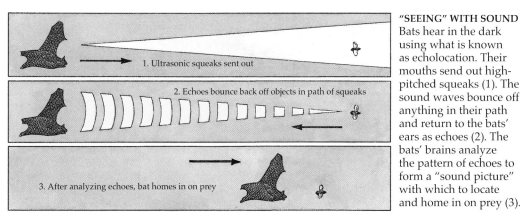

1. Ultrasonic squeaks sent out

2. Echoes bounce back off objects in path of squeaks

3. After analyzing echoes, bat homes in on prey

"SEEING" WITH SOUND
Bats hear in the dark using what is known as echolocation. Their mouths send out high-pitched squeaks (1). The sound waves bounce off anything in their path and return to the bats' ears as echoes (2). The bats' brains analyze the pattern of echoes to form a "sound picture" with which to locate and home in on prey (3).

FUNCTIONAL FACES
The curved flaps on the noses of horseshoe bats and leaf-nosed bats help with echolocation. A long, hairy tongue is useful for catching insects.

Horseshoe bat

Leaf-nosed bat

Bat with hair-fringed tongue

Rodent success

RODENTS ARE GREAT survivors. They have the ability to adapt to changing circumstances and environments, and are very good at protecting and defending themselves. Rodents make up the order Rodentia, which is the largest order of mammals, with more than 1,700 species, including squirrels, chipmunks, rats, beavers, and gerbils. Rodents usually have two incisors in each jaw, short forelimbs for manipulating food, and cheek pouches for storing food. Like other mammals, rodents have furry coats to keep them warm and dry, and they groom themselves and each other regularly to get rid of parasites and dirt. Many rodents live underground in burrows because there temperatures do not fluctuate as much as they do at surface level. Desert rodents, such as the pallid gerbil, escape the extreme heat of the day in a cool burrow, and during the cold desert night, find that the burrow is warmer than outside.

Pallid gerbils have long tails for balance while leaping and running

Chinchilla
Chinchilla laniger

HUNGRY CHINCHILLA
Chinchillas eat nuts, just like the chipmunk below, by turning them over and over in their paws as they nibble. These luxuriously coated creatures live in the high, rocky mountains of South America, where they spend much time and energy grooming their long, thick fur so it will protect them efficiently from the bitter mountain cold and wind.

Shaw's jird
Meriones meridianus

Tail helps jird balance on hind legs

BALANCING ACT
Jirds are related to gerbils. Together they are the largest groups of small mammals living in the dry regions of Africa and Asia. This large jird, its body measuring up to 8 in (20 cm) long, lives in Morocco, Algeria, Tunisia, and Egypt. Jirds are adept at leaping and climbing and balance easily on their hind legs.

Chipmunk
Tamius striatus

Nut is rotated in manipulative forepaws

Distinctive stripes in fur on back

Short, fluffy tail

Strong back paws for climbing

HAND TO MOUTH
The chipmunk, holding food in its handlike forepaws, is a common sight in eastern North America. These naturally curious members of the squirrel family frequent picnic sites and parks in the hope of finding leftover tidbits. The chipmunk manipulates food in a very efficient way. As it feeds, it rotates the food quickly, scraping off loose bits and testing with its teeth to find a weak point where the food, such as a nut, can be cracked. Like many other rodents, it carries surplus food back to its burrow in cheek pouches.

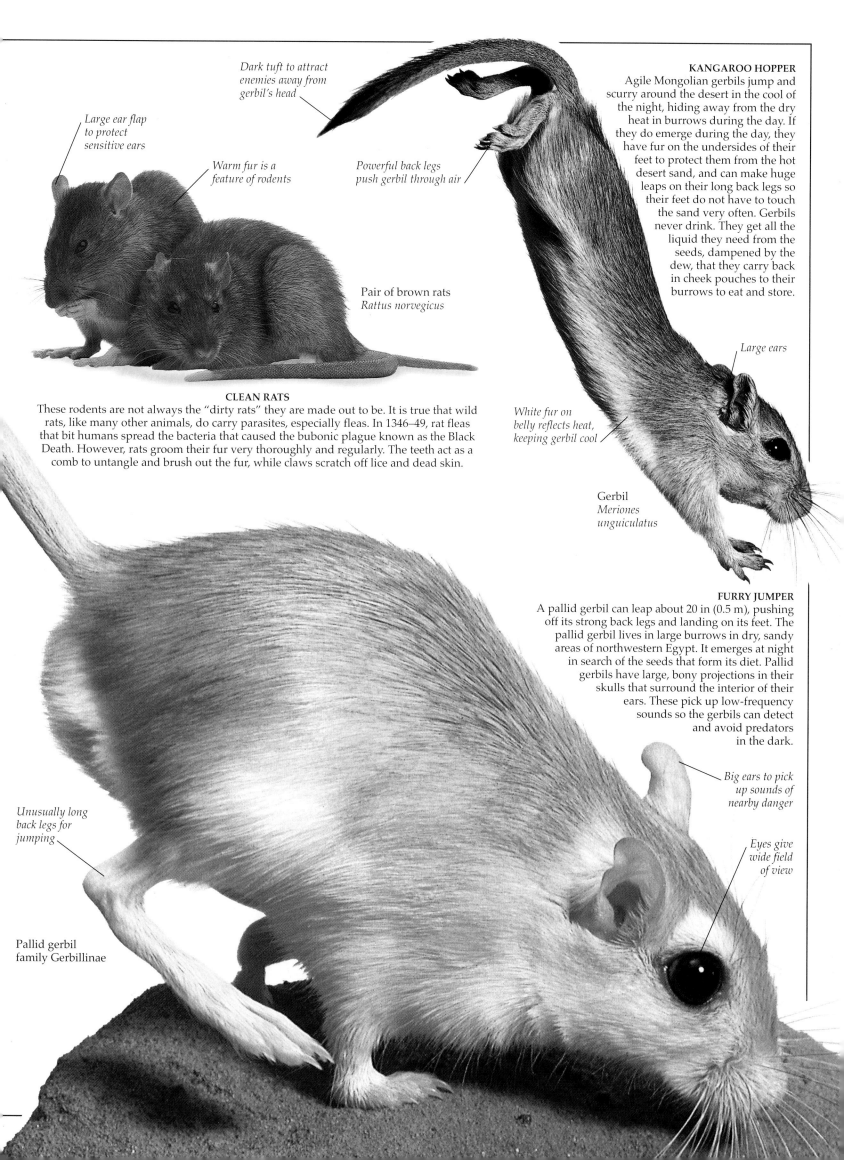

Dark tuft to attract enemies away from gerbil's head

Large ear flap to protect sensitive ears

Warm fur is a feature of rodents

Powerful back legs push gerbil through air

Pair of brown rats
Rattus norvegicus

KANGAROO HOPPER

Agile Mongolian gerbils jump and scurry around the desert in the cool of the night, hiding away from the dry heat in burrows during the day. If they do emerge during the day, they have fur on the undersides of their feet to protect them from the hot desert sand, and can make huge leaps on their long back legs so their feet do not have to touch the sand very often. Gerbils never drink. They get all the liquid they need from the seeds, dampened by the dew, that they carry back in cheek pouches to their burrows to eat and store.

Large ears

CLEAN RATS

These rodents are not always the "dirty rats" they are made out to be. It is true that wild rats, like many other animals, do carry parasites, especially fleas. In 1346–49, rat fleas that bit humans spread the bacteria that caused the bubonic plague known as the Black Death. However, rats groom their fur very thoroughly and regularly. The teeth act as a comb to untangle and brush out the fur, while claws scratch off lice and dead skin.

White fur on belly reflects heat, keeping gerbil cool

Gerbil
Meriones unguiculatus

FURRY JUMPER

A pallid gerbil can leap about 20 in (0.5 m), pushing off its strong back legs and landing on its feet. The pallid gerbil lives in large burrows in dry, sandy areas of northwestern Egypt. It emerges at night in search of the seeds that form its diet. Pallid gerbils have large, bony projections in their skulls that surround the interior of their ears. These pick up low-frequency sounds so the gerbils can detect and avoid predators in the dark.

Big ears to pick up sounds of nearby danger

Unusually long back legs for jumping

Eyes give wide field of view

Pallid gerbil
family Gerbillinae

King of the Arctic

IN EVERY HABITAT there is a dominant predator. In the Arctic, the polar bear is the largest and most powerful hunter. There are probably 20,000 polar bears wandering over the vast Arctic ice floes, some of them even roaming as far as the North Pole. Polar bears are solitary animals except during the breeding season. They do not hibernate, and in the long winter, when the Arctic ice pack extends farther out to sea, they hunt for seals beneath the ice. Their small ears help prevent heat loss, and they have a third eyelid, like a cat, which protects their eyes from snow blindness. Their dense fur keeps them warm even when the temperature drops to –40°C (–40°F). An undercoat of thick fur is protected by an outer coat of long guard hairs. These hairs stick together when wet, forming a waterproof barrier. Under the fur, a thick layer of blubber performs two roles, insulating the bear against the cold and acting as a food store to help the bear survive hard times.

Polar bear
Tharlactos maritimus

Small, rounded ears help prevent heat loss

HEAVYWEIGHT
Polar bears are twice the size of a tiger – an average adult male polar bear measures 8 ft (2.5 m) from head to tail and weighs more than 1,100 lb (500 kg). Female polar bears are much smaller than males, measuring 6.5 ft (2 m) and weighing about 700 lb (320 kg). To maintain this size, polar bears sometimes eat as much 150 lbs (68 kg) of seal blubber and entrails in one sitting. After feeding, they lick their fur and wipe their faces with their paws, very much like cats do.

Air vent scraped in roof lets stale air escape

Polar bears rely on scent and light reflected from the snow to guide them

GARBAGE DISPOSAL
When polar bears find it hard to hunt live food such as seals, they become omnivorous, and are often attracted by human garbage. The dumps on the edge of Churchill, Canada, are a favorite haunt for these enormous animals.

BEAR JOURNEYS
In their quest for food, polar bears make long journeys across the Arctic. In fact, they spend most of their lives walking on pack ice in a world of twilight and darkness. They are expert divers and swimmers, and often hitch rides on ice floes – one was even found swimming 200 miles (320 km) from land. They also dive from the tops of icebergs more than 50 ft (15 m) from the water.

CAVE CUBS
Polar bear cubs are born in December or January in a warm, cozy den dug in the snow by the mother. The cubs – usually two of them, sometimes one or three – grow rapidly on their mother's rich milk, which is about 30 percent fat. While in the ice cave, the mother has nothing to eat, and lives on the stored fat in her body.

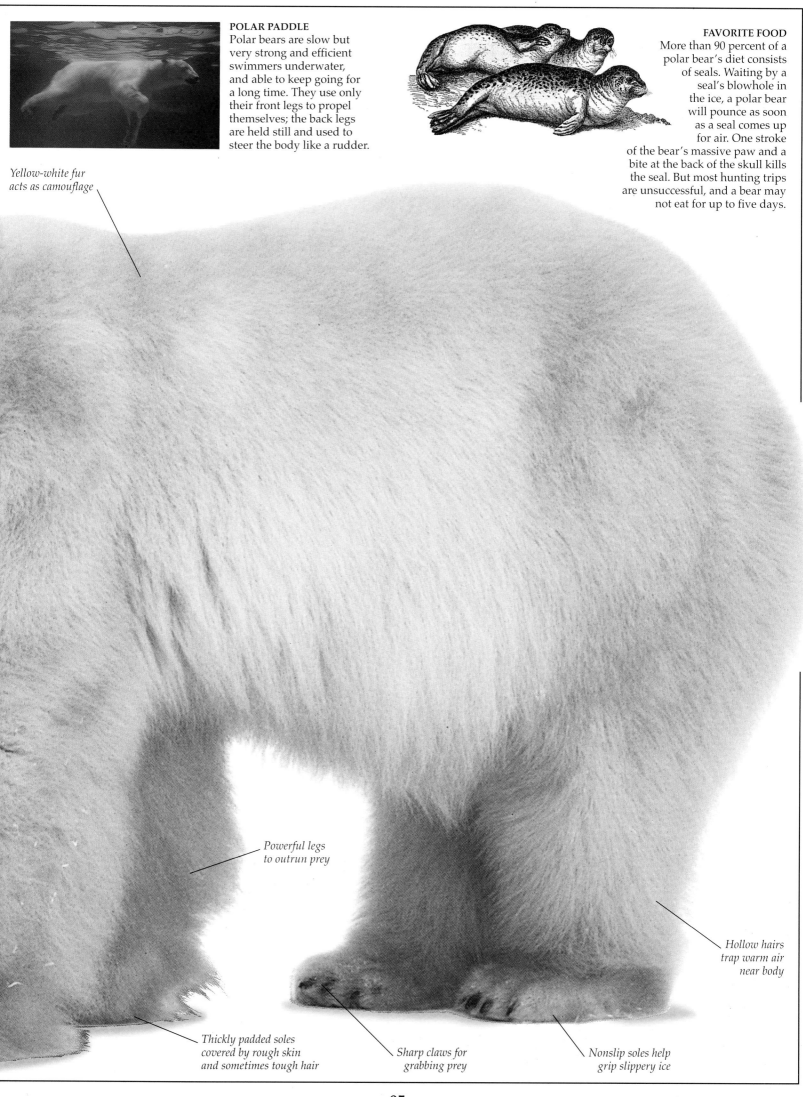

POLAR PADDLE
Polar bears are slow but very strong and efficient swimmers underwater, and able to keep going for a long time. They use only their front legs to propel themselves; the back legs are held still and used to steer the body like a rudder.

FAVORITE FOOD
More than 90 percent of a polar bear's diet consists of seals. Waiting by a seal's blowhole in the ice, a polar bear will pounce as soon as a seal comes up for air. One stroke of the bear's massive paw and a bite at the back of the skull kills the seal. But most hunting trips are unsuccessful, and a bear may not eat for up to five days.

Yellow-white fur acts as camouflage

Powerful legs to outrun prey

Hollow hairs trap warm air near body

Thickly padded soles covered by rough skin and sometimes tough hair

Sharp claws for grabbing prey

Nonslip soles help grip slippery ice

Living in a troop

WESTERN LOWLAND GORILLAS (*Gorilla gorilla gorilla*) live in tropical rain forests in central Africa. A gorilla troop is usually made up of about 5 to 15 animals. The leader of the group is an adult male called a silverback because of his coloring. Apart from the silverback, the troop may include one or two young adult males, several adult females, and a number of juveniles and infants. The gorillas are fruit- and plant-eating, and their day begins just after dawn, when they set off through the forest to find food. The gorillas eat as they walk along, but if they find a ripe fruit tree, the younger ones will clamber into the branches. When they need to digest, the gorillas build day-nests on the ground and sleep for two or three hours. The troop moves off again, eating and traveling until dusk. The silverback decides when it is time to stop for the night and each gorilla then builds a new night-nest.

HIGH CLIMBER
This young zoo gorilla is playing on a climbing frame. For many years, scientists thought that gorillas were too heavy to climb trees. But when they actually studied them in the wild, they found that even adults are surprisingly agile and often climb high into trees to reach ripe fruit.

19th-century engraving of a gorilla family

White tail tuft helps mother locate infant in the jungle

A QUICK BITE
Gorillas sometimes crouch on two feet like this to gather up fallen fruit, or when there is not enough food in one place to make it worth sitting down! It is also a useful posture to adopt when feeding on fierce soldier ants, because it exposes less of the body to their painful bites.

Juvenile has lost its white tail tuft

Nimble fingers pick up fruit

THE FEMALE ROLE
Mature females like this one may be smaller than the males, but their role in the continuation of the group is vital. Female gorillas first give birth when they are eight years old, and the baby gorillas are weaned at the age of two. Females may leave their parents' group and join another group. This avoids inbreeding.

Weight rests on the knuckles while walking

A SLIMMER GORILLA
In the gorilla world it is not unhealthy to have a pot belly. It just means that the owner eats a hearty diet of bulky vegetation. Many zoo gorillas (right) look much slimmer than those in the wild because they are often fed on pellets of concentrated food, and given fewer fruits and vegetables.

LIFE AT THE TOP
The big silverback is lord of all he surveys. In addition to making all the day-to-day decisions for the troop, he can also take his pick of the breeding females. Serious fights among male gorillas are infrequent, but the silverback may take exception to another male when he becomes fully mature at about 11 or 12 years. The younger male may decide to leave the troop, and he will live alone or with other males until he can form his own troop.

Bare chest is a sign of maturity

Young gorilla can watch the world go by from its safe perch

JUNGLE EXPLORER
A gorilla learns to walk at about five to six months. When it is 18 months old, like this young gorilla, it can follow its mother on foot for short distances, often resting one hand on her rump for security. By the time it is two, it has enough confidence to follow the troop on its own. However, the young gorilla stays close to its mother so it can climb on her back if it gets scared or tired.

Mother munches as she walks along

Gorilla leans forward to use his teeth on a stubborn plant

ON THE MOVE
The safest place for a young gorilla when traveling through the jungle is on its mother's back. From here it can watch the other members of the troop as they follow the broad silver back of the dominant male along the forest floor. Infant gorillas depend upon their mothers for transportation until they are about two and a half or three years old, by which time they are strong enough to walk by themselves for long distances.

Food picked from the wayside

Pot belly is not an unhealthy sign

BREAKFAST IN BED
If food is within easy reach when a gorilla wakes up in its night-nest, it will have breakfast in bed before setting off into the forest. The silverback decides the pace and direction of the day's travel and will also indicate when it is time to stop and rest. Although he may look easygoing, the silverback is in fact keeping a constant lookout for dangers along the way.

Adapting to the dark

IN THE DARK OF AN AFRICAN NIGHT, the quiet background of insect noises may be pierced by a strange, childlike cry. This is the call of the bush baby, or galago, a small, nocturnal primate. Bush babies have sensitive, mobile ears to detect moving insects, and large eyes to focus on their prey in moonlight or starlight. They are very agile and move quickly, leaping from branch to branch. At the opposite end of the speed scale, but related to the galago, are the loris, the potto, and the angwantibo. These strange, slow primates are also nocturnal, and creep around the forest in search of fruit and creatures slow enough to be caught. There are no bush babies in Asia, but there is a fast-moving nocturnal primate – the tarsier. With their huge eyes, the three species of tarsier all look like tiny gremlins. In one species, a single eye weighs more than the animal's brain!

PRIMATE OWL
Don't be fooled by their large appealing eyes and cute faces – tarsiers are efficient and ruthless predators. Hunting at night, they silently drop onto large insects, roosting birds, and even venomous snakes. They kill their prey with a nip of their sharp teeth, and meticulously finish off every edible morsel.

SLOW MOVER
A slender loris creeps through the trees, grasping branches with each hand and foot. Lorises eat slow-moving caterpillars, beetles, and millipedes that faster insectivores leave behind.

Nocturnal spectral tarsier

Potto's specialized hand has small bump for second finger

A LEAP IN THE DARK
The nocturnal spectral tarsier is only the size of a squirrel, yet it can leap across gaps of 20 ft (6 m). Tarsiers spend most of their lives holding on to and jumping between upright stems, using the sticky pads on their toes to cling to even the smoothest wood. Using their tails to prop themselves up, they can even sleep clinging to vertical branches.

Enlarged thumb

PINCER FINGERS
This plaster cast of a potto's hand shows how the muscular thumb is set at 180 degrees opposite the other fingers. The hand works just like a pincer, allowing the potto to grasp branches and small trees in a clamplike grip.

Pincer-shaped hand can close tightly around branches

ALL EYES
The main feature of a loris's face are its eyes. Enormous eye sockets, or orbits, are set into the skull and protected by a thick, bony ring called the orbital margin.

Rounded cranium, or brain case

Postorbital bar protects side of eye

CRUNCHY SUPPER
This lesser bush baby is eating a praying mantis. After spending the day asleep, a bush baby sets off to hunt as soon as it is dark. Its large, mobile ears are sensitive to the sounds made by insects, scorpions, spiders, lizards, and nesting birds. Bush babies also eat fallen fruit, petals, nectar, and the sap of some trees.

Large, mobile ears for detecting movement of prey

Enormous eyes for sharp night vision

SCENT SIGNALS
This greater bush baby's powerfully built back legs suggest that it is a vertical clinger and leaper, like a tarsier. But scientists have found that different bush baby species move in different ways. Some bush babies move on all fours, while others seldom leap at all. However they move around their territory, bush babies let others know of their presence by anointing their hands and feet with their own urine. In this way, every hand- and foothold leaves a smelly message that clearly says "I was here."

Long, powerful legs for gripping on to and leaping from branch to branch

Protective pads on palm

Relatively short arms, with hands for grabbing prey

RECOGNIZING THE PATTERN
Zebras live in protective family groups and may recognize family members by their stripe patterns. No two zebras have the same pattern. The black-and-white stripes are confusing to predators. When zebras are moving, their coats blend together, making it difficult for predators to pick a target.

CHAPTER 4

LIFE ON THE LAND

ALTHOUGH LIFE MAY SEEM to be uniformly distributed over the surface of the Earth, in reality it is very uneven. In the extreme heat of some desert areas, and in parts of the frozen continent of Antarctica, there is no life at all. The complexity of life found in other areas reflects the extraordinary variety of habitats in which animals and plants live.

CATCHING THE EYE
To survive, species must procreate, and many animals, birds, and insects have evolved spectacular courtship displays. The male peacock, *Pavo cristatus*, spreads out his long, colorful feathers in a shimmering fan to impress a female. After the breeding season is over, the long tail feathers fall out.

Clouds of all kinds

Ten CATEGORIES OF CLOUDS were identified by the English pharmacist and amateur meteorologist Luke Howard in 1803. All the categories are variations on three basic cloud forms: puffy cumulus clouds, layered stratus clouds, and feathery cirrus clouds. This system proved so simple and effective that it is still used by meteorologists. Clouds form whenever moist air is lifted high enough above the ground to cool and condense. Cumulus clouds form because the Sun heats the ground unevenly, creating bubbles of warm air, or thermals, that drift upward through the cooler air. The bubbles cool as they rise until, high up, water vapor condenses to form a cloud.

FLYING SAUCERS
Lenticular clouds, so-called because they look like lenses, always form on wind-sheltered sides of mountains.

Strong updrafts carry billows of cloud high into atmosphere

Temperature here –40°F (–40°C)

TRANSLUCENT CLOUD
Altostratus are high, thin sheets of cloud that can often completely cover the sky, so that the Sun looks as if it is behind misty glass. Altostratus usually appear at a warm front, where warm, moist air from the tropics slides up over a wedge of cold, polar air. The lower, thicker, nimbostratus rain clouds follow.

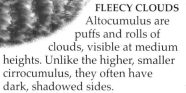

FLEECY CLOUDS
Altocumulus are puffs and rolls of clouds, visible at medium heights. Unlike the higher, smaller cirrocumulus, they often have dark, shadowed sides.

A GREY BLANKET
Stratus is a vast, dull type of cloud that hangs low in the sky and may produce a damp drizzle, but no real rain. Higher up, on hills or viewed from tall buildings, stratus simply appears as fog.

Temperature here 32°F (0°C)

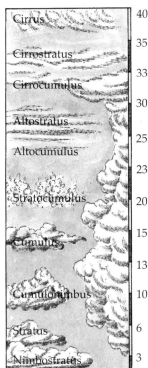

Cirrus	40
Cirrostratus	35
	33
Cirrocumulus	30
Altostratus	25
Altocumulus	23
Stratocumulus	20
	15
Cumulus	13
Cumulonimbus	10
Stratus	6
Nimbostratus	3

Sea level (1,000 ft)

CLOUD HEIGHTS
Cirrus clouds, including cirrocumulus and cirrostratus, form at the top of the troposphere, where it is coldest. Altostratus and altocumulus are found at medium heights; stratocumulus, stratus, nimbostratus, and cumulus form closer to the ground. Cumulonimbus may reach up through the whole troposphere.

TRAILING VIRGA
Rain or ice crystals in cumulus clouds sometimes fall into drier, slower-moving layers of air. The streaks that result, known as virga, evaporate before they reach the ground. From below, they look as if they are vanishing into thin air.

MARES' TAILS
Cirrus clouds form high in the sky where the atmosphere is so cold that they are made entirely from ice crystals. Strong winds blow the crystals into wispy "mares' tails."

AN ICY VEIL
Cirrostratus occur when cirrus clouds spread into a thin, milky sheet. The Sun appears very bright and may have one or more colored rings, or haloes, around it and, occasionally, brilliant "mock suns."

HIGH, FLUFFY CLOUDS
Cirrocumulus are tiny, high clumps of shadowless clouds. Like all cirrus clouds, they consist of ice crystals, and often form in beautiful, regular waves and ripples known as a mackerel sky – because they look like the mottled scales of the mackerel.

Typical anvil shape

Mixture of ice crystals and water

A LAYER OF CUMULUS
Stratocumulus often form when the tops of cumulus clouds rise and spread out into broad sheets. Viewed from an airplane, they appear as an undulating blanket of cloud, with narrow breaks that sometimes allow a glimpse of the ground.

CLOUDS THAT BRING SHOWERS
Bigger and darker than cumulus, cumulonimbus usually bring rain – nimbus means "rain" in Latin. Sometimes they grow huge and unleash sudden, dramatic thunderstorms.

Violent updrafts and downdrafts in front wall of cloud create hailstones

Mainly water droplets

CAULIFLOWER CLOUDS
Cumulus clouds often mass together and grow upward. They have dense, white heads that look just like cauliflowers. If they keep on growing, they may become rain-bearing cumulonimbus.

Air drawn in here

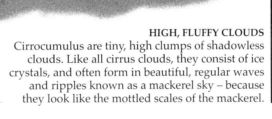

103

Natural signs

SAILORS, FARMERS, AND OTHERS whose livelihood depends on the weather learned long ago that the world around them offers plenty of clues to the weather – as long as they know what to look for. Age-old advice has been passed down from generation to generation on everything from the color of the sky to the feel of your boots in the morning. Of course, most weather lore is little more than superstition and next to useless for weather forecasting. But some is based on close observation of the natural world and can give an accurate prediction of the weather. Tiny variations in the air, which we cannot feel, often affect plants and animals. A change in their appearance or behavior can be the sign of a change in the weather.

WHAT'S THE WEATHER LIKE?
Everyone from travelers to sailors must know about the weather and be aware of natural signs around them.

NOTHING BUT A GROUNDHOG
In the United States, February 2 is Groundhog Day. People say that if a groundhog sees its shadow, the weather will remain cold for six more weeks. Weather records have proved the groundhog wrong many times.

SUNDAY OPENING
The scarlet pimpernel can foretell the weather from a flowerbed. Its tiny blossoms open wide in sunny weather, but close up when rain is coming.

Sunset

Sunrise

SEEING RED
Old sea wisdom says: *Red sky at night, sailors' delight; red sky at morning, sailors take warning.* This means a fiery sunset should be followed by a fine morning, and a fiery dawn by storms. Weather experts are doubtful.

WOOLLY WARNING
Wool is very responsive to the humidity of the air. When the air is dry, wool shrinks and curls up. If rain is on its way, the air is moist, and wool swells and straightens out.

WEATHER WEED
People near the sea often hang out strands of kelp because seaweed is one of the best natural weather forecasters. In fine weather, the kelp shrivels and is dry to the touch. If rain threatens, the weed swells and feels damp.

Kelp is sensitive to changes in humidity

INSECT FORECASTING

Like many small creatures, grasshoppers are sensitive to changes in the weather, chirping louder and louder as the temperature rises. The chirping is not a real song, but the sound of the grasshoppers' hind legs rubbing rapidly against their hard front wings.

Cone in wet weather   Cone in dry weather

WEATHER CONES

A pinecone is a very reliable natural weather indicator. In dry weather, the scales on a pinecone open out; when they close up, it is a good sign that rain is on the way. This is because in dry weather, the scales shrivel and stand out stiffly. When the air is damp, the scales absorb moisture and become pliable again, allowing the cone to regain its normal shape.

Oak   Ash

GLORIOUS MORNING

Like the scarlet pimpernel, morning glory flowers open and shut in response to weather conditions. These wide-open blooms indicate fine weather.

SOAK OR SPLASH?

According to some, natural signs can indicate the weather, not just for the next few hours but for many days to come. There is an old English saying that says:
If the oak flowers before the ash, we shall have a splash (meaning only light rain for the next month or so).
If the ash flowers before the oak, we shall have a soak (meaning very wet weather). There is little evidence, however, to support these long-range predictions.

LYING COWS

When cows lie down in a field, it is often said that rain must be on the way. Apparently, the cows sense the dampness in the air and are trying to preserve their patch of dry ground. While many animals can sense changes in the weather before humans, this particular prediction is wrong as often as it is right.

SPRING IS HERE

Many natural signs are said to herald the end of winter, such as the first blooming of the white flowers of the horse chestnut. It is true that the flowers only appear when the weather is mild – but this is no guarantee that there will be no more winter storms.

WINTER'S TAIL

Some people expect a severe winter if squirrels have very bushy tails in the fall, or if they gather big stores of nuts. But scientists have found no evidence to support this.

Fiery rocks

WHEN VOLCANOES ERUPT, they may spout rivers of red-hot lava or spew great clouds of ash and gas into the atmosphere. Sometimes the lava oozes gently from a hole in the ground. At other times, lava is thrown into the air in spectacular fire fountains that run together when they land. In either case, the lava flows off the volcano in rivers of hot rock that may spread out over a large area before it cools. Fire fountains and lava flows are common in Iceland and Hawaii. They are easy to predict in these areas, and it is often possible to get close to them and take photographs. However, from time to time, volcanic gas that escapes the hot rock may cause explosions that throw out bombs and blocks – chunks of flying lava that litter the ground around the vent.

Weedy, flowering plant

Two species of moss

Lichen

GATHERING MOSS
How quickly plants recolonize lava depends on the nature of the erupted material. Climate and altitude are also important – recolonization is fastest in the tropics, for example. This piece of lava is from a flow on the western slope of Mount Vesuvius in Italy after an eruption in 1944. Some 50 years later, lichen covers much of the flow, and moss, grasses, and weedy, flowering plants are taking root.

BOMBS AND BLOCKS
Bombs and blocks can be as big as houses or as small as tennis balls. Bombs are usually more rounded, and blocks are more dense and angular. Their shapes depend upon how molten or gaseous the lava was during flight. Very liquid chunks of lava plop to the ground; denser, more solid chunks often shatter as they land.

Bomb thrown out by Mount Etna and covered with red crust of hematite

SPITTING MOUNTAIN
One of the highest mountains and most active volcanoes in Europe, Mount Etna rises 11,122 ft (3,390 m) over the Italian island of Sicily. Its barren summit is almost always bubbling with lava. Lava flows from an unusually long eruption destroyed several houses and threatened villages in 1992.

Dense, round bomb

Small, explosive eruption photographed at night on Mount Etna

Odd twists and tails of many bombs formed as they spin through the air

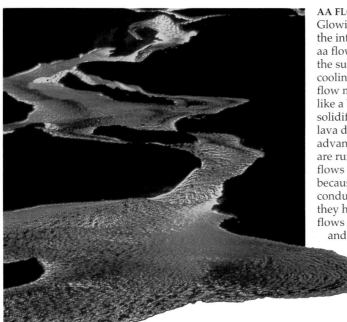

AA FLOWS
Glowing red at night, the intense heat of an aa flow shows through the surface crust of cooling lava. The flow moves forward like a bulldozer, as solidifying blocks of lava drop down the advancing front and are run over. Lava flows cool very slowly because rock is a poor conductor of heat. As they harden, the lava flows slow down and thicken.

Hardened chunk of pahoehoe lava

PAHOEHOE FLOWS
Pahoehoe flows are more fluid than aa flows and contain more gas. As its surface cools, the flow develops a thin, pliable skin. The hot lava on the inside distorts the skin, wrinkling it so that its surface looks like the coil of a rope. The skin of a pahoehoe flow may crust over into a roof thick enough to walk on. Hot lava continues to run in a tunnel or tube only a yard or so beneath the crusty roof.

Lava flows

Lava flows pose little danger to people because they rarely travel faster than a few miles an hour. There are two kinds of flows; they get their names from Hawaiian words. Aa (pronounced *ah-ah*) flows are covered in sharp, angular chunks of lava known as scoria. Pahoehoe (*pa-hoy-hoy*) flows grow a smooth skin soon after they leave the vent. Pahoehoe flows are rarely more than 3.3 ft (1 m) thick, while the thickest aa flows may be 330 ft (100 m) high.

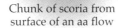

PAHOEHOE TOE
This photo shows red-hot pahoehoe bulging through a crack in its own skin. New skin is forming over the bulge. A pahoehoe flow creeps forward with thousands of little breakouts like this one. The chilled surface of the flow traps gas, keeping the flow in the tunnels hot and mobile. The lava often travels many miles from the vent in this way, engulfing farmland and houses as it goes.

Dribbles of remelted lava from roof of a pahoehoe tunnel

Chunk of scoria from surface of an aa flow

FIRE AND WATER
Volcanic islands like Hawaii and Iceland are usually fringed by black beaches. The sand is formed when hot lava hits the sea and shatters into tiny, glassy particles. It is black because the lava is rich in dark minerals like iron oxides, and low in light-colored ones like quartz.

Black sand from volcanic island of Santorini, Greece

On the mountainside

THE HIGHER THE ALTITUDE at which a plant grows or an animals lives, the colder the temperatures it has to endure. The thin air holds little heat, and on exposed mountainsides, high winds create a chill factor that makes the cold even more penetrating. In addition, low rainfall and thin, frozen soils mean that water is scarce. However, mountain (alpine) plants are generally small and compact, so they can survive on high mountain peaks, often growing in dense cushions or flattened mats to give protection against the cold, drying wind. Animals and insects live on all levels of a mountain, sometimes moving up or down in search of food or greater warmth.

Canada lynx

Western Himalayan spruce
Picea smithiana

HIMALAYAN CONIFER
Above the tropical forests of the southern Himalayan slopes are mixed forests containing many coniferous trees. This elegant spruce is found on the middle slopes. It has a narrow crown and drooping shoots, and the cones have smooth, notched scales.

Large neck ruff

Lady Amherst's pheasant
Chrysolophus Amherstiae

MOUNTAIN RANGES
There are mountains on all the continents. A few form great mountain ranges, such as the Rocky Mountains and the Himalayas. On the highest peaks of mountain ranges, snow lies frozen all year round. Below the high mountaintops with their snowy peaks, alpine meadows and scrub form cool coniferous forests and waterlogged moorlands. On the lower slopes, the warmer, deciduous forests are home to many animals and insects.

SEASONAL MIGRATION
Hardy pheasants such as this spectacular Lady Amherst's pheasant live in the mountain forests of Asia. They move up and down the mountains with the seasons. This shy, secretive bird rarely emerges from the bamboo thickets and dense forest where it lives. It eats bamboo shoots as well as small animals, insects, and spiders, and sometimes fishes under stones in streams for small aquatic animals.

Male has long and colorful tail feathers for display

Himalayan
Mazus reptans
grows in mats

Bhutan Glory
Bhutanitis lidderdalei

*Alpine daphne, or
garland flower, is
miniature shrub*

MOUNTAIN BEAUTY
Many butterflies and moths
have adapted to the harsh
climate of mountains. This
Bhutan glory lives in the
mountain forests of Thailand and
India. It is a dark brown because darker
colors absorb sunlight more easily, so the
insect can warm up rapidly in the early
morning when the air temperature is low.

*Butterfly has prominent
eyespots to startle
predatory birds*

*Moltkias have
small leaves to
withstand high winds*

*Brilliant colors of
North American phlox
stand out to attract
pollinating insects*

Mountain gorilla
*Gorilla gorilla
beringei*

*This St. John's wort
is much smaller than
its lowland relatives*

ALPINE PLANTS
Many plants have adapted to the harsh climate
of mountains. Some of them, such as *Mazus
reptans*, are "prostrate," or mat-forming. Others
are simply smaller than similar species in
warmer habitats. The leaves are often small
and tough to resist sharp frosts, and some are
covered with fine hairs to protect them from the
Sun's ultraviolet rays, which are more intense at
these heights. Mountain summers are short, so
the plants have to flower and produce seeds
quickly before the cold weather returns.

*Weight rests
on knuckles
when walking*

MOUNTAIN APE
Mountain gorillas live in the mountain forests of the Virunga volcanoes in
Africa. Their thick coats keep out the chill, while water runs off the outer
layer of hairs. Mothers like this female wrap their shaggy arms around
their babies to keep them warm and dry. Gorillas spend most of their time
on the ground, but will often climb trees to search for fruit, bark, or leaves.
Today, there are fewer than 650 mountain gorillas left in the world.

Lords of the skies

THE HUGE SUMMER BREEDING COLONIES of birds in both the Arctic and the Antarctic attract a number of predatory birds quick to enjoy easy meals of eggs and chicks. In the Arctic, the small mammals of the tundra lands, such as lemmings and hares, increase the range of food for birds to hunt. The variety of predatory birds is therefore greater in the Arctic than in the Antarctic and includes eagles, skuas, owls, falcons, and buzzards. The predators' breeding cycles are timed to coincide with that of their prey, ensuring that their chicks will always have plenty to eat.

GHOSTLY HUNTER
Snowy owls feed largely on the millions of lemmings living on the Arctic tundra, and their population is closely linked to the cyclical three to four year rise and fall in lemming numbers. Many of these superb owls wander south in winter.

Soapstone and ivory owl carved by Inuit craftsman in Cape Dorset, Canada

Feathers at tips of wings spread out like fingers to help the eagle push and steer through the air

Spread feathers help the bird reduce speed

Powerful wings give both speed and control in flight

Lethal curved talons grip, crush, and carry off prey

Strong legs to cushion impact of landing

The golden eagle slows in midair and spreads out its wings and tail to act as a brake

Eyes firmly focused on its destination, the eagle further brakes its flight by swinging out its lower body and legs

At the last moment, its feet swing down to grip the perch

LOOK OUT BELOW
Golden eagles fly at low altitudes while hunting, then swoop suddenly to pounce on their prey. This swoop-and-grab attack is effective because it happens so swiftly that the prey is often taken by surprise. Here, a golden eagle is landing on a branch in much the same way as it would dive for a meal.

KING OF THE CLOUDS
As the most powerful and majestic bird in the sky, the eagle is featured in countless stories, myths, and legends. Here a magnificent eagle perches in a tree in an illustration by British illustrator Reginald Knowles. It forms the title page of a collection of Norse legends.

Golden eagle
Aquila chrysaetos

Sharp eyesight to spot birds and animals moving on the ground below

Powerful hooked bill to tear flesh from prey

Huge chest muscles drive the enormous wings

Gyrfalcon
Falco rusticolus

A KILLING MACHINE
A magnificent flier, the golden eagle is a fierce predator of ptarmigan and other birds as well as small mammals such as ground squirrels and hares. Golden eagles usually kill their prey before carrying it off in their strong talons. They sometimes hunt in pairs, especially in winter.

BIGGEST AND BEST
The most powerful of the falcons, the gyrfalcon relies on power and speed to catch its victims. It usually kills its prey in flight.

FALCON FOOD
The rock ptarmigan (*Lagopus mutus*) is the gyrfalcon's main prey.

Mountain weather

HIGH UP IN THE ATMOSPHERE, pressure drops, winds are ferocious, and the air is bitterly cold. On mountain peaks like Mount Everest, the air pressure is very low, winds howl through the crags at up to 192 mph (320 km/h), and the temperature often drops to –94°F (–70°C). Because mountains jut so far into the atmosphere, they interfere with wind and cloud patterns, forcing air to move up or down as it passes over the peaks. Air rising up the windward side of a mountain means that the lower summits are often shrouded in mist and rain.

CLOUDS AND SNOW
In many mountain ranges, the highest peaks project above the clouds, basking in bright sunshine while clouds fill the valley below. However, though sunny, the peaks are usually icy cold. Any heat from the Sun is reflected back into the atmosphere by the snow. Near the equator, only the very highest peaks – above 16,400 ft (5,000 m) – are perpetually snow-covered, where it is too cold for rain. Toward the poles, however, the snow line creeps down the mountainside.

HIGH READINGS
Many weather stations are sited on the tops of mountains to record conditions high up in the atmosphere. On the summit of Mount Washington in New Hampshire, winds are frequently over 196 mph (60 km/h) and temperatures are often below –22°F (–30°C).

MEASURING AIR PRESSURE
In 1648, the French scientist Blaise Pascal proved that the atmosphere had its own weight, or pressure. Pascal reasoned that the air pressure would be lower at the top of a mountain because there was less air weighing down on it from above. When he took a barometer up a mountain, the mercury level showing air pressure dropped as he expected.

Barometer used for measuring air pressure

Air pushed up by mountain slopes often fills valleys with clouds

Cloud cover remains on peaks almost year-round

WET AT THE TOP
Even when they are not particularly cold, mountaintops are often wet and misty – especially if they poke up into a moist air stream. Pacific island mountains, like these in Tahiti, are among the dampest places in the world. Hawaii's Mount Wai-'ale-'ale is wreathed in moist clouds for 354 days a year. It is also drenched by more than 457 in (11,600 mm) of rain a year.

Barometer
very low

A little
cloud
cover

Winds of
99 mph
(165 km/h)
or more

ADAPTING
Tiny flowers
called alpines
have been
very successful
in adapting to
the sunny, cold
weather of
mountain ranges
such as the Alps
in Europe,
where they grow
plentifully in spring.

HIGH SIERRA
High up in the mountains, strong winds often
increase the chilling effect, even on sunny
days. Mountaintops are usually much more
windswept than open, low country, partly
because wind strength can be much stronger
at 3,280 ft (1,000 m) than at sea level. Winds
also rush over, rather than around, the tops
of mountains, and gain speed as they go.

*Air warms
and dries as
it descends*

Leeward
(sheltered)
side

Rain on summit

RISING AIR
When a moist air stream meets a
mountain range, it is forced upward, toward the
summit. As it rises, it cools and may condense into clouds
around the top. Higher-level clouds can then act as "feeder"
clouds, letting a little rain fall onto the summit clouds below.
Warm fronts may break up when they run up against a mountain
ridge, while cold fronts may drop so much rain that they die out
quickly on the far side. All this brings rain to the windward side
of mountains, and leaves the sheltered leeward side drier.

Windward
side

*Moist air forced
upward by
mountain range*

*Rising air cools and
condenses into clouds*

In the rain forest

TROPICAL RAIN FORESTS contain more species and a greater diversity of colorful plant and animal life than any other habitat on Earth. These forests are found in permanently wet, warm areas near the equator that get at least 60 in (1.5 m) of rain a year. The jungles have three layers – a layer of smaller plants on the forest floor, an evergreen canopy in the middle, and, towering above, scattered taller trees known as emergents. At all levels of the rain forest there is a host of wary creatures with strong survival instincts. In the canopy, many yards above the ground, harpy eagles swoop down on prey. Lower, hungry pitcher plants digest the insects that fall into their cups. In the dim light of the forest floor, scorpions and other poisonous creatures scuttle and slither their way through the maze of roots, fallen leaves, and branches.

A NASTY SHOCK
There are many ways that rain forest creatures protect themselves. Any predator that tries to sample this spiky leaf insect will receive a painful surprise because the insect has sharp spines all over its body. This female is an immature nymph; its wings are not yet fully formed.

Tomato frogs
Dyscophis antongili

RAIN FORESTS IN DANGER
Madagascar, off Africa's southeastern coast, is the world's fourth largest island. Like many other islands (pp. 122–123), most of its rain forest wildlife has evolved in isolation and is unique. However, many of the plants and animals, such as the rare comet orchid (*Angraecum sesquipedale)* and these tomato frogs, are endangered because their habitat – the rain forest – is being cut down and burned by farmers to clear the way for agriculture.

Four simple eyes on each side of the head

LIVING DANGEROUSLY
Heavy with moisture, the air near the shady forest floor is home to the poisonous tiger centipede, typical of the creatures that lie hidden in the dense vegetation. Tiger centipedes emerge only at night, when the forest grows cool. They have large, poisonous claws, and feed on insects and spiders as well as small toads and mammals.

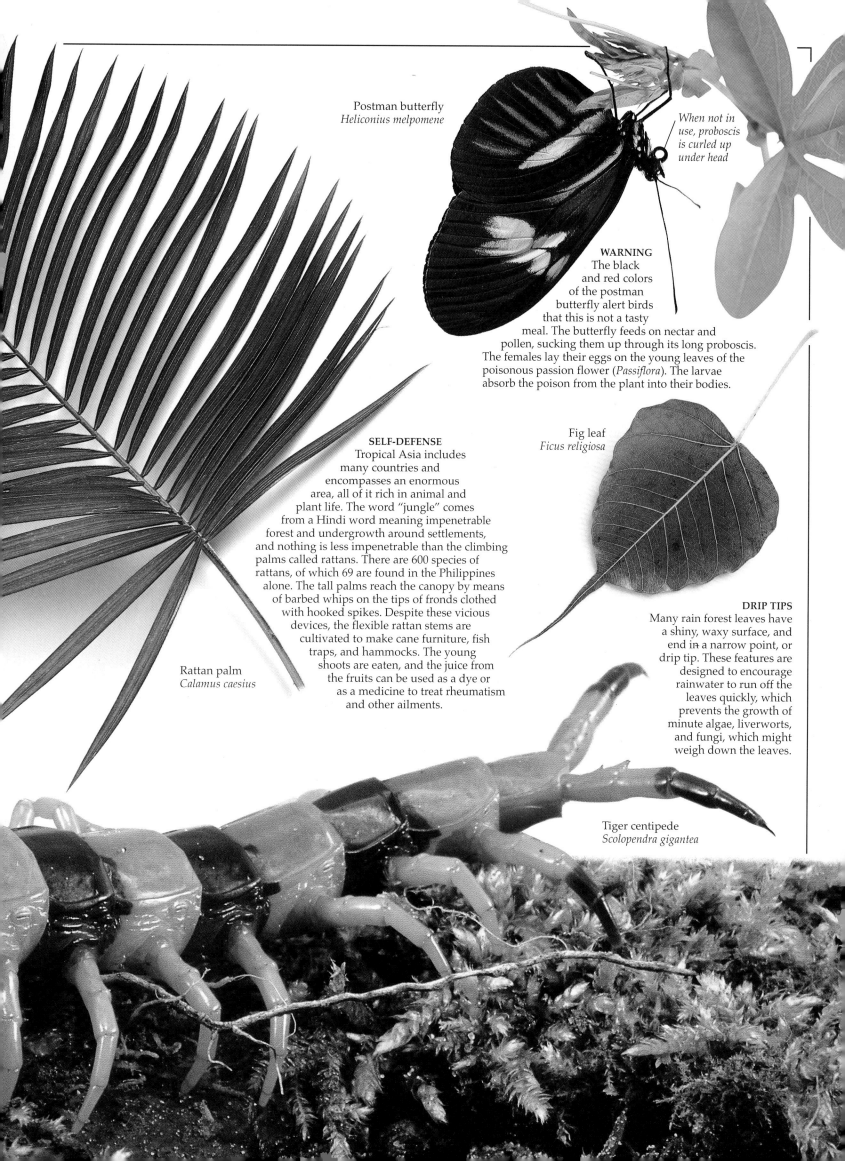

Postman butterfly
Heliconius melpomene

When not in
use, proboscis
is curled up
under head

WARNING
The black
and red colors
of the postman
butterfly alert birds
that this is not a tasty
meal. The butterfly feeds on nectar and
pollen, sucking them up through its long proboscis.
The females lay their eggs on the young leaves of the
poisonous passion flower (*Passiflora*). The larvae
absorb the poison from the plant into their bodies.

Fig leaf
Ficus religiosa

SELF-DEFENSE
Tropical Asia includes
many countries and
encompasses an enormous
area, all of it rich in animal and
plant life. The word "jungle" comes
from a Hindi word meaning impenetrable
forest and undergrowth around settlements,
and nothing is less impenetrable than the climbing
palms called rattans. There are 600 species of
rattans, of which 69 are found in the Philippines
alone. The tall palms reach the canopy by means
of barbed whips on the tips of fronds clothed
with hooked spikes. Despite these vicious
devices, the flexible rattan stems are
cultivated to make cane furniture, fish
traps, and hammocks. The young
shoots are eaten, and the juice from
the fruits can be used as a dye or
as a medicine to treat rheumatism
and other ailments.

Rattan palm
Calamus caesius

DRIP TIPS
Many rain forest leaves have
a shiny, waxy surface, and
end in a narrow point, or
drip tip. These features are
designed to encourage
rainwater to run off the
leaves quickly, which
prevents the growth of
minute algae, liverworts,
and fungi, which might
weigh down the leaves.

Tiger centipede
Scolopendra gigantea

Living on the grasslands

MUCH OF THE AFRICAN continent is grassland, and most areas are hot savanna plains lying between tropical forests and desert land. Grasses, small trees, and shrubs are scattered across the savanna, with tall, thick grasses growing near the forests, and shorter, thinner grasses near the deserts. Grazing animals such as zebras, antelope, and wildebeests live in large herds that wander the plains, cropping the grass as they go. The trees and shrubs, such as acacias, have deep roots to reach water sources underground, and provide nourishment for many of the herbivores that live on the grasslands. Large browsing animals use their different heights to reach different parts of the foliage. Giraffes eat the tasty shoots at the treetops, elephants eat the leaves, twigs, and bark, and black rhinoceroses eat the lower branches. The water in the plants keeps these animals hydrated in this dry area – the animals may go up to a week without drinking.

Males' skulls strengthened for fighting

Small horns

Patas monkey
Erythrocebus patas

Cloven hoof like that of a cow

Males are twice as big as females

Long legs for sprinting

LIVING IN A HERD
Giraffes live in herds of up to 12 individuals, which may be spread out over a wide area, but always move together across the plains. The males average 16 ft (5 m) in height and weigh 3,080 lb (1,400 kg), while the females are usually 14 ft (4.3 m) tall and around 1,760 lb (800 kg). Giraffes move with some difficulty. They have trouble getting up from the ground, for instance, but when they gallop away, few predators can catch them. Unlike most large animals, they move with both legs on the same side working together, and they can gallop for hours without getting tired.

PLAINS MONKEY
The patas monkey, also known as the military monkey because of its reddish coat and impressive white mustache, lives on the dry plains of Africa in troops of about 15 to 20. It lives on the ground and its long legs let it bound along at 33 mph (55 km/h) if necessary. Patas troops spend most of the day moving around looking for leaves, fruit, and flowers to eat. At night, the monkeys climb into trees to sleep.

Spongy blood vessels near brain prevent blood pressure problems when giraffe bends down to drink

Reticulated giraffe
Giraffa melopardis

Because of its long neck, giraffe has to lower or raise its head slowly

Common zebra
Equus burchelli

RECORD HEIGHTS
No animal alive today is as tall as a giraffe. The long neck evolved to enable the animal to browse on the foliage of trees on the wide plains of the savanna. The extraordinary thing about a giraffe's neck is that it contains only seven vertebrae – exactly the same number as in the necks of other mammals, including our own. The vertebrae are simply long – 1 ft (0.3 m) long. When it reaches into the treetops, a giraffe's long tongue grasps leaves and twigs and pulls them within reach. Its canine teeth have two deep grooves to strip the leaves from their twigs.

HERDING TOGETHER
The main threat to the large herds of zebras on the African plains, apart from drought, is the efficient hunting of the large cats: the lion, leopard, and cheetah. Lions hunt in groups. The lionesses do most of the work, picking out and attacking the weakest animals in a herd. Zebras stay together for protection. Zebra herds contain family groups of about 12 females and their foals, led by a dominant male. By day, they graze on the long coarse grass and drink from waterholes regularly. They migrate to find water in the dry season.

Ostrich
Struthio camelus

Flexible neck

BIG BIRD
The ostrich is the heaviest bird, 200–345 lb (90–157 kg), the tallest bird, 7–9 ft (2.1–2.7 m), and the fastest two-legged animal, up to 45 mph (75 km/h), in the world. It also lays the largest egg, which has an incredible average weight of 3.3 lb (1.5 kg). The ostrich lays between 6 and 20 eggs at one time, and incubates them for up to 48 days. Ostriches are omnivorous, eating grass, seeds, insects, and small animals.

How plants survive in the desert

PLANTS THAT LIVE IN DESERTS either spring up from dormant seeds after rain, or stay alive all year by adapting to the meager supply of water. The more permanent plants have a variety of methods of obtaining water. Some have long roots to reach moisture deep in the soil; some spread their roots to collect water over a wide area; others absorb dew through their leaves. Many desert plants, including cacti, are succulents, which are able to store water. A thick waxy layer on the succulents' stems and leaves also helps retain moisture and protects tissues from the Sun's intense heat. Growing smaller leaves, shedding leaves in times of drought, or even having no leaves at all, also helps reduce water loss by keeping the surface area of the plant to a minimum.

DATE PALMS
This grove of date palms is at an oasis in Oman. Only female trees produce dates, so just a few male trees are grown to produce pollen. Palm trees can live for up to 200 years.

FRESH DATES
There are many different varieties of dates. The most familiar are the ones that are dried and packed in boxes for export around the world. Dried dates are also part of the staple diet of villagers and desert nomads such as the Bedouin. They are very nutritious and do not rot easily.

Very long roots to seek out water

FLESHY LEAF
Haworthias grow in places with some shade, usually next to rocks. Only the tips of the leaves poke above the surface of the soil, the rest stays out of the sun. But leaves need light in order to make food by photosynthesis. This leaf has a translucent (clear) window in the tip to allow light through the leaf.

These agaves with varied patterns have been specially bred

CENTURY PLANTS
It takes 20 to 50 years for the century plant to produce flowers on a stem up to 30 ft (9 m) tall, growing out of the center of the plant. The flowers are pollinated by nectar-seeking bats. After flowering and producing seeds, the plant dies. The century plant belongs to the agave family, members of which are a source of sweet sap for drinks and of fibers for ropes and other products.

FIRETHORN BRANCH
Also called the ocotillo, or candlewood plant, the firethorn grows in the deserts of the southwestern US. In dry times, it sheds its leaves to conserve moisture. After rain, new leaves grow among the spines; if the ground is wet enough, the firethorn flowers.

WELWITSCHIA
This bizarre plant has only two frayed, straplike leaves, and a huge taproot that may be up to 3.3 ft (1 m) wide at the top. It grows on the gravel plains in the Namib Desert. Welwitschia is actually a dwarf tree, and may live for 100 years or more, each leaf growing about 2 in (5 cm) a year.

Leaf absorbs dew

Welwitschia leaves usually split into many strips

When spread out, each leaf reaches up to 6.5 ft (2 m) long

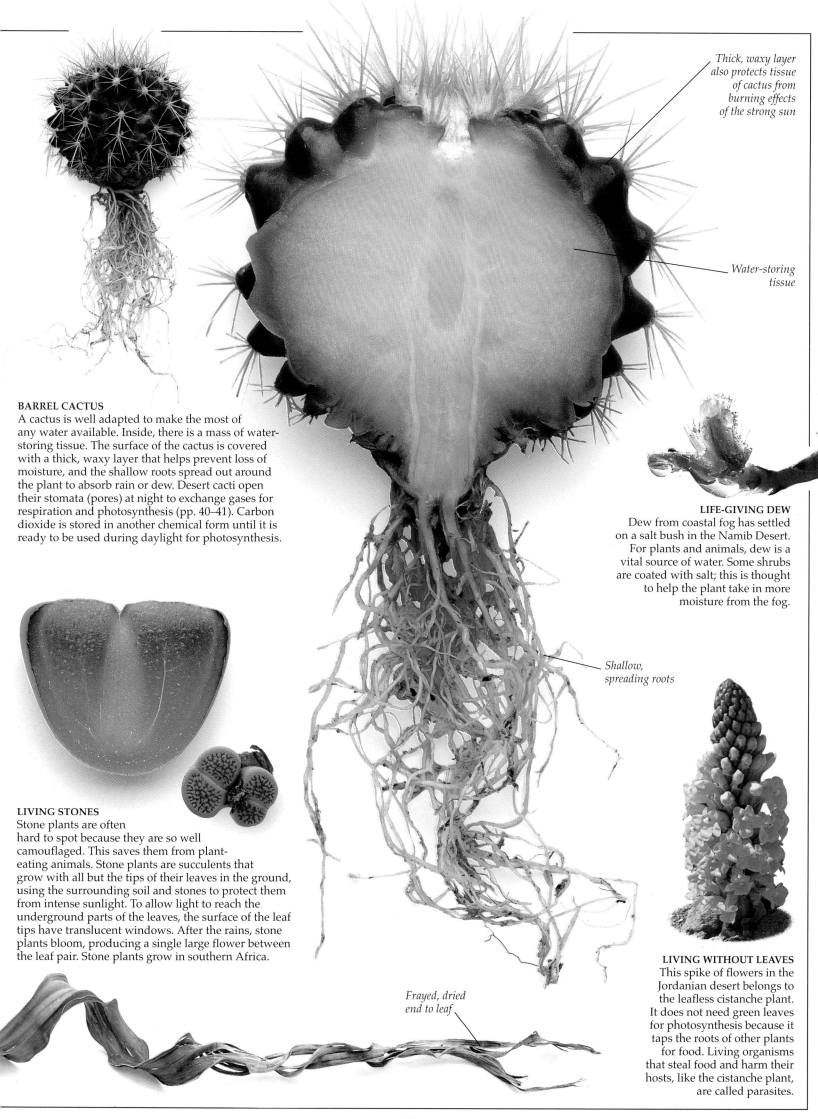

Thick, waxy layer
also protects tissue
of cactus from
burning effects
of the strong sun

Water-storing
tissue

BARREL CACTUS

A cactus is well adapted to make the most of any water available. Inside, there is a mass of water-storing tissue. The surface of the cactus is covered with a thick, waxy layer that helps prevent loss of moisture, and the shallow roots spread out around the plant to absorb rain or dew. Desert cacti open their stomata (pores) at night to exchange gases for respiration and photosynthesis (pp. 40–41). Carbon dioxide is stored in another chemical form until it is ready to be used during daylight for photosynthesis.

LIFE-GIVING DEW

Dew from coastal fog has settled on a salt bush in the Namib Desert. For plants and animals, dew is a vital source of water. Some shrubs are coated with salt; this is thought to help the plant take in more moisture from the fog.

Shallow,
spreading roots

LIVING STONES

Stone plants are often hard to spot because they are so well camouflaged. This saves them from plant-eating animals. Stone plants are succulents that grow with all but the tips of their leaves in the ground, using the surrounding soil and stones to protect them from intense sunlight. To allow light to reach the underground parts of the leaves, the surface of the leaf tips have translucent windows. After the rains, stone plants bloom, producing a single large flower between the leaf pair. Stone plants grow in southern Africa.

Frayed, dried
end to leaf

LIVING WITHOUT LEAVES

This spike of flowers in the Jordanian desert belongs to the leafless cistanche plant. It does not need green leaves for photosynthesis because it taps the roots of other plants for food. Living organisms that steal food and harm their hosts, like the cistanche plant, are called parasites.

Desert wildlife

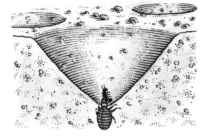

Animals in the desert have a difficult problem to solve – they must find water in a dry, dusty environment. Some herbivorous animals and insects feed on fresh green plants that spring up after rain. Others get moisture and food from prey or from water and dew. To conserve water and avoid the drying effects of the Sun, many desert creatures are only active at night. Desert hedgehogs and foxes spend the heat of the day in burrows, emerging when it is dark to search for food. Members of the cat family that live in desert regions often hunt at night, sheltering in rocky lairs or any available shade during the day. There are desert animals that avoid the driest times, only becoming active after occasional rains. The eggs of desert crustaceans, such as brine and tadpole shrimps, need water just to bring them to life, and spadefoot toads remain inactive during the dry season, buried in the soil, only emerging when they hear rain falling above.

THE ANT LION
The larva of this winged insect is called an ant lion. As soon as it hatches, it digs a pit in the sand and hides at the bottom with only its jaws exposed, waiting for an insect such as an ant to come into the pit. When prey gets close enough, the ant lion flicks sand at it to make it lose its footing and slide down to certain death.

Long antenna

Shield

Series of limbs push food into mouth

Tadpole shrimps are 1.2 in (3 cm) in length

Jewel wasp

JEWEL OF THE DESERT
Hunting jewel wasps are solitary wasps, living on their own rather than in colonies. The adults feed on nectar from flowers, but their young eat cockroaches caught for them by the adult female. She hunts down the cockroach, stings it to paralyze it, and then drags the insect into a hole where she lays an egg on it. When the young hatches, it feeds on the paralyzed but alive cockroach.

THIRSTY SHRIMPS
The eggs of these tadpole shrimps can survive in dry sands for ten years or more, waiting for rain to bring them to life. The shrimps must grow quickly to reach maturity and produce eggs before the desert pool in which they live dries up and they die. Not all the eggs hatch the first time around. Some eggs are left for the next rain in case the pools dry out and the first shrimps die before they can complete their life cycle.

Distinctive ear tuft similar to that of lynx

Caracal
Lynx caracal

DESERT CAT
The caracal lives in a wide range of habitats, including the deserts of Africa and Asia. These soft-footed cats are adept at catching birds, and can even leap into the air to swat a bird in flight. They also hunt reptiles, small mammals, and even larger prey such as gazelles. Caracals sleep in caves, rocky crevices, and the abandoned burrows of other animals.

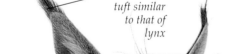

Desert hedgehog
Paraechinus aethiopicus

Meerkat
Suricata suricatta

A group of meerkats is capable of warding off a jackal or cobra

LIVING TOGETHER
Meerkats live in the Kalahari and Namib deserts, and in dry open country in other parts of southern Africa. They work together as a group. A meerkat with its head down looking for food in the wide open desert is an easy target for a bird of prey, so one member of each group scans the horizon from a high place – on a raised sandbank, or in a bush or tree. If a predator is spotted, the guard barks in alarm and the group races to the safety of a burrow. There are "nanny" meerkats in each group that take turns looking after the young while the mothers are out feeding with the rest of the group.

DESERT HEDGEHOG
This spiny creature lives in the dry regions of northern Africa, the Arabian peninsula, and Iraq. When threatened, it rolls up to expose the spines of its coat, like other species of hedgehog, protecting its vulnerable underparts. Desert hedgehogs dig individual burrows that they live in during the day. In the breeding season, the female looks after the young in the burrow, suckling them for two months. Adult hedgehogs eat birds, eggs, scorpions, and small mammals.

Enlarged glands secrete a strong poison to deter predators

Green toad
Bufo viridis

TOADS IN THE HEAT
Green toads live in oases where there is a permanent water supply in which to lay their eggs. During the day, they hide away from the heat of the desert under stones. At night, they emerge to hunt insects near water holes and around palm trees. They have enlarged glands that secrete a strong poison to deter predators.

Island life

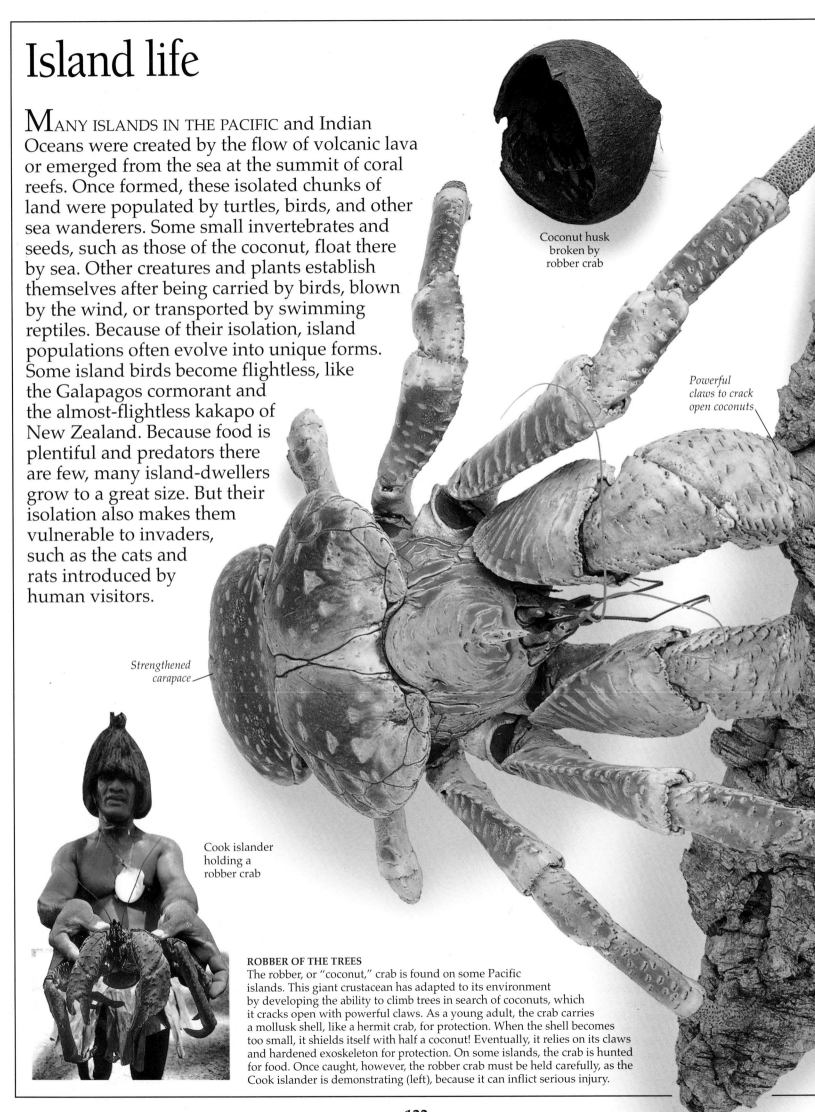

MANY ISLANDS IN THE PACIFIC and Indian Oceans were created by the flow of volcanic lava or emerged from the sea at the summit of coral reefs. Once formed, these isolated chunks of land were populated by turtles, birds, and other sea wanderers. Some small invertebrates and seeds, such as those of the coconut, float there by sea. Other creatures and plants establish themselves after being carried by birds, blown by the wind, or transported by swimming reptiles. Because of their isolation, island populations often evolve into unique forms. Some island birds become flightless, like the Galapagos cormorant and the almost-flightless kakapo of New Zealand. Because food is plentiful and predators there are few, many island-dwellers grow to a great size. But their isolation also makes them vulnerable to invaders, such as the cats and rats introduced by human visitors.

Coconut husk broken by robber crab

Powerful claws to crack open coconuts

Strengthened carapace

Cook islander holding a robber crab

ROBBER OF THE TREES
The robber, or "coconut," crab is found on some Pacific islands. This giant crustacean has adapted to its environment by developing the ability to climb trees in search of coconuts, which it cracks open with powerful claws. As a young adult, the crab carries a mollusk shell, like a hermit crab, for protection. When the shell becomes too small, it shields itself with half a coconut! Eventually, it relies on its claws and hardened exoskeleton for protection. On some islands, the crab is hunted for food. Once caught, however, the robber crab must be held carefully, as the Cook islander is demonstrating (left), because it can inflict serious injury.

Leaf insect is 2.75 in (7 cm) long

Leg

LEAF WITH LEGS
This leaf insect lives on the island of Java and is very well camouflaged. Its skin has both the color and texture of a real leaf. There are marks that resemble the midrib and veins of a typical leaf, and it even has brown markings that make it look like an unappetizing, dying leaf.

Chameleon protected by ability to change color to match background

Toes of front foot grouped with two on outside and three on inside

Toes of back foot grouped with three on outside and two on inside

Cassowaries make a threatening, booming noise to scare invaders

FLIGHTLESS
Cassowaries, like many island birds, have lost the ability to fly. They have powerful legs for running and fighting, and daggerlike claws for defense, and so do not need to fly. These solitary birds blend easily into the dense jungles of New Guinea, where they feed on fruit, supplementing their diet with occasional reptiles, small birds, or mammals.

LIFE IN THE TREES
Chameleons have remarkable toes that are specialized for life in trees. The toes are arranged so the feet are able to grip branches securely while the tail offers extra support, twisting and twining itself around small twigs. This Madagascan chameleon has a sticky tipped tongue, which it is able to extend farther than the length of its body, guaranteeing it a good diet of insects and other small invertebrates.

In the outback

AUSTRALIA IS HOME to some of the most extraordinary animals in the world. It has been an island continent for millions of years, and its wildlife has developed in a very individual way. There are more than 150 kinds of pouched mammals, or marsupials, in Australia, and only 70 other such species in other parts of the world. Marsupials, including the largest, the kangaroo, are born tiny, naked, and blind, and wriggle from the birth opening to a teat in the mother's pouch. They stay in the pouch, well protected, feeding on the mother's milk until they are large enough to survive outside. In the case of the kangaroo, when it is big enough, the young, or joey, hops in and out of the pouch while its mother grazes. There are many other animals that live only in Australia, including some of the most poisonous snakes in the world.

TREE BOUND
The koala, *Phascolarctos cinereus*, is a marsupial and eats only the tough, leathery leaves of 12 species of eucalyptus gum tree. It is totally arboreal, only able to live in trees, because it has four hands to grip branches, and no feet suitable for walking.

Large, broad bill to catch and swallow prey

Large head with brown ear patch

Warm fur

Laughing kookaburra
Dacelo novaeguineae

BIRD WITH A SENSE OF HUMOR
The laughing kookaburra is named after its chuckling territorial calls, which are sometimes loud and booming, and sometimes quiet. It is a giant kingfisher that lives in the eastern half of Australia in family groups. The kookaburra has a very varied diet, pouncing on snakes, mammals, birds, and invertebrates. Despite the fact that it is a kingfisher, it only occasionally dives into water after fish. It is 16–18 in (40–45 cm) in length and has a large head and bill relative to its body size.

Stiff tail used as support

IN LEAPS AND BOUNDS
There are more than 40 species in the kangaroo and wallaby family. There is no real difference between a kangaroo and a wallaby: larger species tend to be called kangaroos, and smaller ones wallabies. The family name is Macropodidae, which means "big feet," and they certainly do have big feet, which they use to bound along in great leaps, while the tail acts as a counterbalance. Some large kangaroos can travel at nearly 40 mph (60 km/h)! These marsupials are herbivorous, grazing on plants as they move along slowly, resting their heavy tails and front paws on the ground for balance and swinging their back legs forward.

White's tree frog
Litoria caerulea

Doria's tree kangaroo
Dendrolagus dorianus

STICKY-TOED AMPHIBIAN
White's tree frog has round toe-pads that are sticky with mucus. It lives in forests, although it is familiar to many Australians because it also lives in water barrels and lavatories. It is 2–4 in (5–10 cm) long and feeds on any moving creature small enough to be swallowed. These frogs spawn in water, producing 200 to 2,000 eggs.

Large ears

Sharp eyesight

UP A TREE
Tree kangaroos have evolved from ground-living ancestors. They climb trees to browse on foliage, but most species can still hop over the ground. Doria's tree kangaroo is the most arboreal. It has strong forelegs, broad hind feet, and sharp claws, and can no longer hop like other kangaroos. It lives in the cooler forests of the New Guinea highlands and has a thick fur coat to keep warm.

Powerful shoulders

Long tail acts as counterbalance when kangaroo climbs trees

Hands used for pulling down vegetation and sparring with other males

Powerful claws

Deadly sting in the tail

DANGER UNDERFOOT
There are many poisonous creatures to be found in the outback. The marbled scorpion *Lychas marmoreus* lurks under bark and among leaf litter, where it hunts for small invertebrates. These are usually overpowered by its front claws and jaws, and it saves the venomous sting in its tail for defense.

Penguins of the Antarctic

THERE ARE 18 DIFFERENT SPECIES of penguins, all found south of the equator. Some live in cool waters off the coasts of New Zealand, South Australia, and South Africa. Others live off the west coast of South America and in the Galapagos Islands in the Pacific. But the vast majority prefer to live in the far south, in the frozen seas and islands off the coast of Antarctica. These flightless birds divide their time between the sea and the land. They travel up to 500 mi (800 km) in the winter months in search of krill, fish, and squid to eat, returning to rookeries on land to breed during the warmer summer months. A penguin has a thick, waterproof coat, with short, oily-tipped feathers that overlap to stop water from soaking through. Underneath is a thick layer of down that traps the warm air near the penguin's body. A layer of fat immediately under the skin also stops heat loss from the penguin's body.

KEEPING WARM
Emperor penguins are able to raise only one chick a year because the female lays the egg in the depths of winter on the icy surface of the Antarctic. The male penguin then incubates the egg under a brood patch, or flap of skin. The resulting chick – this one is about eight weeks old – benefits from the same extra warmth and protection as it grows.

The birds in the center are the warmest

Heat loss can be reduced by as much as 50 percent

Birds take turns in the most exposed positions

Incubating male Emperor penguins
Aptenodytes forsteri

Emperors often turn their backs to the constantly shifting wind

TOGETHERNESS
Incubating male Emperor penguins huddle together for warmth, moving very little to conserve energy. Even when the chicks are born, the birds still huddle together as much as possible. Some Emperor colonies contain more than 20,000 pairs.

After the females return from fishing, the hungry males head for the open sea

Penguin "flies" out of water to breathe

Penguin catches fish and krill in its beak

Penguin shoots onto land or ice in giant leap of up to 6.5 ft (2 m)

DUCKING AND DIVING
Over a long time, penguin wings have evolved to form flippers with which they "fly" through the water. When they are swimming fast, they often use a technique called porpoising, leaping out of the water like dolphins or porpoises. Air offers less resistance to movement than water, so porpoising penguins can travel at speeds of up to 18 mph (30 km/h).

Under the water, penguin steers with its feet and tail

Bill is small to cut down on heat loss

King penguin
Aptenodytes patagonica

KING OF ALL THEY SURVEY
Nearly as big as an Emperor, at 3.3 ft (1 m) tall, the handsome King penguin breeds in huge colonies of thousands and thousands of birds. It breeds on Antarctica and the sub-Antarctic islands, but because it relies on a warmer breeding climate than the Emperor, it only raises, on average, two chicks every three years. The chicks take 10 to 13 months to fledge. When the chick has hatched, the parent birds go on fishing trips that last between four and eight days. The youngsters wait, huddled together in enormous outdoor nurseries or crèches. The average weight of an adult King penguin is 33 lb (15 kg), so parents need to catch between 50 and 90 squid or fish on each trip to the sea.

Penguin feeds chick by regurgitating catch

Overlapping, closely packed feathers cover a thick layer of blubber

King penguins lay only one egg, carrying around on their feet, covered by a brood patch

Small feet cut down on heat loss

Adaptable animals

To SURVIVE THE CHANGING SEASONS in some parts of the world, animals have to change, too. As winter approaches, some mammals grow thick fur coats, which may be white for camouflage against snow. They store a thick layer of fat in their skin to trap extra warmth and to act as a food supply in lean times. Some birds also gain layers of fat and a set of dense, fluffy feathers to keep out the cold. For many birds and mammals, the severe winter weather is just too much. They migrate south to warmer places, returning again in spring. Insects rest in soil over the winter, usually in the form of larvae, and are able to withstand the freezing temperatures. As summer arrives, birds and mammals molt, or shed, their thick coats. Animals that turn white in winter turn brown for summer camouflage.

FINE FURS
People in cold countries always wore fur clothes to keep warm through the coldest winters. They usually obtained them by snaring their original owners in traps.

Arctic fox
Alopex lagopus

DRESSED FOR SUMMER
In summer, the Arctic fox grows a thinner coat of brownish-gray fur over most of its body. These colors match the brownish-gray rocks of the tundra landscape, making the fox hard to see, so it can creep up on its prey, such as a lemming, without being spotted. The fox stores food under rocks during the summer and comes back to eat it in the winter months when food is hard to find. Arctic foxes have a varied diet, eating anything from berries, shells, and dead animals to garbage, birds, and eggs. But lemmings are vital to their diet and Arctic foxes will endure many weeks of starvation if few lemmings are available.

The chest and belly are usually a pale gray-white in color

Short legs lose less heat than long ones because there is less surface area exposed to the air

Thick, bushy tail can be curled around the body for warmth during blizzards or when resting

Antarctic ice fish
Chaenocephalus aceratus

ANTIFREEZE IN ITS VEINS
Many Antarctic fish have antifreeze molecules in their bodies that enable them to live in a "supercooled" state; their body fluids remain liquid at temperatures below the point at which ice forms. Antarctic ice fish (such as the fish to the left) have almost translucent blood.

Hair under paws stops the fox from sinking in snow; the fox's Latin name is Alopex lagopus – lagopus *means "hairy foot"*

A BIRD FOR ALL SEASONS
Ptarmigans change their plumage twice a year so that they are always well camouflaged. Their feather density also increases in winter. When resting overnight, ptarmigans sometimes burrow in snow to reduce heat loss.

Rock ptarmigan
Lagopus mutus

Dense fur coat with long hairs traps body warmth

Ears are furry inside and out for extra warmth

KEEPING WARM WITH FAT
Whales and seals are kept warm by a layer of thick fat called blubber. This fat walrus is in no danger of getting cold. Walruses can weigh up to 1.8 tons (1,600 kg), and have tusks 3.3 ft (1 m) long.

Small, round ears and a short muzzle cut down on heat loss; foxes from warmer places have larger ears and longer muzzles

Sharp, pointed teeth to grab animals such as lemmings

INSULATED FUR
The Arctic fox's white winter fur is made up of hairs that are hollow inside and full of air. The air in the hairs traps body warmth from the fox in much the same way as an insulated window traps warmth from a house. Air is a good insulator and does not let heat pass through it easily. The Arctic fox can tolerate temperatures of –40°F (–40°C), or even lower, quite comfortably.

Sharp claws used to dig through snow to find food

GIANT WEED
Many species of coastal kelps are found around the world. Some are very large indeed – hundreds of feet long. Waves and water currents pull on the enormous fronds with great force, so the kelp is fastened to the rocks of the shoreline by gnarled, rootlike structures called holdfasts. These hold tight to the rock, like a tree's roots in soil. Well-anchored kelp protects many ocean dwellers from the Sun and lessens the force of waves and winds, so many smaller plants and shore animals, such as crabs, fish, prawns, and mollusks, take advantage of the calmer conditions in forests of kelp.

CHAPTER 5
LIFE IN THE WATER

In FRESHWATER rivers and lakes, and in saltwater seas
and oceans, a multitude of habitats exist. Water is a
rich environment, teeming with life, but tides, winds,
waves, water currents, temperature, and climate
can make it a difficult one in which to live.

SHAGGY SHELLS
Gaping file shells move by expelling
water from their shells and using their
masses of orange tentacles like oars.
They cannot withdraw the
tentacles inside the two
halves of their shells
for protection, so the
tentacles produce a sour-
tasting, sticky substance to
deter predators. Gaping file
shells build homes in
seaweeds, such as this maerl,
a chalky, red seaweed that
grows along the
stony seabed.

Freshwater fish

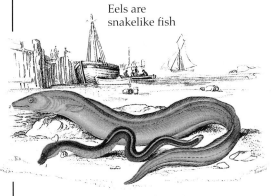

Mᴏsᴛ ᴘᴇᴏᴘʟᴇ ᴏɴʟʏ ᴇᴠᴇʀ sᴇᴇ freshwater fish as dark torpedo shapes cruising silently below the surface of a river or pond. Their ability to remain elusive has served freshwater fish well, and an amazing variety of species are supremely suited to underwater life. They swim by flexing powerful muscles that move their bodies back and forth. This produces a thrashing motion and propels the fish along. The fins are used chiefly for stabilizing, steering, and braking. The stripe along a fish's side is called the lateral line. It is a groove of specialized tissue that detects vibrations in the water, in effect allowing the fish to "hear" and "feel" water movements. Most of the fish on these two pages demonstrate a clever camouflage trick called countershading. Their backs are dark and dull, so when viewed from above, they blend in with the murky water of their pond or riverbed. Their bellies are shiny and silvery, so that when seen from below, they merge with the ripples and flashes on the underside of the water's surface.

Lateral line for detecting water movements

Roach has red iris

RUDD
This fish likes still water, and the more weeds, the better. The rudd can be distinguished from the roach (above right) by its fins: in the rudd, the front edge of the dorsal (back) fin is farther back than the base of the ventral (belly) fin, while in the roach, these are in line. In some areas, rudd interbreed with roach or bream (bottom right). Rudd reach about 4.5 lb (2 kg) in weight.

Rudd
Scardinius erythrophthalmus

Rudd has orange iris

Ventral fins are bright orange

Young roach

Tench
Tinca tinca

Medieval ailments were treated with slime from tench skin

Unforked tail

YOUNG ROACH
When they are young, fish are very difficult to identify. This one is probably a young roach and bears very little resemblance to the older roach shown above.

TENCH
Tiny scales, a greenish sheen, an almost unforked tail, and a bulky, muscular body are characteristics of this still-water, bottom-feeding member of the carp family. A good-sized tench weighs around 9 lb (4 kg), and the fish is a powerful fighter.

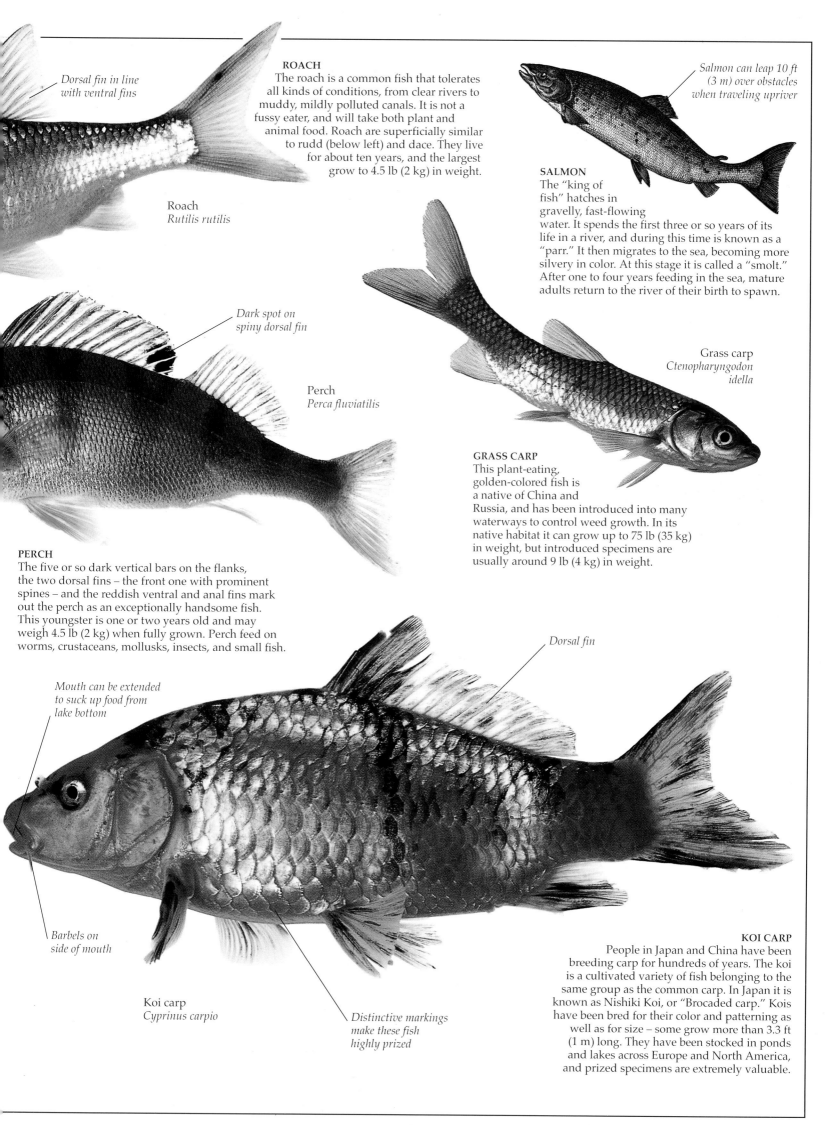

Dorsal fin in line with ventral fins

ROACH

The roach is a common fish that tolerates all kinds of conditions, from clear rivers to muddy, mildly polluted canals. It is not a fussy eater, and will take both plant and animal food. Roach are superficially similar to rudd (below left) and dace. They live for about ten years, and the largest grow to 4.5 lb (2 kg) in weight.

Roach
Rutilis rutilis

Salmon can leap 10 ft (3 m) over obstacles when traveling upriver

SALMON

The "king of fish" hatches in gravelly, fast-flowing water. It spends the first three or so years of its life in a river, and during this time is known as a "parr." It then migrates to the sea, becoming more silvery in color. At this stage it is called a "smolt." After one to four years feeding in the sea, mature adults return to the river of their birth to spawn.

Dark spot on spiny dorsal fin

Perch
Perca fluviatilis

Grass carp
Ctenopharyngodon idella

GRASS CARP

This plant-eating, golden-colored fish is a native of China and Russia, and has been introduced into many waterways to control weed growth. In its native habitat it can grow up to 75 lb (35 kg) in weight, but introduced specimens are usually around 9 lb (4 kg) in weight.

PERCH

The five or so dark vertical bars on the flanks, the two dorsal fins – the front one with prominent spines – and the reddish ventral and anal fins mark out the perch as an exceptionally handsome fish. This youngster is one or two years old and may weigh 4.5 lb (2 kg) when fully grown. Perch feed on worms, crustaceans, mollusks, insects, and small fish.

Dorsal fin

Mouth can be extended to suck up food from lake bottom

Barbels on side of mouth

Koi carp
Cyprinus carpio

Distinctive markings make these fish highly prized

KOI CARP

People in Japan and China have been breeding carp for hundreds of years. The koi is a cultivated variety of fish belonging to the same group as the common carp. In Japan it is known as Nishiki Koi, or "Brocaded carp." Kois have been bred for their color and patterning as well as for size – some grow more than 3.3 ft (1 m) long. They have been stocked in ponds and lakes across Europe and North America, and prized specimens are extremely valuable.

Underwater weeds

Submerged weeds grow in ponds and rivers like trees in a miniature underwater forest. They provide shelter for some animals and hiding places for others from which to pounce on unwary victims. Underwater weeds are food for many creatures, from pond snails to ducks, and provide vital oxygen. As a plant carries out photosynthesis (pp. 40–41), released oxygen is the essential by-product. The oxygen diffuses into the water and is used by both plants and animals for respiration. On a sunny day, tiny oxygen bubbles coat the leaves of underwater plants and occasionally rise to the water's surface.

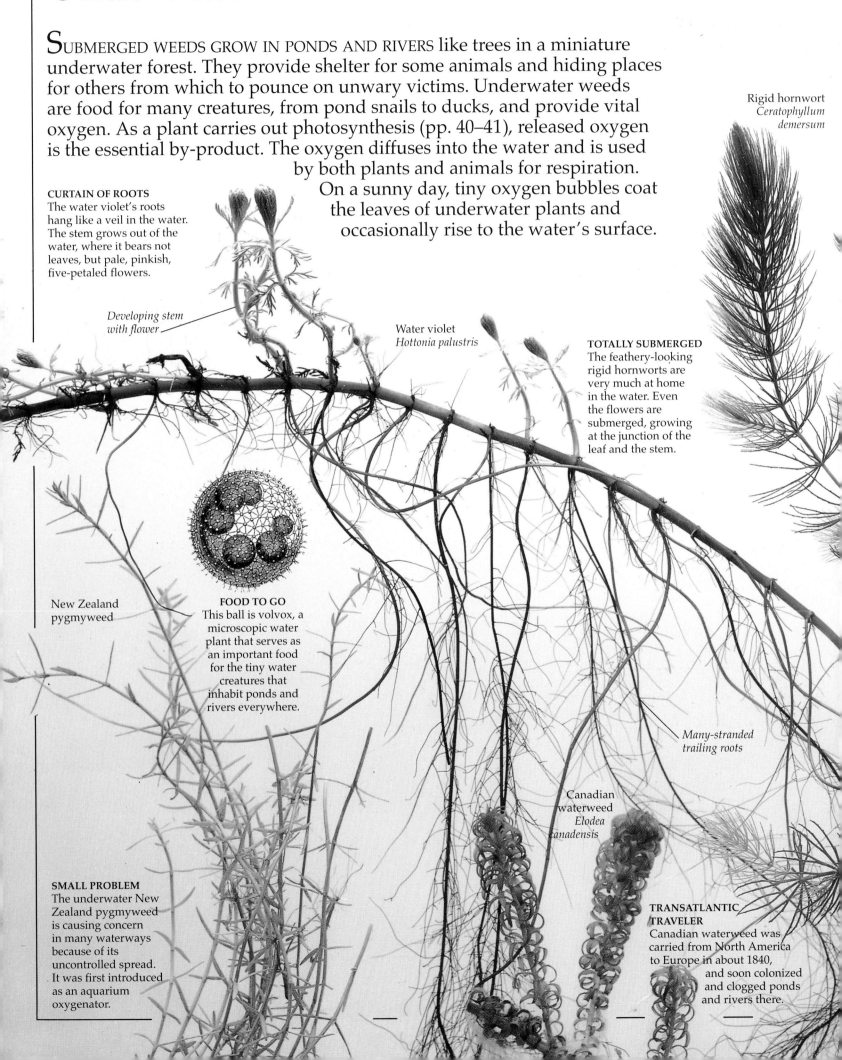

Rigid hornwort
Ceratophyllum demersum

CURTAIN OF ROOTS
The water violet's roots hang like a veil in the water. The stem grows out of the water, where it bears not leaves, but pale, pinkish, five-petaled flowers.

Developing stem with flower

Water violet
Hottonia palustris

TOTALLY SUBMERGED
The feathery-looking rigid hornworts are very much at home in the water. Even the flowers are submerged, growing at the junction of the leaf and the stem.

New Zealand pygmyweed

FOOD TO GO
This ball is volvox, a microscopic water plant that serves as an important food for the tiny water creatures that inhabit ponds and rivers everywhere.

Many-stranded trailing roots

Canadian waterweed
Elodea canadensis

SMALL PROBLEM
The underwater New Zealand pygmyweed is causing concern in many waterways because of its uncontrolled spread. It was first introduced as an aquarium oxygenator.

TRANSATLANTIC TRAVELER
Canadian waterweed was carried from North America to Europe in about 1840, and soon colonized and clogged ponds and rivers there.

INVISIBLE TO THE EYE
At 25 x magnification, the microscopic world of underwater plants is revealed. This drop of pond water is teeming with plankton.

Narrow leaves resemble needles of a fir tree

Tape grass
Vallisneria spiralis

Bulbous rush

PERCH IN THE GRASS
Tape grass is one of the popularly named "river grasses." It provides a hideout for many fish, particularly the perch, which is well camouflaged by the vertical stripes on its sides.

Tall, grasslike stems grow close together

SLENDER WATERWEED
The pale green water starwort sways in large clumps in the water. Water starwort is a favorite shelter for the shy loach, which only emerges to forage for food at dusk.

RUSHED GROWTH
The bulbous rush is usually rooted on the pond side, but sometimes it grows underwater, becoming very elongated.

Water starwort
Callitriche stagnalis

Floating flowers

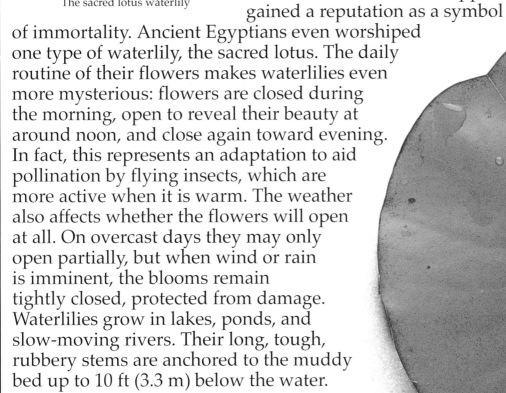

The sacred lotus waterlily

IN ANCIENT TIMES, people saw that when a previously dry watercourse filled with rain, the lush blooms of waterlilies would soon appear. These aquatic plants gained a reputation as a symbol of immortality. Ancient Egyptians even worshiped one type of waterlily, the sacred lotus. The daily routine of their flowers makes waterlilies even more mysterious: flowers are closed during the morning, open to reveal their beauty at around noon, and close again toward evening. In fact, this represents an adaptation to aid pollination by flying insects, which are more active when it is warm. The weather also affects whether the flowers will open at all. On overcast days they may only open partially, but when wind or rain is imminent, the blooms remain tightly closed, protected from damage. Waterlilies grow in lakes, ponds, and slow-moving rivers. Their long, tough, rubbery stems are anchored to the muddy bed up to 10 ft (3.3 m) below the water.

NUISANCE OR FRIEND?
The flowering water hyacinth floats freely on the surface of the water, carrying its roots below. It is borne along by the water currents and breezes, spreading rapidly – and often clogging rivers and canals. However, the roots are good at trapping the harmful substances that pollute rivers and lakes. They are often planted by scientists to "strain" water and clean it of toxins.

Waxy coating repels water droplets

Red hybrid – "Escarboucle"

Yellow waterlily leaves are patterned with a red tinge

Silky hairs cover leaf surfaces, preventing them from becoming waterlogged and sinking underwater

Leaves may be heart-shaped, oval, or round

Conspicuous yellow stamens

LILIES AND THEIR HYBRIDS

There are more than 60 species of waterlilies around the world. In some areas thay are known as lotuses. Their magnificent waxy-looking flowers and bold circular leaves have made them favorites for growing in ponds, ornamental water gardens, and lakes. A wide variety of different-colored flowers known as hybrids have been bred by horticulturalists.

Waxy petals

Yellow hybrid –
"Chromatella"

FLOATING SAUCERS

The Amazonian waterlily has some of the largest leaves in the plant world. A single leaf may measure more than 5 ft (1.5 m) across and has an upturned rim with reinforcing ribs beneath.

WATER LILY LEAF CASE

The china mark moth caterpillar cuts out an oval of leaf and fastens to the underside with silk thread to form a case in which it stays, underwater, until it emerges as a moth.

Waterlily leaf

WELL-USED LEAVES

The leaves, also known as lily pads, are used by many creatures that live in the water. In the spring, pond snails lay their speckled, jellylike egg masses on the undersides of lily pads. Frogs rest on or under them, waiting to snap up unwary insects. Lily pads can grow dense enough to allow some creatures to walk across them. The African jaçana, a bird with long, widespread toes, is known as the "lily trotter" because it steps delicately from pad to pad as it searches for insects and seeds.

Waterfowl

WATER AND ITS RESIDENT WILDLIFE attract an amazing variety of birds. There are about 150 species of wildfowl, including swans, geese, and ducks, which are quite at home on the ponds, lakes, rivers, and seashores of the world. These generally heavy-bodied birds have webbed feet for swimming, and long, mobile necks for dabbling in the water and rummaging in the muddy bed for food. During spring, the dense bank vegetation provides many species with safe and sheltered nesting sites. In summer, the proud parents can be seen leading their fluffy chicks across the surface of the water. Aquatic plants and animals are a ready source of food for most of the year. In winter, when ponds and some lakes freeze over, many wildfowl fly south, often covering vast distances to find a more favorable climate in which to spend the winter. Others retreat to parks and gardens where they feast on scraps donated by well-wishing humans.

Nest and eggs of
eider duck
Somateria mollisima

Soft down feathers
insulate eggs in nest

Nest and eggs
of Common teal
Anas crecca

TEAL NEST
The teal makes its nest in dense undergrowth, using twigs and grasses. The female is very careful not to attract predators when visiting her chicks.

SPECIALLY GROWN DOWN
Ultrasoft eiderdown feathers grow on the female eider duck's breast. She plucks them to cocoon her eggs as she nests on sea- or lakeshore, or on the riverbank.

TUFTED DUCK EGG
The six to fourteen eggs of the tufted duck are laid in a nest close to the water's edge. The chicks hatch after 25 days and are swimming within a day.

Teal is one of the smallest ducks

MUTED COLORS
Out of the breeding season, the pintail drake molts to the inconspicuous "eclipse" plumage, resembling the female's colors.

Pintail wing

PLUMAGE
In the breeding season, most male ducks, like the pintail (far right), sport bright plumage to catch the eye of the female. The female (right) is a duller color for camouflage on the nest.

TUFTED DUCK FOOD
The tufted duck feeds on freshwater mussels, as well as small fish, frogs, and any insects it can catch.

Tufted duck
Aythya fuligula

Tufted duck skull

ON THE WING
Pintails, like most ducks, can escape danger with a twisting and turning flight. They open and close their pointed wings (right) to change direction. All wildfowl are strong fliers, many covering vast distances during annual migrations.

MUSCOVY DUCK BILL *below*
This native of Central and South American ponds and marshes has a broad bill that allows it to feed on aquatic plants and animals.

Muscovy duck
Cairina moschata

Muscovy duck skull

MUTE SWAN THREAT
The mute swan's bill (below) is normally covered by an orange sheath. Male swans can be extremely vicious, particularly in the breeding season, when defending territory.

Outer vane (windward edge of feather)

Mute swan
Cygnus olor

Broad bill of swan suitable for dabbling for water vegetation

Flight feathers

Long quill

Mute swan skull

FEATHER CARE
Water-dwelling birds rely on feathers to stay dry. They spend a lot of time preening their feathers to keep them in good condition and free of parasites.

River life

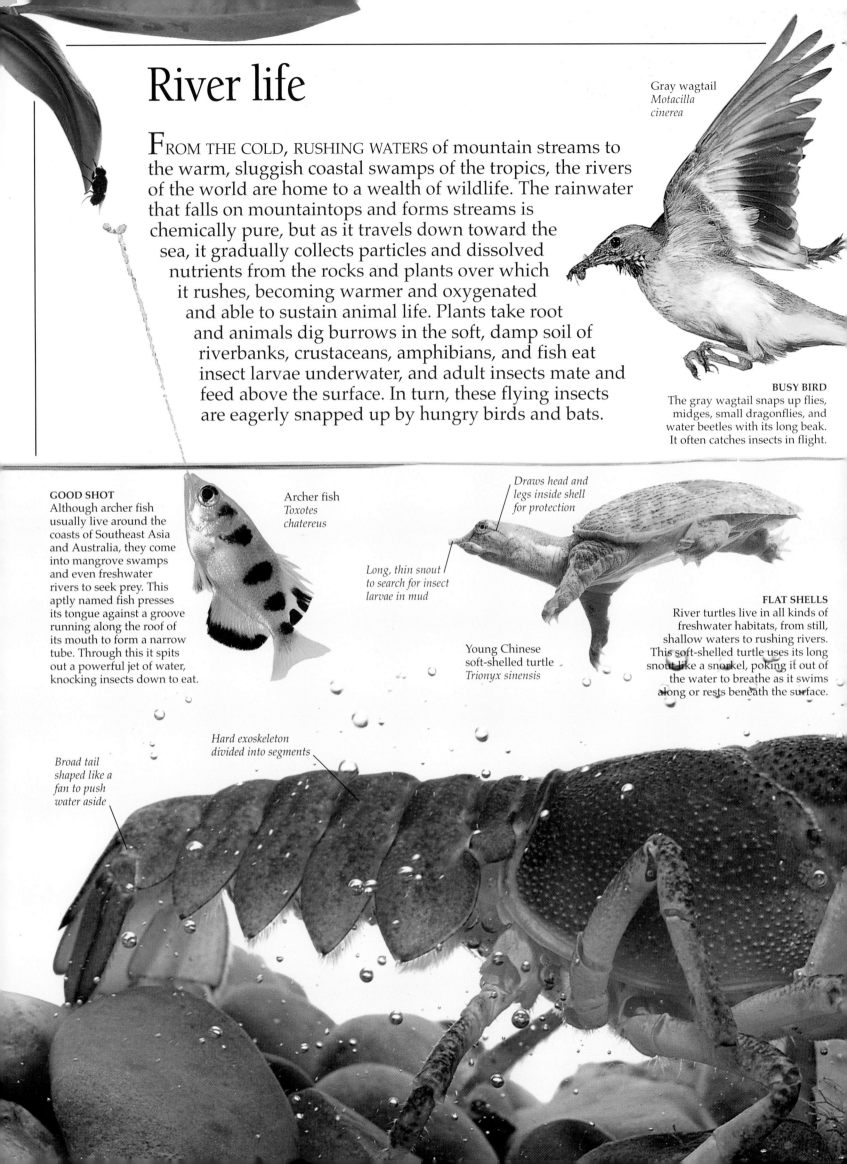

FROM THE COLD, RUSHING WATERS of mountain streams to the warm, sluggish coastal swamps of the tropics, the rivers of the world are home to a wealth of wildlife. The rainwater that falls on mountaintops and forms streams is chemically pure, but as it travels down toward the sea, it gradually collects particles and dissolved nutrients from the rocks and plants over which it rushes, becoming warmer and oxygenated and able to sustain animal life. Plants take root and animals dig burrows in the soft, damp soil of riverbanks, crustaceans, amphibians, and fish eat insect larvae underwater, and adult insects mate and feed above the surface. In turn, these flying insects are eagerly snapped up by hungry birds and bats.

Gray wagtail
*Motacilla
cinerea*

BUSY BIRD
The gray wagtail snaps up flies, midges, small dragonflies, and water beetles with its long beak. It often catches insects in flight.

GOOD SHOT
Although archer fish usually live around the coasts of Southeast Asia and Australia, they come into mangrove swamps and even freshwater rivers to seek prey. This aptly named fish presses its tongue against a groove running along the roof of its mouth to form a narrow tube. Through this it spits out a powerful jet of water, knocking insects down to eat.

Archer fish
*Toxotes
chatereus*

Draws head and legs inside shell for protection

Long, thin snout to search for insect larvae in mud

Young Chinese soft-shelled turtle
Trionyx sinensis

FLAT SHELLS
River turtles live in all kinds of freshwater habitats, from still, shallow waters to rushing rivers. This soft-shelled turtle uses its long snout like a snorkel, poking it out of the water to breathe as it swims along or rests beneath the surface.

Broad tail shaped like a fan to push water aside

Hard exoskeleton divided into segments

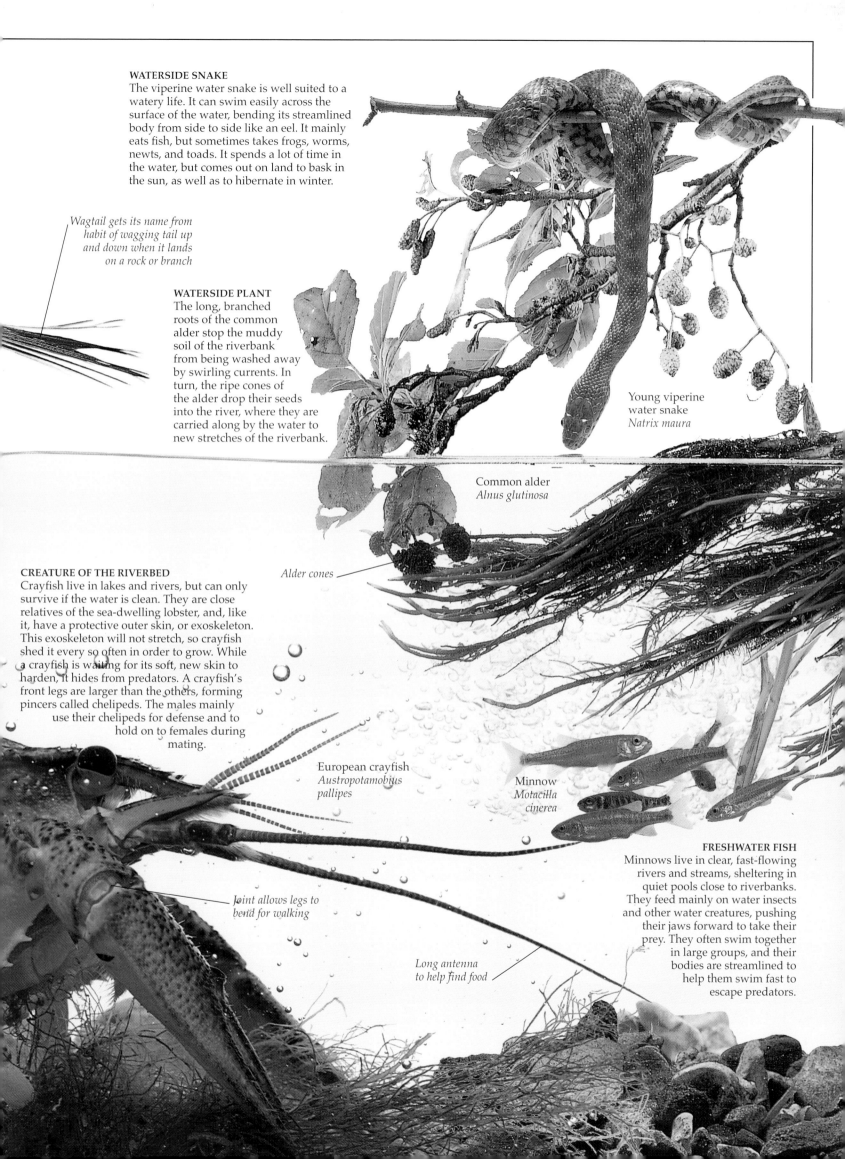

WATERSIDE SNAKE
The viperine water snake is well suited to a
watery life. It can swim easily across the
surface of the water, bending its streamlined
body from side to side like an eel. It mainly
eats fish, but sometimes takes frogs, worms,
newts, and toads. It spends a lot of time in
the water, but comes out on land to bask in
the sun, as well as to hibernate in winter.

*Wagtail gets its name from
habit of wagging tail up
and down when it lands
on a rock or branch*

WATERSIDE PLANT
The long, branched
roots of the common
alder stop the muddy
soil of the riverbank
from being washed away
by swirling currents. In
turn, the ripe cones of
the alder drop their seeds
into the river, where they are
carried along by the water to
new stretches of the riverbank.

Young viperine
water snake
Natrix maura

Common alder
Alnus glutinosa

Alder cones

CREATURE OF THE RIVERBED
Crayfish live in lakes and rivers, but can only
survive if the water is clean. They are close
relatives of the sea-dwelling lobster, and, like
it, have a protective outer skin, or exoskeleton.
This exoskeleton will not stretch, so crayfish
shed it every so often in order to grow. While
a crayfish is waiting for its soft, new skin to
harden, it hides from predators. A crayfish's
front legs are larger than the others, forming
pincers called chelipeds. The males mainly
use their chelipeds for defense and to
hold on to females during
mating.

European crayfish
*Austropotamobius
pallipes*

Minnow
*Motacilla
cinerea*

*Joint allows legs to
bend for walking*

*Long antenna
to help find food*

FRESHWATER FISH
Minnows live in clear, fast-flowing
rivers and streams, sheltering in
quiet pools close to riverbanks.
They feed mainly on water insects
and other water creatures, pushing
their jaws forward to take their
prey. They often swim together
in large groups, and their
bodies are streamlined to
help them swim fast to
escape predators.

The salt marsh

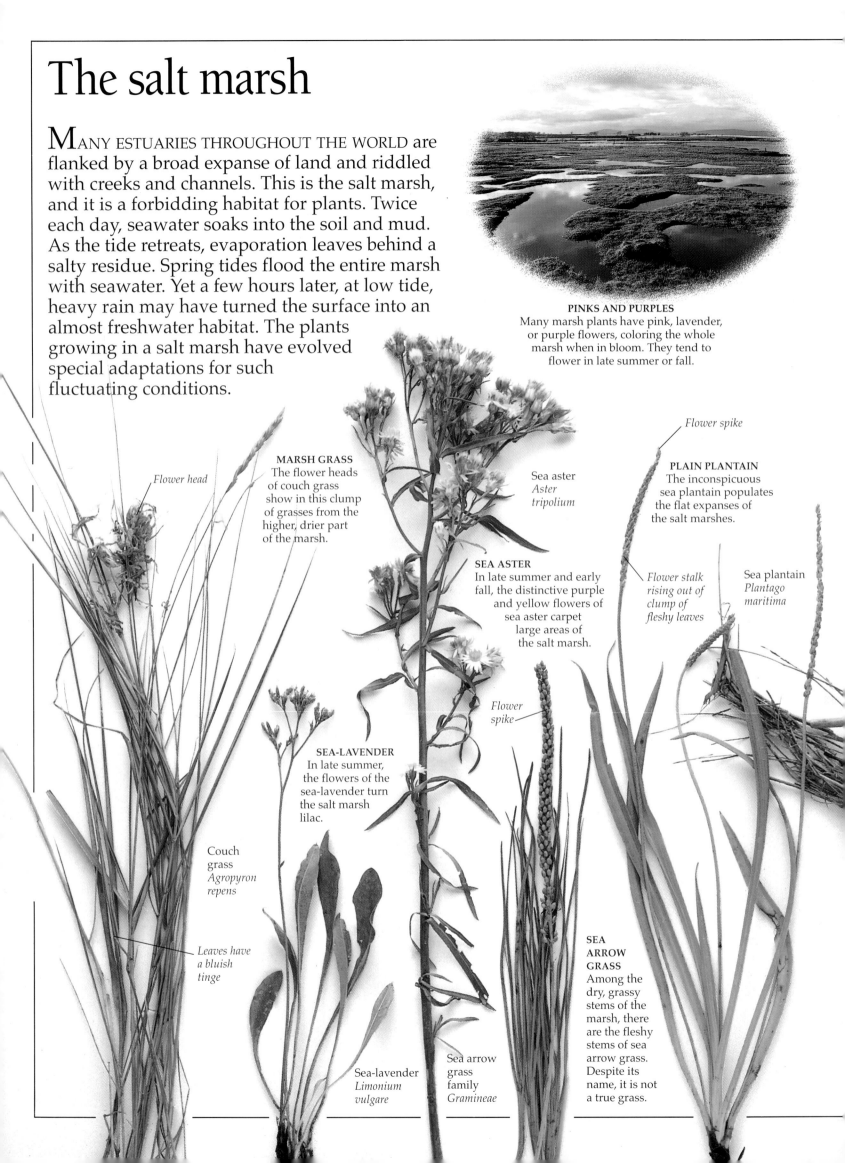

MANY ESTUARIES THROUGHOUT THE WORLD are flanked by a broad expanse of land and riddled with creeks and channels. This is the salt marsh, and it is a forbidding habitat for plants. Twice each day, seawater soaks into the soil and mud. As the tide retreats, evaporation leaves behind a salty residue. Spring tides flood the entire marsh with seawater. Yet a few hours later, at low tide, heavy rain may have turned the surface into an almost freshwater habitat. The plants growing in a salt marsh have evolved special adaptations for such fluctuating conditions.

PINKS AND PURPLES
Many marsh plants have pink, lavender, or purple flowers, coloring the whole marsh when in bloom. They tend to flower in late summer or fall.

Flower head

MARSH GRASS
The flower heads of couch grass show in this clump of grasses from the higher, drier part of the marsh.

Sea aster
Aster tripolium

Flower spike

PLAIN PLANTAIN
The inconspicuous sea plantain populates the flat expanses of the salt marshes.

SEA ASTER
In late summer and early fall, the distinctive purple and yellow flowers of sea aster carpet large areas of the salt marsh.

Flower stalk rising out of clump of fleshy leaves

Sea plantain
Plantago maritima

Flower spike

SEA-LAVENDER
In late summer, the flowers of the sea-lavender turn the salt marsh lilac.

Couch grass
Agropyron repens

Leaves have a bluish tinge

Sea-lavender
Limonium vulgare

Sea arrow grass family
Gramineae

SEA ARROW GRASS
Among the dry, grassy stems of the marsh, there are the fleshy stems of sea arrow grass. Despite its name, it is not a true grass.

SEA PURSLANE
The silver-green leaves of the sea purslane are covered with minute, air-filled, protective scales. Sea purslane grows along the edges of the channels and creeks within the salt marsh.

Ripening seed heads

Sea purslane
Halimione portulacoides

Leaves absorb or lose water as salinity changes

ANNUAL SEABLITE
The thick, fleshy leaves of this annual seablite are typical of many plants of the salt marsh. The succulent leaves store water until it is needed.

BINDING IN THE MARSH
Cord grass, an early colonizer of bare mud, is often planted on the lower parts of marshes and estuaries to stabilize the ground with its underground stems and thick root system.

Cord grass
Spartina anglica

Annual seablite
Suaeda maritima

The leaves secrete salt crystals to rid the plant of excess salt

Thick roots supply plant with nutrients

RICH PICKINGS
Knots and many other wading birds probe the mud of the salt marsh channels for plants and insects.

Glasswort
Salvornia europaea

Swollen, jointed stems store water

SALT MARSH STABILIZER
Glasswort is one of the first plants to colonize the estuary mud. Its delicate roots begin the stabilizing process.

TIDAL DEBRIS
Each tide sweeps old stems, bits of crab, and other debris along the water channels that riddle the marsh.

MARSH MUD
Squelching, oozing mud, rich in organic matter, is the stuff of life in the salt marsh and estuary.

Roots bind the slippery mud

Crabs

Empty shells

CAST-UP REMAINS
Young shore crabs and cockles, and a whelk's spongy, empty egg case are some of the items found when "marsh-combing" along the channel edges.

Whelk egg case

Swamp life

DEEP LAYERS of mud and silt accumulate along sheltered tropical coastlines and in river estuaries. A number of different kinds of trees colonize these areas of still or slow-moving water. They are collectively known as mangroves and form swampy forests. Mangroves are the only trees that can live in the saltwater that is carried in and out of swamps by the tide twice a day. Among the mangroves' tangled roots live an amazing variety of animals that have adapted to the tidal ebb and flow of these thick jungles. Snapping turtles feed on water plants and carrion, while fiddler crabs emerge from muddy burrows to gather food. Water lettuces and water hyacinths provide food for the hungry herbivores, while overhead, iguanas and mangrove snakes sun themselves in the leafy branches.

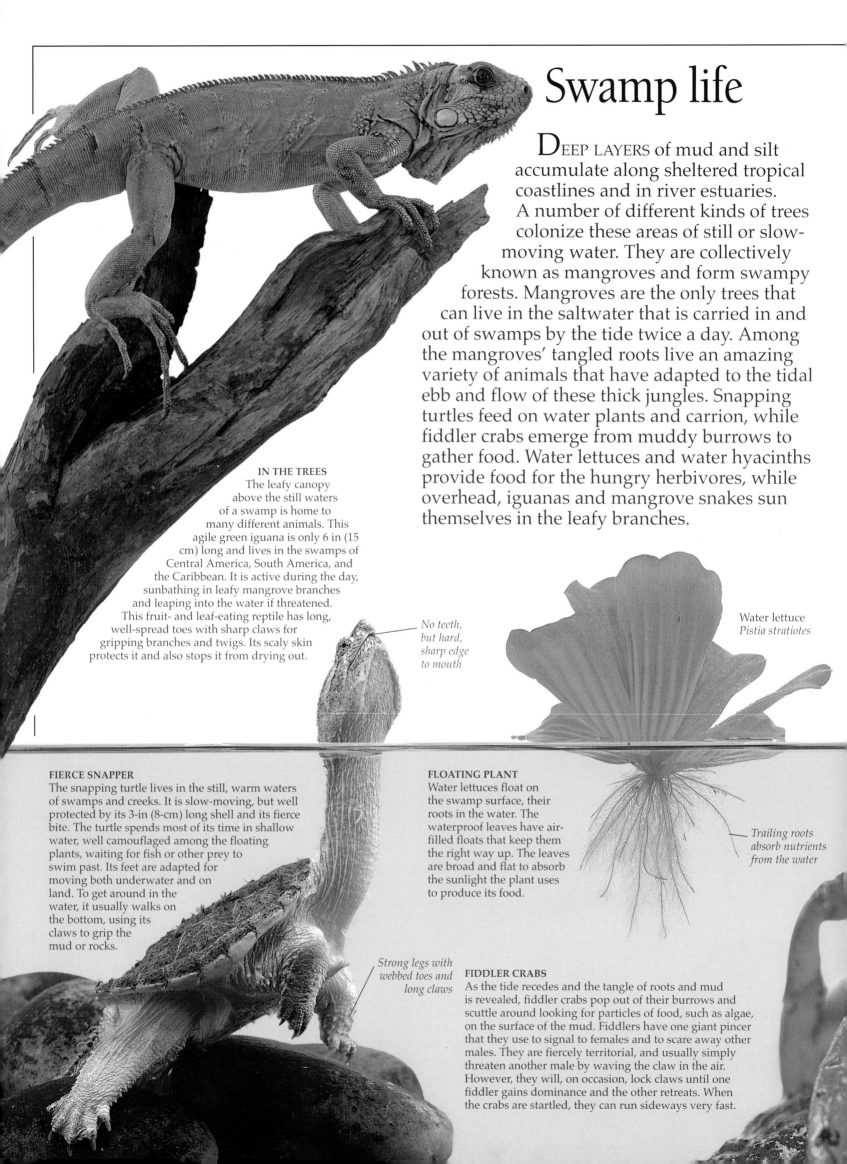

IN THE TREES
The leafy canopy above the still waters of a swamp is home to many different animals. This agile green iguana is only 6 in (15 cm) long and lives in the swamps of Central America, South America, and the Caribbean. It is active during the day, sunbathing in leafy mangrove branches and leaping into the water if threatened. This fruit- and leaf-eating reptile has long, well-spread toes with sharp claws for gripping branches and twigs. Its scaly skin protects it and also stops it from drying out.

No teeth, but hard, sharp edge to mouth

Water lettuce
Pistia stratiotes

FIERCE SNAPPER
The snapping turtle lives in the still, warm waters of swamps and creeks. It is slow-moving, but well protected by its 3-in (8-cm) long shell and its fierce bite. The turtle spends most of its time in shallow water, well camouflaged among the floating plants, waiting for fish or other prey to swim past. Its feet are adapted for moving both underwater and on land. To get around in the water, it usually walks on the bottom, using its claws to grip the mud or rocks.

FLOATING PLANT
Water lettuces float on the swamp surface, their roots in the water. The waterproof leaves have air-filled floats that keep them the right way up. The leaves are broad and flat to absorb the sunlight the plant uses to produce its food.

Trailing roots absorb nutrients from the water

Strong legs with webbed toes and long claws

FIDDLER CRABS
As the tide recedes and the tangle of roots and mud is revealed, fiddler crabs pop out of their burrows and scuttle around looking for particles of food, such as algae, on the surface of the mud. Fiddlers have one giant pincer that they use to signal to females and to scare away other males. They are fiercely territorial, and usually simply threaten another male by waving the claw in the air. However, they will, on occasion, lock claws until one fiddler gains dominance and the other retreats. When the crabs are startled, they can run sideways very fast.

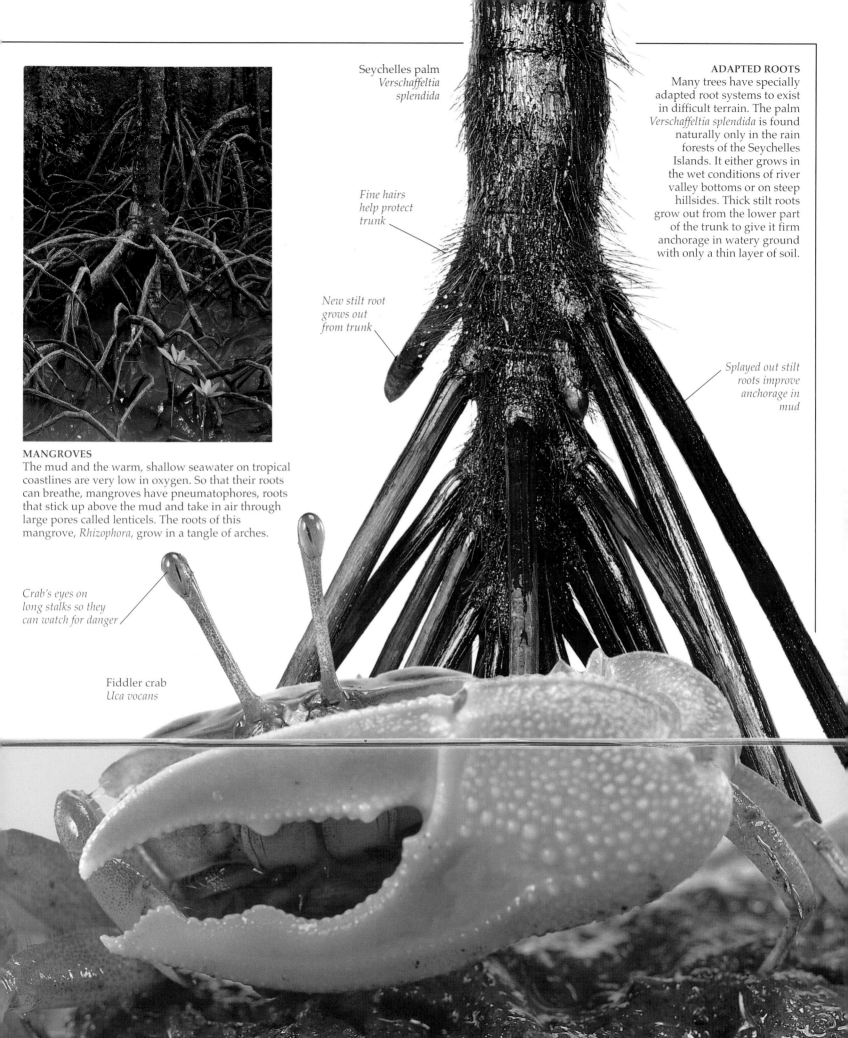

Seychelles palm
*Verschaffeltia
splendida*

Fine hairs
help protect
trunk

New stilt root
grows out
from trunk

ADAPTED ROOTS
Many trees have specially
adapted root systems to exist
in difficult terrain. The palm
Verschaffeltia splendida is found
naturally only in the rain
forests of the Seychelles
Islands. It either grows in
the wet conditions of river
valley bottoms or on steep
hillsides. Thick stilt roots
grow out from the lower part
of the trunk to give it firm
anchorage in watery ground
with only a thin layer of soil.

Splayed out stilt
roots improve
anchorage in
mud

MANGROVES
The mud and the warm, shallow seawater on tropical
coastlines are very low in oxygen. So that their roots
can breathe, mangroves have pneumatophores, roots
that stick up above the mud and take in air through
large pores called lenticels. The roots of this
mangrove, *Rhizophora*, grow in a tangle of arches.

Crab's eyes on
long stalks so they
can watch for danger

Fiddler crab
Uca vocans

Inside a tide pool

A TIDE POOL IS A miniature natural world – a specialized habitat shared by plants and animals. There is usually a wide range of plants, ranging from the film of microscopic algae coating almost any bare surface to wracks and other large seaweeds. These plants capture light energy from the Sun (pp. 12–13) and obtain nutrients from seawater. The plants in turn provide food for winkles, limpets, and other marine plant eaters. Flesh-eating animals – sea stars, small fish, whelks, and other creatures – eat the plant eaters. Tide pool scavengers such as crabs and prawns eat both plants and animals.

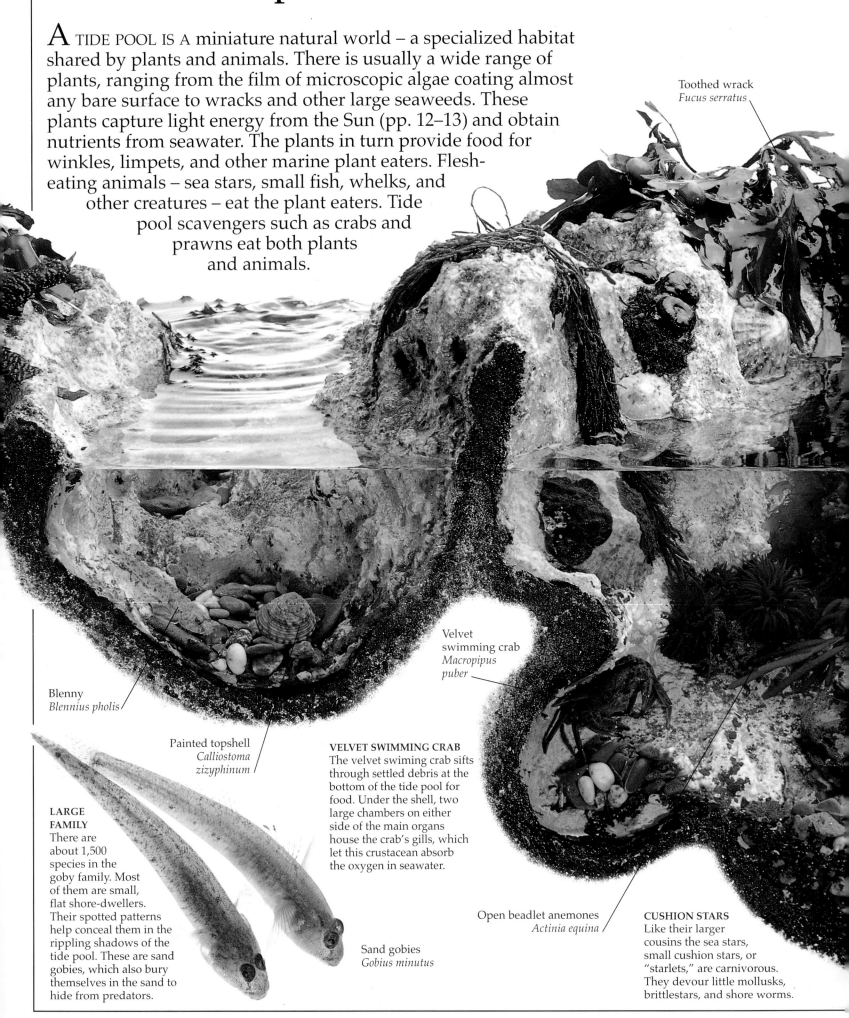

Toothed wrack
Fucus serratus

Velvet
swimming crab
*Macropipus
puber*

Blenny
Blennius pholis

Painted topshell
*Calliostoma
zizyphinum*

**LARGE
FAMILY**
There are
about 1,500
species in the
goby family. Most
of them are small,
flat shore-dwellers.
Their spotted patterns
help conceal them in the
rippling shadows of the
tide pool. These are sand
gobies, which also bury
themselves in the sand to
hide from predators.

VELVET SWIMMING CRAB
The velvet swiming crab sifts
through settled debris at the
bottom of the tide pool for
food. Under the shell, two
large chambers on either
side of the main organs
house the crab's gills, which
let this crustacean absorb
the oxygen in seawater.

Sand gobies
Gobius minutus

Open beadlet anemones
Actinia equina

CUSHION STARS
Like their larger
cousins the sea stars,
small cushion stars, or
"starlets," are carnivorous.
They devour little mollusks,
brittlestars, and shore worms.

CLINGING TO THE ROCKS
Many animals found in tide pools are gastropods (snaillike mollusks), and they cling to the tide pool walls. The common limpet can only be pried loose if taken by surprise, before its muscular foot "cements" it to the rock. Winkles, topshells, conches, cowries, cone shells, and whelks all patrol the shoreline looking for food.

ANEMONES
When they are immersed in water, anemones protect themselves with tiny stinging cells in their tentacles. They also use these stinging cells to paralyze prey. However, when the tide retreats, this gem anemone folds in its 48 tentacles. It cannot feed when the tide is out and folding inward stops its tentacles from drying out.

Red dulse seaweed
Rhodymenia palmata

Edible periwinkle
Littorina littorea

Common limpet
Patella vulgata

Common prawn
Leander serratus

SHRIMP OR PRAWN?
These ten-limbed crustaceans look very similar. In general, shrimps have fatter bodies, blunt claws on only the first pair of limbs, and they live mostly in sand. Prawns (shown here) are thinner, have small, narrow pincers on the first two pairs of limbs, and live in pools and among seaweed.

Breadcrumb sponge
Halichondria panicea

BREADCRUMB SPONGE
The deep green sponge attached to the rock is the common breadcrumb sponge, often found in shady gulleys and under boulders on the lower shore. Sponges are primitive animals that draw in water from which they extract oxygen and floating particles of food.

Snakelocks anemone
Anemonia sulcata

Common prawn

Waders

In the soda lakes of Africa's Great Rift Valley, flamingos flock in hundreds of thousands, forming a sea of deep pink. They owe their color to the pink pigment in the small shrimps that they sift and eat from the lake-bottom mud. Flamingos nest on the ground in large colonies. Adults fly away every day to find more food and water. Flamingos' long legs allow them to wade in deep water as they search for food. Where rivers meet the sea, the shallow, muddy waters of estuaries teem with a wealth of food, and these are rich waters for other long-legged wading birds, too, such as stilts, dunlins, and oystercatchers.

Large bill

Flamingos feed their young on a rich "milk" produced in the crop, part of the esophagus

Lesser flamingo
Phoenicopterus minor

The more shrimps the flamingo eats the pinker the feathers become

Long neck

Slender bill

ESTUARY BIRD
The black-necked stilt lives in North America and northern South America, breeding in colonies on marshy ground or on the bare mud of the salt pans. In flight, their legs stick out 7 in (18 cm) beyond their tail to counterbalance the long neck and the weight of the head. The very long legs allow the stilt to feed on small creatures that it takes from the mud in deep water on shores and estuaries.

Black-necked stilt
Himantopus mexicanus

Long legs to wade through deep water while feeding

LONG LEGS
The long legs of the flamingo enable it to reach deep water, helping it avoid competition for the available food from other, shorter-legged birds. Like ducks and geese, flamingos have webs of skin between their toes. The webs work like paddles when the bird is in water. They are also useful when the flamingo is walking on soft, marshy ground, as they spread the flamingo's weight evenly over the boggy surface.

Marabou stork
*Leptoptilos
crumerniferus*

*Characteristic
hunched shoulders*

*Long bill for
seizing prey*

*Adult has
large throat
pouch for inflation
in courtship rituals*

*Flexible
neck*

*Marabou has
longest legs
of any stork*

*Lesser flamingos
are the smallest of the
six species of flamingo*

LARGE SCAVENGER
The Marabou stork of East
Africa scavenges on the
carcasses of large grazing
animals and human garbage
dumps. It also feeds on fish
and frogs, which it finds
while wading in the shallow
waters of riverbeds, and
sometimes eats sick or injured
birds, and flamingo eggs and
chicks. The Marabou stork is
also called the "adjutant" or
"adjutant stork" because of its
hunched military bearing.
It is the largest species
of stork, growing to a
height of 5 ft (1.5 m).

*Sievelike edges
on top bill to
filter food*

*Large,
splayed
feet*

FILTER FEEDING
The flamingo has a unique method
of feeding. Sievelike edges on its
top bill filter out tiny plants and
invertebrates from the surface of
the water. The bottom bill and
tongue move up and down to
pump water through comb-like
fringes on the sides of the top bill.

Weather by the sea

THE PRESENCE OF SO MUCH WATER gives weather by the sea its own particular characteristics. Winds blowing in off the sea naturally carry more moisture than those blowing off the land, so coastal areas tend to be noticeably wetter than inland areas – especially if they face into the wind. They can be cloudier, too. Cumulus clouds, for instance, usually form inland only during the day, but on coasts facing the wind, they drift overhead at night as well, when cold winds blow in over the warm sea. Sometimes these clouds bring localized showers to coastal areas. Fogs can form at sea in the same way, and creep slightly inland. At daybreak the sea is often shrouded in a thick mist that disperses only as the wind changes or as the Sun's heat begins to dry the atmosphere. The overall effect of all this water is to make weather in coastal areas generally less extreme than it is farther inland. Because the sea retains heat well, nights tend to be warmer on the coast, and winters are generally milder, summers slightly cooler.

OUT FOR A BLOW
Seaside resorts are often very windy, as depicted by this early 20th-century postcard. The open sea provides no obstacle to winds blowing off it, and temperature differences between land and sea can generate stiff breezes as well.

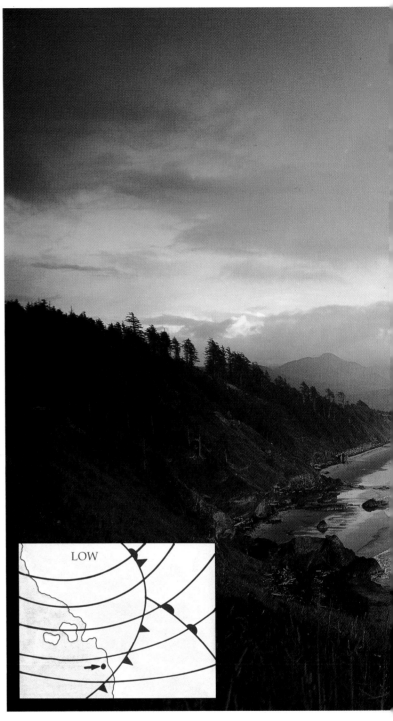

CLEAR COAST
This picture shows the coast of Oregon, but it is typical of west coasts everywhere in the midlatitudes. Deep depressions are common at this latitude, and here a cold front has just passed over, moving inland. An overhang of cloud lingers in the upper air from the front itself, and cumulus clouds are still growing in its wake. More showers are clearly on the way. As the front moves inland, it may produce progressively less rain, because there is less moisture available to feed its progress.

COASTAL FOG
Sea fog is an advection fog, which means that it occurs where a warm, moist wind blows over a cooler surface. Sea fog often happens off the coast of Newfoundland, in Canada (left), where warm westerly winds blow over a sea cooled by currents flowing down from the Arctic. Sometimes thick fogs linger there for days on end.

1000 mb

A little
cloud
cover

Strong
wind

WIND AND WAVES
The winds that help windsurfers skim across the
surface of the sea are often locally generated sea
breezes. But the waves they ride may be created
by winds thousands of miles away. Waves are
whipped up by the wind when air turbulence
over the water creates little pockets of low and
high pressure that suck and push on the water.
Just how big the waves are depends on the
strength of the wind, how long it blows, and
the "fetch," or how far it blows over the water.

Nighttime land breeze

*Warmer air from over sea pushes
cool air over land downward*

Land cools quickly

*Sinking air over land
drives air seaward,
creating land breeze*

Sea cools slowly

*Air rising over warm sea pushes
air at high altitude toward land*

Daytime sea breeze

*Air sinks over
the cool sea*

*Air pushed out to sea at
high altitude increases
air pressure over cool sea*

*Air rises over warm
land about 0.6 mile
(1 km) over ground*

Land and sea breezes

A marked characteristic of coastal areas
is the frequent occurrence of land and sea
breezes. Both occur because land and water
absorb and lose heat from the Sun at different
rates. During the day, the land heats up far
more quickly than the sea, and air begins to
rise. As warm air rises above the land, cool
air from the sea is drawn in underneath,
creating a stiff sea breeze blowing inland. At
night, the situation is reversed. The land
cools more quickly, and air begins to sink.
The cool air pushes out under the warm air
over the sea. This is called a land breeze.

*Land warms up quickly
in the warmth of the Sun*

*Sea warms
up very slowly*

*Sea air driven shoreward
creates stiff sea breeze at surface*

Turtles and tortoises

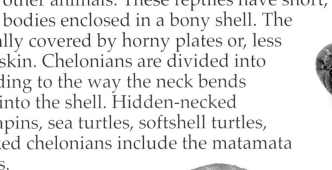

REPTILES WITH SHELLS are found in most warm areas of the world. There are more than 250 species, and they live in saltwater, freshwater, and on land. Turtles, also known as chelonians, make up most of the species. All chelonians lay eggs on land – some in sand, some in leaf litter, and some in the burrows of other animals. These reptiles have short, broad bodies enclosed in a bony shell. The bone of the shell is usually covered by horny plates or, less commonly, by leathery skin. Chelonians are divided into two main groups according to the way the neck bends when the head retreats into the shell. Hidden-necked chelonians include terrapins, sea turtles, softshell turtles, and tortoises. Side-necked chelonians include the matamata and African mud turtles.

ALLIGATOR SNAPPING TURTLE
This turtle is ferocious both in appearance and its habits. It spends nearly all its time in water, lying motionless on the riverbed, its mouth wide open, its knifelike jaws ready to scythe through its prey.

MIGRATING TURTLE
Some marine turtles have developed incredible migratory habits, traveling hundreds of miles from their feeding grounds to lay their eggs on the beaches where they were born. The green turtle travels to its nesting ground every two or three years.

Green turtle
Chelonia mydas

Turtles are air breathers, so must come to the surface regularly

LEATHER SHELLED
The largest of all turtles, this giant leatherback has a leathery, ridged skin above and below its body, instead of the usual horny plates. It usually lives in the mid-depths of ocean waters, breeding in the warm waters of the Caribbean.

RED-EARED TERRAPIN
This chelonian gets its name from the broad, red stripe that runs along the side of its head. Because they are gentle and attractive creatures, these terrapins are very popular as pets. Found in North America, they live in ponds and rivers, but frequently climb out of the water to bask.

Red-eared terrapin
Pseudemys scripta elegans

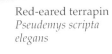

HERMANN'S TORTOISE
Different lifestyles lead to alterations in shell structure. Very few land tortoises have the speed or agility to escape a predator, so they usually have high-domed or knobby shells as a defense against predators' strong jaws. Turtles tend to have flatter shells that are streamlined for easy movement through the water. Soft-shelled tortoises have the flattest shells, allowing them to hide easily beneath sand and mud.

Hermann's tortoise
Testudo hermanni

High-domed shell

Swimming sequence
of green turtle

Front flippers
help turtle "fly"
through water

Stinkpot
turtle

Painted
turtle

Color of shell is
green, brown,
or black

Red-eared
slider

BASKING TERRAPINS
Terrapins live in freshwater habitats
and can often be seen basking in the
sun on rocks or riverbanks. Usually
smaller than either tortoises or
turtles, they are often kept as
pets in freshwater tanks.

Back pair of
flippers used
as rudders
to steer

Smooth sections
do not overlap

Streamlined shell

GREEN TURTLE
Green turtles live in
the warm waters of the
Atlantic, Pacific, and Indian
Oceans. Like all chelonians, they
come ashore to lay their eggs. First,
the females mate in shallow water
with the waiting males. Later, under
cover of darkness, the females crawl
up the beach to lay their eggs in the
sand before heading back to the water.
They may return several times in one
breeding season to lay more batches.

Life on the rocks

ROCKY SHORES provide a diverse and complex environment for many types of marine creatures. The types of rocks from which a beach is made, its position relative to the sea, and the range of tide levels it receives all play a part in determining the variety of creatures that live there. The tide may expose a rocky shore for several hours each day, and some creatures can tolerate living without water for extended periods. Those that cannot, and fail to reach deeper waters or find tidal pools when the water recedes, will dry out and die from exposure to the air and Sun. The pounding of powerful waves erodes the rocks themselves. Many animals have evolved very strong shells to withstand the force of the waves and have also developed ways of anchoring themselves firmly to the surface of rocks so they are not washed away.

TIDE POOLS
Life can be hard in the shallow water pools left by receding tides. Many creatures that prefer less light and warmth are left stranded and must try their best to find shelter.

New Zealand mussel

Bearded ark shell

BOUVIER'S CRAB
Like many small crabs, this one lives between or under rocks, and only emerges to scavenge for food at night.

BEARDED ARK SHELL
This bivalve gets its name from the tiny hairs that cover it. It lives in rock crevices and attaches itself by means of a broad byssus (see left). The shell often gets distorted as it grows to fit snugly into its rocky niche.

Mussel with byssal threads

Tail fan

Common blue mussels

ANCHORED
Mussels are common inhabitants of many rocky shores, often living in massive clusters high on the shore. Mussels anchor themselves to rocks and other surfaces by means of byssal threads – strong, thin filaments secreted by a gland in their feet.

JEWEL IN A SHELL
This rough star-shell lives on the rocky shores of the Mediterranean, but is found below tide level. The shell is often encrusted with marine growths. The bright red operculum, or gill cover, is sometimes used to make jewelry.

Operculum

WINKLES ON THE WEEDS
Tiny periwinkles are among the most common inhabitants of rocky shores. They tend to live high up on the shore, where they cling to rocks and clumps of seaweed.

Rough periwinkles

Antenna

Left large pincer, or cheliped, is larger and stronger than right

Common shore crab

Antennule

Eyes tucked in under carapace

One of four pairs of walking legs

ELUSIVE LOBSTER
The common lobster is highly prized as a food and is a favorite catch for divers. Lobsters can be difficult to find as they blend in well with their surroundings and often hide in crevices during the day, with only their claws and antennae exposed.

SHORE CRAB
The shore crab is one of the most common European crabs and is often found lurking under rocks and seaweed on the seashore.

STONY-SHELLED CRAB
The Mediterranean stone crab is so-called because of its heavy-looking, irregular shell.

Clever disguises

A CASUAL GLANCE into a tide pool may reveal only a few strands of seaweed and some dead-looking shells. But wait patiently, sitting still to avoid being seen, and watch carefully. A dark patch of rock may suddenly glide forward: it is a blenny, on the lookout for food. A slightly hazy-looking area of sand may walk away: it is a prawn, adjusting the spots and lines on its body to blend perfectly with the background. A small pebble may slip: it is a winkle grazing on algae. A patch of gravelly bottom ripples and two eyes may appear: a flatfish is wafting small pebbles and shell fragments over its body to hide its outline. All these creatures use camouflage to help conceal themselves from voracious predators – and to catch prey themselves.

PALE UNDERSIDE
Flatfish are well camouflaged when viewed from the surface of the water. The underside, flat against the seabed, has no need of special coloring, so it is white or pale in many flatfish species.

WEED LOOKALIKE
The leafy sea dragon, from the coastal waters of southern Australia, is a type of sea horse. Its loose lobes of skin resemble the seaweed fronds in which it hides.

Urchins graze on the rocks and weeds, eating small algal growths and animals

URCHIN COVER-UP
Several species of sea urchins grasp pebbles, shells, and pieces of seaweed with their long "tube feet" and hold them over their bodies. A well-draped urchin can be difficult to spot. These are green sea urchins, which are found on the lower shore and in inshore waters.

Dab larvae move to depths of up to 230 ft (70 m) before becoming "flat"

A DAB WILL DO
Many flatfish can change color to match the surface on which they are resting. A few minutes earlier, this young dab was a light sandy color. It became several shades darker when placed on selected dark pebbles, and the marks on its upper side became almost black. The largest dabs reach about 16 in (40 cm) in length.

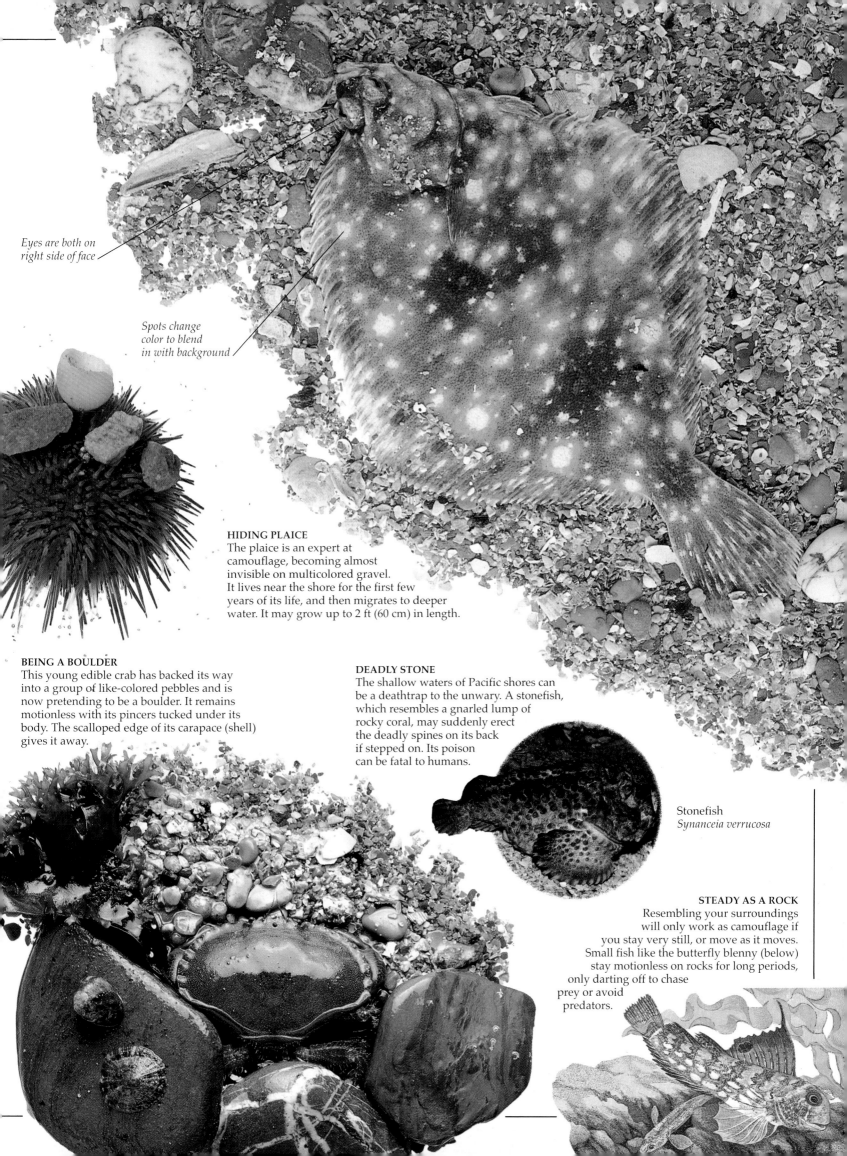

Eyes are both on right side of face

Spots change color to blend in with background

HIDING PLAICE
The plaice is an expert at camouflage, becoming almost invisible on multicolored gravel. It lives near the shore for the first few years of its life, and then migrates to deeper water. It may grow up to 2 ft (60 cm) in length.

BEING A BOULDER
This young edible crab has backed its way into a group of like-colored pebbles and is now pretending to be a boulder. It remains motionless with its pincers tucked under its body. The scalloped edge of its carapace (shell) gives it away.

DEADLY STONE
The shallow waters of Pacific shores can be a deathtrap to the unwary. A stonefish, which resembles a gnarled lump of rocky coral, may suddenly erect the deadly spines on its back if stepped on. Its poison can be fatal to humans.

Stonefish
Synanceia verrucosa

STEADY AS A ROCK
Resembling your surroundings will only work as camouflage if you stay very still, or move as it moves. Small fish like the butterfly blenny (below) stay motionless on rocks for long periods, only darting off to chase prey or avoid predators.

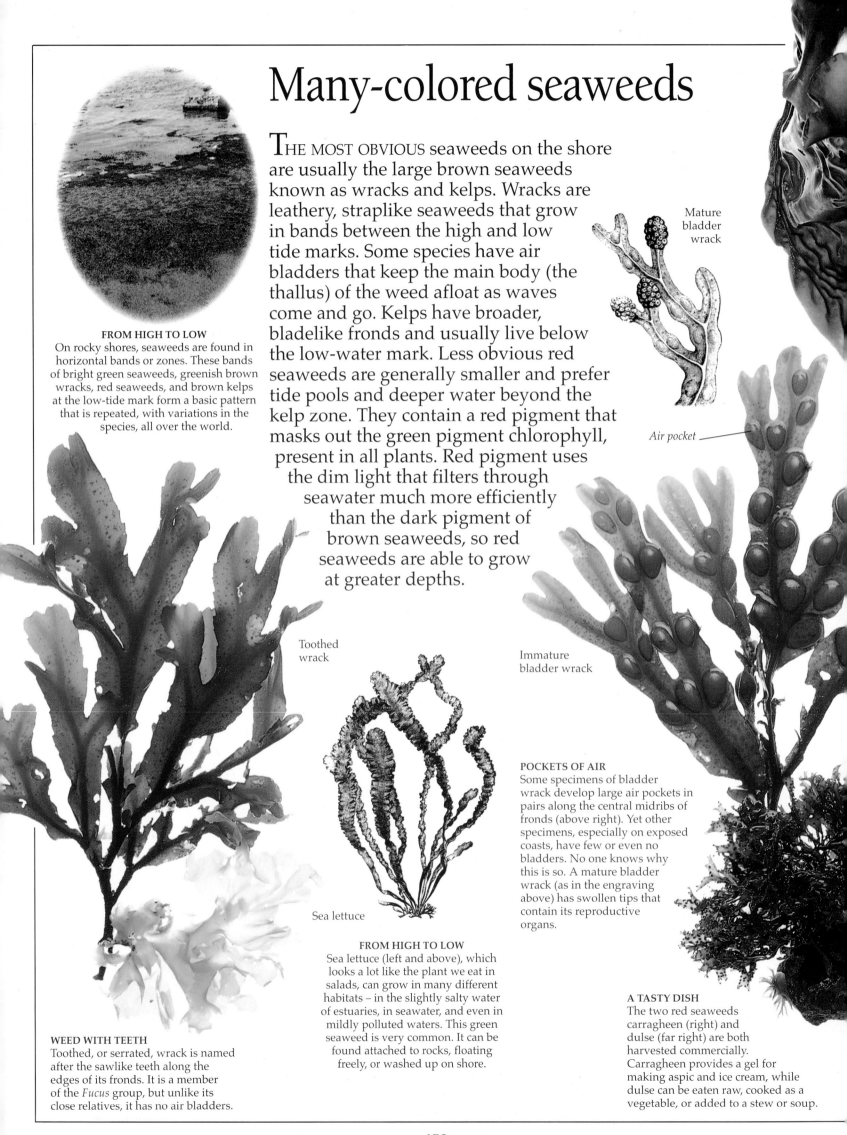

Many-colored seaweeds

THE MOST OBVIOUS seaweeds on the shore are usually the large brown seaweeds known as wracks and kelps. Wracks are leathery, straplike seaweeds that grow in bands between the high and low tide marks. Some species have air bladders that keep the main body (the thallus) of the weed afloat as waves come and go. Kelps have broader, bladelike fronds and usually live below the low-water mark. Less obvious red seaweeds are generally smaller and prefer tide pools and deeper water beyond the kelp zone. They contain a red pigment that masks out the green pigment chlorophyll, present in all plants. Red pigment uses the dim light that filters through seawater much more efficiently than the dark pigment of brown seaweeds, so red seaweeds are able to grow at greater depths.

FROM HIGH TO LOW
On rocky shores, seaweeds are found in horizontal bands or zones. These bands of bright green seaweeds, greenish brown wracks, red seaweeds, and brown kelps at the low-tide mark form a basic pattern that is repeated, with variations in the species, all over the world.

Mature bladder wrack

Air pocket

Toothed wrack

Sea lettuce

Immature bladder wrack

POCKETS OF AIR
Some specimens of bladder wrack develop large air pockets in pairs along the central midribs of fronds (above right). Yet other specimens, especially on exposed coasts, have few or even no bladders. No one knows why this is so. A mature bladder wrack (as in the engraving above) has swollen tips that contain its reproductive organs.

FROM HIGH TO LOW
Sea lettuce (left and above), which looks a lot like the plant we eat in salads, can grow in many different habitats – in the slightly salty water of estuaries, in seawater, and even in mildly polluted waters. This green seaweed is very common. It can be found attached to rocks, floating freely, or washed up on shore.

WEED WITH TEETH
Toothed, or serrated, wrack is named after the sawlike teeth along the edges of its fronds. It is a member of the *Fucus* group, but unlike its close relatives, it has no air bladders.

A TASTY DISH
The two red seaweeds carragheen (right) and dulse (far right) are both harvested commercially. Carragheen provides a gel for making aspic and ice cream, while dulse can be eaten raw, cooked as a vegetable, or added to a stew or soup.

SUGAR IN THE SALT
The sugar kelp, or sugar wrack, is a big brown seaweed of the low-water level and below. Its crinkly fronds and wavy edges are distinctive, as is the sweet taste of the white powder that forms on its drying surface. It is eaten as a delicacy in the Far East.

LONG THONGS
Thongweed is a leathery, strap-like brown seaweed found near the low-water level. Its narrow fronds may grow more than 10 ft (3 m) long. Like many seaweeds, its tough and rubbery texture protects it from the pounding of waves on rocks.

Thongweed

Sugar kelp

BUTTON-SHAPED BASE
The button-, or mushroom-, shaped base is one stage in the life cycle of the thongweed. In the plant's second year of growth, the thongs develop from this base. They contain the reproductive structures.

Nutrients are absorbed through the whole surface of the seaweed

Holdfasts (root-like structures) anchor brown seaweeds to rocks

Dulse

Carragheen

Oceans of the world

Leafy sea
dragon

THE EARTH'S SEAWATER IS ONE CONTINUOUS MASS. Each body of
water is linked to another, all around the world. The largest expanses
of water are called oceans and the smaller areas (usually close to, or partly
enclosed by, land) are called seas. Two-thirds of the Earth's surface is covered by
seawater, and this saltwater makes up 97 percent of our planet's entire water supply.
The temperature of seawater varies in different areas – it is colder at the surface in
polar regions than in the tropics, and it usually gets colder with depth. The salinity (how much
salt there is in the water) varies, too. In the saltiest water, such as in the Red Sea, there is a high
evaporation rate and very little freshwater flowing in from rivers. The least
salty water, such as in the Baltic Sea, has a large influx of freshwater.
Nor is the seafloor the same everywhere. There are undersea
mountains, plateaus, plains, and trenches, making
the ocean floor at least as complex as
geological formations found on land.

Haiti/Dominican
Republic

Tobago

Trinidad

North coast
of Venezuela

South America

Continental shelf

Guiana Plateau

Model (right) of a
section of the seafloor
east of the Caribbean,
as shown in red square
on map (below)

Continental
slope

Arctic
Ocean

Pacific
Ocean

Sargasso
Sea

Arabian
Sea

Baltic Sea

Mediterranean
Sea

Indian
Ocean

Coral
Sea

Tasman
Sea

Antarctic
Ocean

Caribbean
Sea

Atlantic
Ocean

OCEANS OF OCEANS
The world's five oceans,
from the largest to the smallest,
are the Pacific, the Atlantic, the
Indian, the Antarctic, and the Arctic.
The Pacific Ocean covers 64 million sq.
miles (166 million sq. km) and is about 13 times
the size of the Arctic Ocean. The Arctic Ocean's center is
permanently covered by a layer of sea ice that grows larger in
winter and shrinks in summer, when some of it melts. More than
half of the Antarctic Ocean is also frozen in winter, and sea ice still
fringes the continent of Antarctica during the summer. The average depth
of all the oceans is 12,000 ft (3,650 m), with the deepest part in the Pacific
Ocean, at 36, 000 ft (10,920 m) in the Mariana Trench, east of the Philippines.

FLOATING MEAL
The sea otter will float on its back in the calm of a kelp bed by the coasts of the Pacific Ocean rather than come ashore. It feeds on sea urchins and crustaceans floating in this position, crushing the hard shells with a stone.

GOD OF THE SEA
Neptune, the Roman god of the sea, seen here with a sea nymph, is usually depicted carrying a pronged trident or spear and riding a dolphin. He was also thought to control freshwater supplies, so offerings were made to him during the driest months of the year.

FORMING A TRENCH
The gigantic plates on the Earth's crust move like a conveyor belt. As new areas of ocean floor form, old areas disappear into the molten heart of the planet. This diagram shows one oceanic plate being forced under another to form the Mariana Trench. This process is called subduction, and here it creates an island arc.

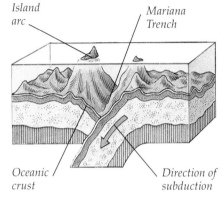

Island arc

Mariana Trench

Oceanic crust

Direction of subduction

Formation of Mariana Trench

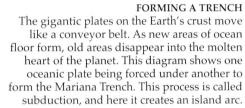

Hatteras Abyssal Plain

Puerto Rico Trench

Nares Abyssal Plain

Mid-Atlantic Ridge

Kane Fracture Zone

Vema Fracture Zone

Demerara Abyssal Plain

OCEAN LANDSCAPE
This model shows the features on the bottom of the Atlantic Ocean off the northeastern coast of South America, from Guyana to Venezuela. Off this coast is the continental shelf, a region of relatively shallow water about 660 ft (200 m) deep. Here the continental shelf is about 125 miles (200 km) wide, but off the coast of northern Asia it is as much as 1,000 miles (1,600 km) wide. At the outer edge of the continental shelf, the ocean floor drops steeply away to form the continental slope. Sediments eroded from the land and carried by rivers like the Orinoco accumulate at the bottom of the slope. The ocean floor then opens out in almost flat areas called abyssal plains, which are covered with a deep layer of soft sediments. The Puerto Rico Trench formed where one of the Earth's plates, the North American Plate, is sliding past another, the Caribbean Plate. An arc of volcanic islands has also been created where the North American Plate is forced under the Caribbean Plate.

The coral kingdom

I N THE CRYSTAL-CLEAR, WARM WATERS of the tropics, coral reefs flourish, covering vast areas. The largest stony coral structure, Australia's Great Barrier Reef, stretches for 1,260 miles (2,027 km). Made of the skeletons of stony corals, coral reefs are cemented together by chalky algae. Most stony corals are colonies of many tiny, anemonelike individuals called polyps. Each polyp makes its own hard limestone cup (skeleton), which protects its soft body. To make their skeletons, the coral polyps need the help of microscopic, single-celled algae that live inside them. The algae need sunlight to grow, which is why coral reefs are found only in sunny surface waters. In return for giving the algae a home, corals get some food from them, but they also capture plankton with their tentacles. Only the upper layer of a reef is made of living corals, which build upon skeletons of dead polyps. Coral reefs are also home to soft corals and sea fans, which do not have stony skeletons.

Tentacle's stings catch food

Mouth also expels waste

Hard plates of stony skeleton

Baglike stomach

INSIDE A CORAL ANIMAL
In a stony coral, a layer of tissue joins each polyp to its neighbor. To reproduce, they divide in two or release eggs and sperm into the water.

Black coral's horny skeleton looks like a bunch of twigs

Orange sea fan, Indian and Pacific Oceans

STINGING CORAL
Colorful hydrocorals are related to sea firs and, unlike horny and stony corals, produce jellyfishlike forms that carry their sex organs. Known as fire corals, they have potent stings on their polyps.

BLACK CORAL
In living black corals, the skeleton provides support for the living tissues and the branches bear rows of anemonelike polyps. Black corals are mainly found in tropical waters, growing in the deep part of coral reefs. Although they take a long time to grow, the black skeleton is sometimes used to make jewelry.

Intricate mesh developed to withstand strong currents

Stem of sea fan

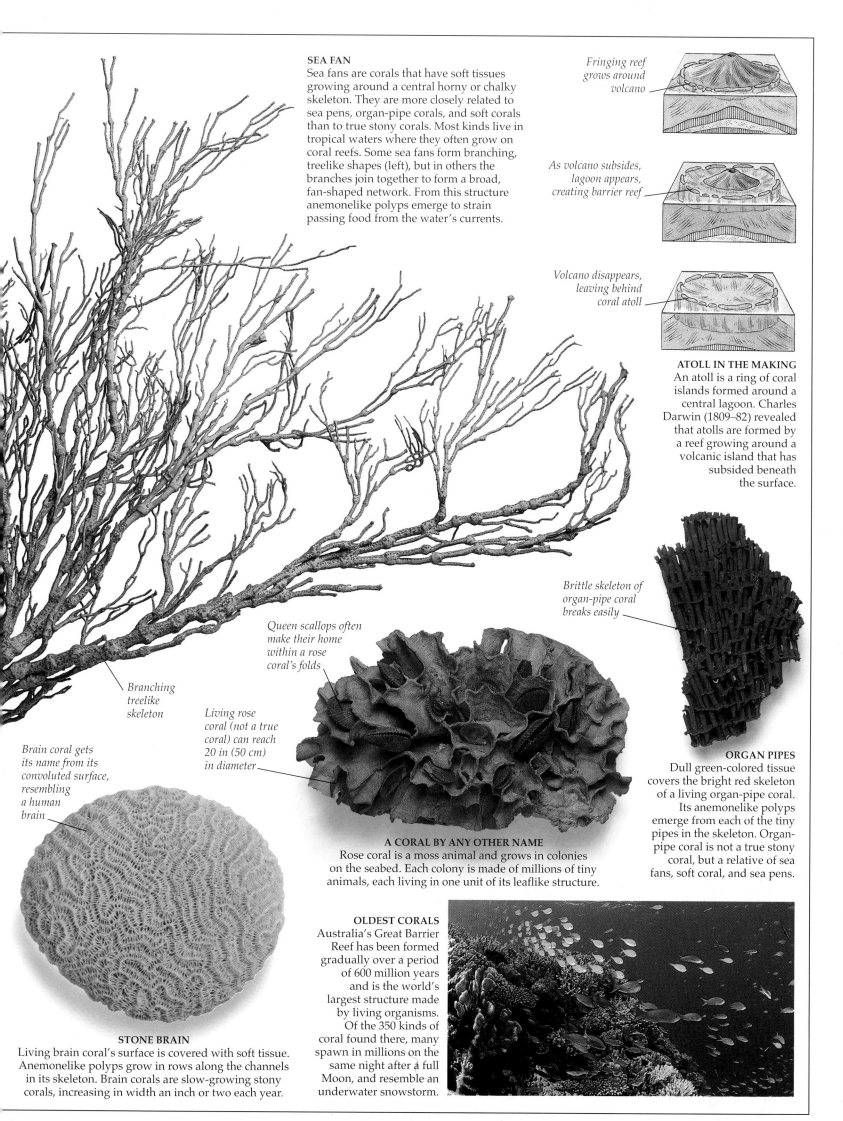

SEA FAN
Sea fans are corals that have soft tissues growing around a central horny or chalky skeleton. They are more closely related to sea pens, organ-pipe corals, and soft corals than to true stony corals. Most kinds live in tropical waters where they often grow on coral reefs. Some sea fans form branching, treelike shapes (left), but in others the branches join together to form a broad, fan-shaped network. From this structure anemonelike polyps emerge to strain passing food from the water's currents.

Fringing reef grows around volcano

As volcano subsides, lagoon appears, creating barrier reef

Volcano disappears, leaving behind coral atoll

ATOLL IN THE MAKING
An atoll is a ring of coral islands formed around a central lagoon. Charles Darwin (1809–82) revealed that atolls are formed by a reef growing around a volcanic island that has subsided beneath the surface.

Branching treelike skeleton

Queen scallops often make their home within a rose coral's folds

Brittle skeleton of organ-pipe coral breaks easily

Brain coral gets its name from its convoluted surface, resembling a human brain

Living rose coral (not a true coral) can reach 20 in (50 cm) in diameter

ORGAN PIPES
Dull green-colored tissue covers the bright red skeleton of a living organ-pipe coral. Its anemonelike polyps emerge from each of the tiny pipes in the skeleton. Organ-pipe coral is not a true stony coral, but a relative of sea fans, soft coral, and sea pens.

A CORAL BY ANY OTHER NAME
Rose coral is a moss animal and grows in colonies on the seabed. Each colony is made of millions of tiny animals, each living in one unit of its leaflike structure.

STONE BRAIN
Living brain coral's surface is covered with soft tissue. Anemonelike polyps grow in rows along the channels in its skeleton. Brain corals are slow-growing stony corals, increasing in width an inch or two each year.

OLDEST CORALS
Australia's Great Barrier Reef has been formed gradually over a period of 600 million years and is the world's largest structure made by living organisms. Of the 350 kinds of coral found there, many spawn in millions on the same night after a full Moon, and resemble an underwater snowstorm.

Clown fish
Amphiprion
species

Yellow
anemone

Clown anemone

Dangers of the reef

CORAL REEFS TEEM WITH LIFE. Bright fish and sea slugs dart in and out of the jagged landscape, shrimps hide in the coral's natural crevices, and sea horses cling to the seaweeds and sponges of the reef. Yet a coral reef is a dangerous place. Its changing surfaces provide shelter and opportunity for prey and predator alike. Most of the hunted sea creatures, like small wrasse, must feed out in the open. However, at a second's notice, they can dart out of harm's way by digging themselves into loose sand or mud or diving into a narrow cleft in the rocks. Hunters like the mandarin fish and the common octopus (pp. 78–79) are content to lurk inside coral caves, watching for unsuspecting victims. And there are other dangers – many sea creatures have to avoid the deadly embrace of poisonous sea anemones and carnivorous corals. Sometimes, however, a dangerous situation can be advantageous, too. The clown fish lays its eggs and even rears its young safely among the tentacles of the clown anemone, which catches, poisons, and eats other small fish.

CLOWNING AROUND
On many tropical reefs, bright-colored clown fish dart among the tentacles of a sea anemone whose venomous sting would paralyze other small fish in seconds. Clown fish have an especially thick body covering that lacks the usual substances that stimulate the anemone to sting. The anemone absorbs pieces of food dropped by its colorful visitors.

Eyespots give impression of huge "face"

Loose gravel for wrasse to dive into

1 SELF-PROTECTION
The twinspot wrasse has two large eyespots on its dorsal fin. If this huge false "face" fails to frighten predators, the twinspot uses alternative means to avoid danger. A threatening sound, worrying scent, or an actual sighting of a predator makes the twinspot tilt its head down. As it dives, it searches out a bare patch of shell fragments and gravel for refuge.

2 TESTING THE BED
As the twinspot reaches the seabed, it swerves up to a horizontal position and thrusts its sensitive snout and chest into the gravel. Sometimes this turns out to be only a shallow layer on top of solid rock – no use for hiding.

Ray of dorsal fin

Sea horse
*Hippocampus
kuda*

Sea horse's eyes
move independently

Long, hollow
snout to suck
up shrimps

Mandarin fish
*Synchiropus
splendidus*

FOUL FINERY

The brilliant colors of its skin warn other sea
creatures that the mandarin fish tastes foul. Its skin
produces a slimy mucus that smells and tastes unpleasant.
The mucus helps protect the fish from attack by bacteria and
fungi, as well as larger fish. The mandarin fish lives near the
seabed and feeds on smaller fish and other creatures that
float past. It also nibbles at the algae on the coral reef.

CHANGING COLOR

Sea horses cannot swim quickly to escape danger, but
they can change color to match their background and
hide from enemies. They anchor themselves with their
strong, supple tail, to coral or seaweeds and wait for
food, such as prawns, to swim past. The
sea horse straightens its tail to rise up,
and curls it to sink. The fin on its back
bends backward and forward to push
it through the water.

Loose gravel
flung upward
by wrasse's
activity

3 DIGGING IN
Hurling its body into S-shaped curves, and
digging down in a diagonal direction, the twinspot
"swims" headfirst into the loose gravel and stones.
Its fins and tail fling the gravel up and out of the way.
Within seconds, the fish settles into the surface layer of
stones, and the falling gravel rains back down to add
to its covering. The twinspot stays still until it senses
that things above are back to normal. Many species of
wrasse, especially near the Pacific coral islands, bury
themselves in the gravel each night and "sleep" there.

Strawberry
shrimp
*Lysmata
debelius*

SHY SHRIMP

The strawberry shrimp hides
in natural crevices in coral or
digs a burrow in the sand with its
chelipeds (claws). The shrimp grows
in spurts, increasing in size each
time it molts. It has to hide
from enemies, such as fish
and crabs, while the
soft, new exoskeleton
stretches and hardens.

Complete layer of
gravel hides wrasse
from predators

Tropical storms

K NOWN AS TYPHOONS IN THE PACIFIC and as tropical cyclones by meteorologists, hurricanes claim more lives each year than any other storms. When a full-blown hurricane strikes, trees are uprooted and buildings flattened by raging winds that gust at up to 220 mph (360 km/h). Vast areas are swamped by torrential rain, and coastal regions can be overwhelmed by the "storm surge." This is a wall of water up to 26 ft (8 m) high sucked up by the storm's "eye" – the ring of low pressure at the storm's center – and topped by giant waves whipped up by the winds. Hurricanes begin as small thunderstorms over warm, tropical oceans. If the water is warm enough (over 75°F or 24°C), several storms may whirl around as one, encouraged by strong winds high in the atmosphere. Soon they drift westward across the ocean, drawing in warm, moist air and spinning in tighter circles. At first, the center of the storm may be more than 200 miles (330 km) across and the winds at gale force. As it moves west, it gains energy from the warm air it sucks in. By the time the storm reaches the far side of the ocean, the eye may have shrunk to 30 miles (50 km) across, pressure may have dropped, and the winds may be howling around at hurricane force.

Hurricane force winds often damage buildings

ANATOMY OF A HURRICANE
The air in the eye of the hurricane is at low pressure. As the eye passes over, the winds may drop altogether, and a small circle of clear sky become visible for a while. The lull is short-lived as torrential rains fall around the eye, and raging winds, drawn in from hot air that spirals up its wall, circulate at speeds of 30 mph (50 km/h). Spiraling bands of rain and wind can occur up to 240 miles (400 km) away. It can be 18 hours or more before the storm passes over.

MIXED BLESSING
The vegetation and agriculture on many tropical islands depend on the torrential rains brought by hurricanes. But the terrible winds can also ravage crops, and only a few – like bananas – recover quickly.

Winds of more than 100 mph (165 km/h) occur over a large area beneath the storm

HURRICANE WATCH
Thanks to satellite images, meteorologists can detect hurricanes when they are far from land and track them as they approach. Special aircraft repeatedly fly through the storm to obtain accurate measurements that help predict its violence and likely path. Since 1954, names have been given to all tropical storms to prevent confusion when issuing forecasts and evacuation warnings.

 **1** Day 1: Thunderstorms develop over the sea.

 **2** Day 2: Storms group to form a swirl of cloud.

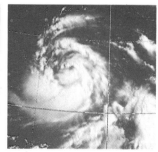 **3** Day 4: Winds grow; center forms in cloud swirl.

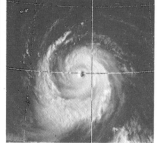 **4** Day 7: Eye forms; typhoon is at its most dangerous.

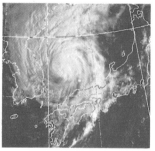 **5** Day 11: Eye passes over land; typhoon starts to die.

PACIFIC HURRICANE
The sequence above shows satellite images of a typhoon passing over the Pacific Ocean. It begins when water evaporates in the tropical sun over vast areas of the ocean to produce huge cumulonimbus clouds and bands of thunderstorms (1). A swirl of clouds develops and the growing storm looks like a vigorous, ordinary depression (2). The winds become even stronger and rotate around a single center (3). Eventually, an eye develops just inside the ring of the most destructive and violent winds (4). When such a storm passes over land – in this case, Japan – or over cold seas, it loses its source of energy and the winds drop rapidly (5).

Warm, moist air spirals up around the eye inside the hurricane

Hurricanes are enormous; some may be as much as 480 miles (800 km) across

The heat contained by the warm sea provides the energy needed to drive the whole system

Air descends in the eye, leaving it clear of cloud

The strongest winds, with gusts up to 220 mph (360 km/h), are found beneath the eye wall, immediately outside the eye

ALBANY HURRICANE
Hurricanes were far more dangerous before the strength of their approach could be predicted. In 1940, the fringes of a hurricane struck Albany, Georgia, without adequate warning, killing several people and wrecking large numbers of buildings, including big hotels. Two years before, 600 people were killed in New England by a sudden, fast-moving storm.

Ocean giants

THE BIGGEST WHALE – and the biggest animal that has ever lived – is the blue whale. Only other baleen whales and sperm whales come anywhere near its enormous size. The largest living land animal, the bull elephant, could stand on a blue whale's tongue! Even the biggest dinosaur weighed less than a quarter of a large blue whale. Such size has its benefits – big animals are less likely to be attacked by predators and it is easier for them to keep warm. Their main problem is to find enough food to nourish their awesome bulk.

Pectoral fin

Tail flukes

WHALE LICE
A number of animals make their homes on the great expanse of a whale's skin. Some are harmless hangers-on, but others, like this whale louse, probably irritate the skin.

TALL TAIL
Unlike some baleen whales, blue whales raise their tails in the air when they dive.

Stubby dorsal fin

A WHALE OF AN APPETITE
It is no coincidence that whale sharks, the world's largest fish, are also filter feeders. Because animals that feed on plankton do not need to chase individual prey, they do not have to be agile. This has allowed some to grow to great sizes. Whale sharks do not have baleen plates. Instead, they filter food from the water with their gills.

THE WORLD'S BIGGEST BABY
The day it is born, a baby blue whale is already as big as an elephant. It has no baleen plates, and relies entirely on its giant mother's milk. Like seal milk, this is very high in fat. Every day the growing whale drinks about 175 pints (100 liters) of milk and puts on another 200 lb (90 kg). By the time it is weaned, at the age of six or seven months, the young blue whale is already 52 ft (16 m) long.

Baby blue whales often breach when only a few weeks old

Adult blue whales can weigh 200 tons

WHALE OUT OF WATER
Whales can only reach such incredible sizes because
their weight is supported by the water. When a
large whale like this sperm whale is stranded,
it cannot support its own weight and
its internal organs are crushed.

BLUE SPLASH
No one knows why whales breach, or leap out of the
water. Adults often breach in the company of other
whales, and this suggests that the big splash is a way
of communicating. Young animals like this baby blue
whale may start breaching when they are only a few
weeks old. Perhaps by playing they are learning
skills that will be important to them as adults.

Paired blowholes

THE BIG BLUE
Blue whales grow to more than 104 ft (32 m) and
can weigh up to 220 tons (200 tonnes). They have
been hunted mercilessly in the southern oceans,
and most information about them comes from
the whaling industry, which estimated
weights by measuring chopped-off chunks
and adding a few tons to make up for lost
blood. Lengths may be incorrect as
well, since the whales could have
been stretched by towing. Blue
whales theoretically received
complete protection from
whalers in 1966. But there are
no signs that numbers have
increased, and there may
be only a few hundred
left in the entire
southern oceans.

*Throat
grooves allow
baleen whales to
gulp down huge
amounts of water*

PILOT STUDY
Measuring a stranded
whale is easy. But how do you
measure a live whale at sea? One way
is to take a series of photos as the whale
surfaces. By lining them end to end, scientists
can piece together the animal's entire length.

Vents and smokers

IN PARTS OF THE OCEAN FLOOR, there are deep cracks that let very hot, mineral-rich water gush into the ocean. These dramatic vents, or hot springs, exist at the spreading centers where the gigantic plates that make up the Earth's crust are moving apart. Cold seawater sinks deep into cracks in the crust where it is heated, and, in the process, collects dissolved minerals. At temperatures of up to 752°F (400°C), hot water spews out. Some of the minerals form chimneys known as black or white smokers. Water heated by the vents helps bacteria grow, and they create food from the hydrogen sulfide in the water. Extraordinary animals crowd around the cracks and rely on these microbes for food. The vents are independent of energy from the Sun, relying instead on chemosynthesis from sulfur-fixing bacteria. As recently as the late 1970s, scientists using submersibles found the first vent communities in the Pacific. Since then, vents have been found in other spreading centers in the Pacific Ocean and the Mid-Atlantic Ridge.

A CHANGING OCEAN
New areas of ocean floor are continually being created at spreading centers between two crustal plates. When hot, molten lava (rock) emerges from within the crust, it cools and solidifies along the edge of each adjoining plate.

Spreading center *Solidified lava*

Magma *Crustal plate*

SEEPING LAVA
Under the huge pressure of the ocean water, lava from vents or hot springs erupts constantly and gently, like toothpaste squeezed from a tube, and cools to form rounded shapes known as pillow lava (above). Where there is a spreading ridge, the water is hot, acidic, and dark, with sulfides of copper, lead, and zinc. These valuable metals come from the new oceanic plate that is formed at the ridges. The minerals are dissolved out by seawater that percolates through the cooling rock.

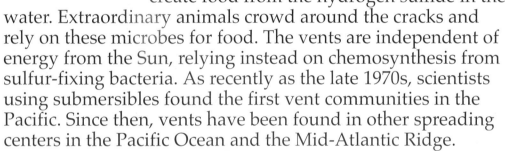

DEEP SEA PRAWNS
Animal life abounds at an active vent site. If the vent stops producing sulfur-rich water, the community is doomed. This new species of prawn was found at the Galápagos Rift in the Pacific Ocean in 1979.

Model of hydrothermal vents found in the eastern Pacific

VENT COMMUNITIES
This model shows the vent communities that have been found in the eastern Pacific, where giant clams and tube worms are the most distinctive animals. Vents in other parts of the world have different groups of animals, such as the hairy snails from the Mariana Trench, and eyeless shrimps from vents along the Mid-Atlantic Ridge.

Giant clams in the eastern Pacific can grow to 12 in (30 cm) long

Some animals graze on mats of bacteria covering rocks near a vent

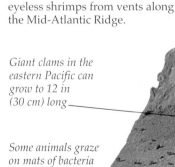

Fish predators nibble tops off tube worms

Plumes of hot water rich in sulfides and poisonous to most animals

Black smoker chimney can reach 33 ft (10 m)

Chimney made from mineral deposits

Dense collection of animals crowds around a vent

THE MID-ATLANTIC RIDGE
The rocks that make up the ocean floor are all relatively young – nowhere older than 200 million years – because new ocean plates are constantly being made by volcanic eruptions deep below the ocean waters. A long range of mountains snakes through the oceans, cut at its heart by a rift valley. The volcanoes in this valley erupt constantly, producing new volcanic rock. The new rock fills in the widening rift as the plates pull apart. The Mid-Atlantic Ridge (above), running the length of the Atlantic Ocean between Europe and Africa on the east and the Americas on the west, is part of the largest mountain range in the world.

Tube worms, Riftia pachyptila, can grow to 10 ft (3 m) long

Giant tube worm has bacteria inside its body to provide the worm with food

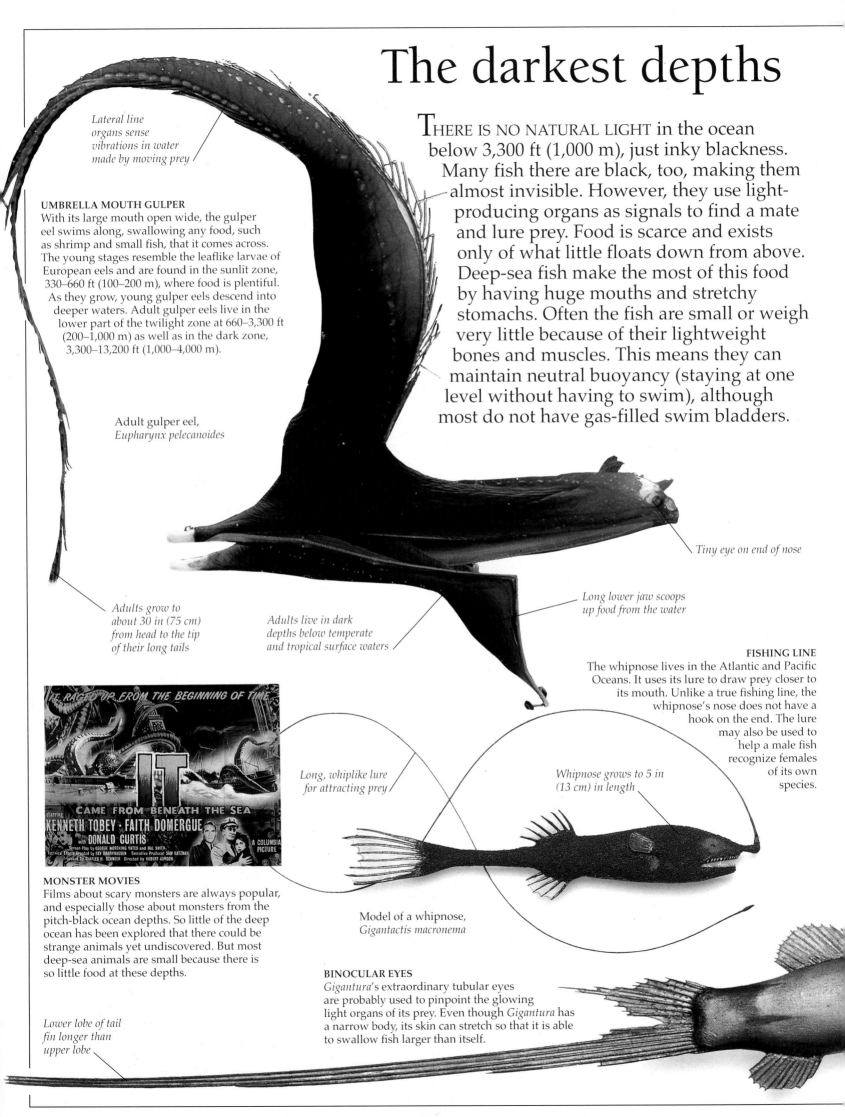

The darkest depths

THERE IS NO NATURAL LIGHT in the ocean below 3,300 ft (1,000 m), just inky blackness. Many fish there are black, too, making them almost invisible. However, they use light-producing organs as signals to find a mate and lure prey. Food is scarce and exists only of what little floats down from above. Deep-sea fish make the most of this food by having huge mouths and stretchy stomachs. Often the fish are small or weigh very little because of their lightweight bones and muscles. This means they can maintain neutral buoyancy (staying at one level without having to swim), although most do not have gas-filled swim bladders.

Lateral line organs sense vibrations in water made by moving prey

UMBRELLA MOUTH GULPER
With its large mouth open wide, the gulper eel swims along, swallowing any food, such as shrimp and small fish, that it comes across. The young stages resemble the leaflike larvae of European eels and are found in the sunlit zone, 330–660 ft (100–200 m), where food is plentiful. As they grow, young gulper eels descend into deeper waters. Adult gulper eels live in the lower part of the twilight zone at 660–3,300 ft (200–1,000 m) as well as in the dark zone, 3,300–13,200 ft (1,000–4,000 m).

Adult gulper eel, Eupharynx pelecanoides

Tiny eye on end of nose

Long lower jaw scoops up food from the water

Adults grow to about 30 in (75 cm) from head to the tip of their long tails

Adults live in dark depths below temperate and tropical surface waters

FISHING LINE
The whipnose lives in the Atlantic and Pacific Oceans. It uses its lure to draw prey closer to its mouth. Unlike a true fishing line, the whipnose's nose does not have a hook on the end. The lure may also be used to help a male fish recognize females of its own species.

Long, whiplike lure for attracting prey

Whipnose grows to 5 in (13 cm) in length

MONSTER MOVIES
Films about scary monsters are always popular, and especially those about monsters from the pitch-black ocean depths. So little of the deep ocean has been explored that there could be strange animals yet undiscovered. But most deep-sea animals are small because there is so little food at these depths.

Model of a whipnose, Gigantactis macronema

Lower lobe of tail fin longer than upper lobe

BINOCULAR EYES
Gigantura's extraordinary tubular eyes are probably used to pinpoint the glowing light organs of its prey. Even though *Gigantura* has a narrow body, its skin can stretch so that it is able to swallow fish larger than itself.

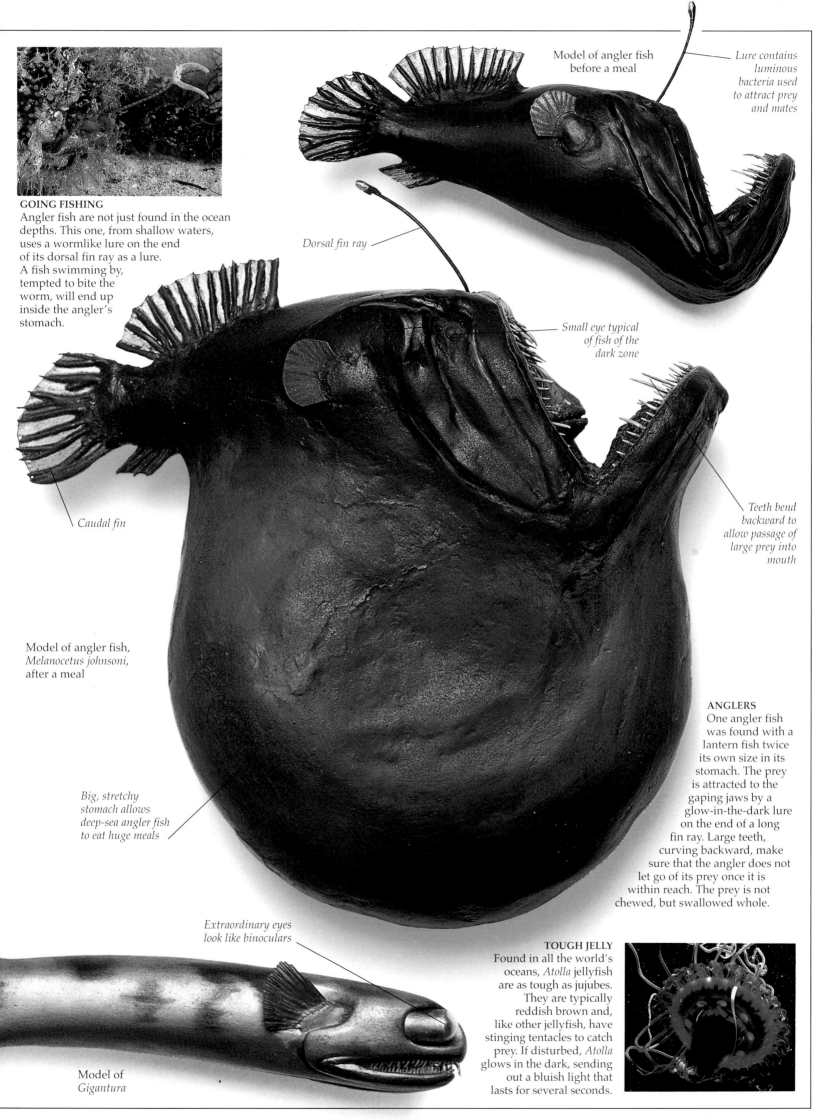

Model of angler fish before a meal

Lure contains luminous bacteria used to attract prey and mates

Dorsal fin ray

GOING FISHING
Angler fish are not just found in the ocean depths. This one, from shallow waters, uses a wormlike lure on the end of its dorsal fin ray as a lure. A fish swimming by, tempted to bite the worm, will end up inside the angler's stomach.

Small eye typical of fish of the dark zone

Caudal fin

Teeth bend backward to allow passage of large prey into mouth

Model of angler fish, *Melanocetus johnsoni*, after a meal

Big, stretchy stomach allows deep-sea angler fish to eat huge meals

ANGLERS
One angler fish was found with a lantern fish twice its own size in its stomach. The prey is attracted to the gaping jaws by a glow-in-the-dark lure on the end of a long fin ray. Large teeth, curving backward, make sure that the angler does not let go of its prey once it is within reach. The prey is not chewed, but swallowed whole.

Extraordinary eyes look like binoculars

TOUGH JELLY
Found in all the world's oceans, *Atolla* jellyfish are as tough as jujubes. They are typically reddish brown and, like other jellyfish, have stinging tentacles to catch prey. If disturbed, *Atolla* glows in the dark, sending out a bluish light that lasts for several seconds.

Model of *Gigantura*

Ocean wanderers

THE HUGE, GENTLE ALBATROSS of the Antarctic seas come ashore only to breed. They do not breed on the Antarctic land mass itself but on islands such as South Georgia, just north of the pack ice, the main advantage of these isolated locations being safety from predators. There are six species of albatross breeding in the Antarctic: black-browed, gray-headed, wandering, yellow-nosed, sooty, and light-mantled sooty. Probably about 750,000 pairs of birds breed each year. Albatross raise only one chick at a time and the chick takes a long time to mature, sometimes remaining in the nest for up to a year. Chicks are protected from the intense cold by thick down feathers and an insulating layer of fat or blubber. When winter sets in, most albatross set off over the southern oceans once more.

A man weighed down by more than grief: albatross can weigh up to 25 lb (12 kg)

DEAD WEIGHT
Sailors believed that albatross brought them bad luck. In Coleridge's *The Rime of the Ancient Mariner,* the unlucky mariner is forced to wear an albatross he has killed.

Wings very long and slender, for effortless gliding above the ocean

Black-browed albatross
Diomedea melanophris

Webbed feet held wide to push against the air and act as brakes

BUMPY LANDING
Landing is a difficult task for a bird so well adapted to flying over the sea. When albatross approach their nest site, they circle around several times before putting their legs down like the landing gear on an aircraft. They often land with a bump.

Gray-headed albatross
Diomedea chrysostoma

Large eyes indicate sharp eyesight needed for spotting food in the sea

BIRD MAN
People have always wanted to fly like birds, but this design for an early flying machine was no challenge to the albatross's mastery of the air. For birds, as with planes, takeoff and landing are the most dangerous parts of flying. Like planes, albatross need a runway to gather enough speed for takeoff. Without this, their enormous wingspan and body weight ensure that they remain earthbound.

Tube-shaped nostrils have glands at the base that excrete excess salt

Bill has razor-sharp edges to catch fish and squid

LIVING THE HIGH LIFE
Gray-headed albatross live on the sides of steep cliffs because they need the strong winds rising up over the cliffs to help them take off. Although gray-headed albatross weigh half as much as wandering albatross, only half of their chicks survive because many of the parent birds cannot find and bring back enough food to keep the young alive.

During courtship the bird points its beak to the sky and moos like a cow

FAITHFUL FLYING ACE

The wandering albatross has the greatest wingspan of any living bird. Its wing power enables the bird to cover as much as 300 miles (500 km) a day, landing on the sea in calm weather and to feed. Like all albatross, it comes ashore only to breed. The breeding cycle is exceptionally long, taking a year to complete. It therefore breeds only every two years. It precedes breeding with an elaborate courtship display in which the two birds dance face to face making a variety of sounds and clapping their beaks together loudly. Wandering albatross usually pair for life. The most elaborate displays take place among newly formed pairs; old, established partners are more discreet.

Wingspan may be 8 ft 4 in– 11 ft 10 in (254–360 cm)

SECONDHAND FOOD

Parent albatross feed their young by regurgitating (bringing up) the seafood they eat in the form of a sticky, oily mixture. This takes place when they return to the nest after many hours, or even days, fishing out at sea. Both adults and young can use this smelly and sticky oil in defense, ejecting it with reasonable accuracy over a 6-ft (2-m) range. Predators, such as skuas, may be repelled by the foul smell or immobilized if the sticky oil saturates their feathers.

Mother feeds regurgitated food to chick

Nest is lined with grass and feathers

Nest is about 12 in (30 cm) high

BARREL NEST

The black-browed albatross makes a raised nest of mud and straw among tussock grass.

Wandering albatross
Diomedea exulans

Strong legs and wide feet help in landing and swimming

GENTLE GIANT
The largest of all the land mammals, the elephant has the longest of all pregnancies – 22 months – and gives birth to only one calf at a time. Like many other large mammals, elephants spend considerable energy and time in nurturing their young, a strategy that helps ensure that the calf survives to breed. Unfortunately, the continued existence of the African elephant is threatened because elephants and people are often competing for the same territory.

CHAPTER 6
PRESERVING LIFE

OVER MILLIONS OF YEARS, fluctuations in the Earth's climate have changed the conditions in which animals and plants live. Some of these changes have been minor, and nature has adapted. Some have been devastating, and whole species have disappeared forever. Today, there is justifiable fear that human activity is changing the climate – and threatening life as we know it on Earth.

UNIQUE EVOLUTION
The golden mantella is threatened by the destruction of its habitat, as are many other species of animals. Many brightly colored mantellas live on the island of Madagascar off the eastern coast of Africa. The island has a high level of "endemism"– that is, most of the species found there are found nowhere else in the world. The bright colors of the mantellas help them defend their territories and warn predators that they have poisonous chemicals in their skin.

In danger

Swallow-tailed
manakin
*Chiroxiphia
caudata*

EVERY MINUTE OF THE DAY, 100 acres (40 hectares) of tropical rain forest are destroyed. The trees are felled for wood, burned to make way for farming, and damaged by pollution. If the clearance continues, 15 percent of plant species and 12 percent of bird species in the American rain forests alone could become extinct by the year 2000. This alarming pattern is being repeated all over the world, and not only in the rain forests. Scientists believe that humans are affecting the atmosphere so much that the world is steadily warming up (global warming). By releasing gases such as methane, CFCs, and carbon dioxide into the air, we have upset the balance in the atmosphere. In the right quantities, these gases are beneficial, trapping heat and keeping the Earth warm. But too many may make the Earth too warm, with terrible repercussions.

VULNERABLE
Manakins live in the thickest forests and are not endangered at present. However, they eat small, soft fruits, and, like many other creatures, are vulnerable to any disturbance of their forest habitat.

GOING, GOING, GONE
Gatherings like this group of male golden toads in the Monteverde Cloud Forest Reserve in Costa Rica in 1985 may be a thing of the past. Golden toads have not been seen at all in this region since 1990, and are believed to be extinct.

A leopard kills quickly, with a swift bite to the neck

KILLER CAT
The most versatile of the big cats, leopards occupy woodland habitats in places from west Africa to Korea and Southeast Asia. Leopards often relax under shady rocks or lie on branches high in the trees – exactly the places frequented by monkeys and the occasional young ape. Like other soft-footed members of the cat family, leopards are stealthy and deadly predators, as this unlucky vervet found out.

Diplazium proliferum

UNDER THREAT
There are many species of plants under threat, including the shade-loving aroid *Alocasia thibautiana*, which grows in the gloomiest parts of the jungles of Southeast Asia. The fern *Diplazium proliferum* thrives best on the jungle floor, where it is warm and damp. This fern produces bulbils on its fronds. Bulbils sprout and take root either when they are knocked off the fern, or when the frond dies.

Alocasia thibautiana

WALLS OF DEATH
Drift nets are like invisible curtains. In the open ocean, big fishing boats use drift nets up to 30 miles (50 km) long. If the nets get tangled, the fishermen often just cut them and let them drift off. Huge numbers of whales, dolphins, and seals are killed when they swim into these free-floating traps. The United Nations has banned long drift nets, but some countries are not members of the UN, and the laws are impossible to enforce in the open ocean.

Dense, waterproof coat turns gray-white in winter

Velvet contains blood vessels to nourish the growing antlers

Reindeer or caribou
Rangifer tarandus

Sensitive nose helps reindeer find food, even under snow

IN THE SNOW
Many animals and plants live in difficult habitats, where food and water are hard to find. Reindeer feed mainly on lichens, one of the few foods available throughout the Arctic winter. Some reindeer will also eat seaweed. Calves are born in June and grow fast on their mothers' rich milk, which is four times as nutritious as cow's milk. Although their thick coats insulate reindeer from the Arctic cold, they still migrate south in the winter to find food.

Sharp hooves grip ice and dig through snow for food

Studying populations

THE WAYS IN WHICH animal and plant populations change tell scientists a lot about specific species and their methods of survival. Lemmings provide a vivid example. These small rodents inhabit the coldest regions of the northern hemisphere. Every three to four years, the lemming population grows so large scientists believe it outstrips its food supplies. The lemmings then migrate in large numbers. The result is a form of population control – lemmings swim across rivers in search of food, so on migration, when they reach the sea, they attempt to swim across it, and drown. This kind of natural population control affects other animals as well; in this case, the snowy owl.

White feathers for winter camouflage

Snowy owl
Nyctea scandiaca

PREDATOR AND PREY
The snowy owl, seen here swooping down on a vole, lives mainly in the tundra of North America and Eurasia, where it is normally a rare sight. However, every three or four years, snowy owls suddenly appear in large numbers and invade towns across the United States, going as far south as Georgia. This strange phenomenon appears to be linked to the population changes of the lemming, on which the snowy owl feeds. As the lemmings reach plague proportions, the snowy owls, provided with a plentiful food supply, increase rapidly in numbers. When the lemmings migrate, the owls also migrate, searching for food, and disperse over a wide area. Their numbers drop to low levels over the next few years.

Owl looks for movement of prey before swooping

Powerful claw with long talons for gripping

MIGRATION PATTERNS
Voles in northern latitudes (left) have a similar population cycle to the lemming, perhaps based on the cycle of plant growth. As the size of the population increases, more and more of the vital nutrients in the environment become locked up in the form of droppings. In the cold conditions of the Arctic, where decomposition takes a long time, these nutrients are released slowly. Plant growth suffers, and the rodents must leave the area to look for food. The vegetation can only begin to recover when the voles migrate.

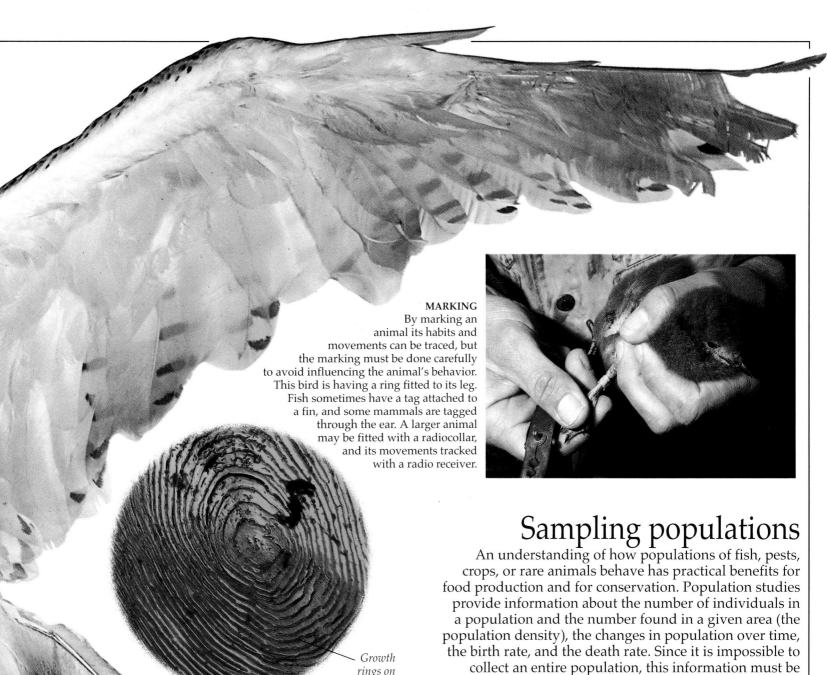

MARKING

By marking an animal its habits and movements can be traced, but the marking must be done carefully to avoid influencing the animal's behavior. This bird is having a ring fitted to its leg. Fish sometimes have a tag attached to a fin, and some mammals are tagged through the ear. A larger animal may be fitted with a radiocollar, and its movements tracked with a radio receiver.

Growth rings on magnified fish scale

SIGNS OF GROWING

An animal's age can be figured out in several ways, such as looking at the wear on a mammal's teeth. In the case of fish, the scales provide a useful indication of age, revealing dark rings that are formed each year during the winter, when growth is at its slowest. Ecologists use this information to determine the age structure of a fish population, calculate how it will change over a period of time, and decide how many fish can be caught without putting the population at risk.

Sampling populations

An understanding of how populations of fish, pests, crops, or rare animals behave has practical benefits for food production and for conservation. Population studies provide information about the number of individuals in a population and the number found in a given area (the population density), the changes in population over time, the birth rate, and the death rate. Since it is impossible to collect an entire population, this information must be gained by capturing a few members and estimating figures from this sample. Such samples are the basis for much of our scientific understanding of populations.

Number of animals (in thousands)

160
140
120
100
80
60
40
20

1845 1855 1865 1875 1885 1895 1905 1915 1925 1935

Snowshoe hare

Lynx

TRAPS AND TRAPPING

Nets are used to catch birds and fish for study, but mammals such as this Australian bandicoot must be attracted to elaborate traps if they are to be released unharmed. The animal's favorite food is usually placed in the trap as bait.

BOOM OR BUST

Gathering long-term data about populations can take many years. Ecologists were able to use historical records from the Hudson's Bay Company to produce this population graph of two species in the Canadian Arctic. It shows that every nine or ten years, the number of snowshoe hares rises to a peak and then drops dramatically. The lynx population follows closely behind that of the snowshoe hare – the lynx depends on it for food. This "boom and bust" cycle, which is still not fully understood, is characteristic of several animal species living in extreme environmental conditions.

Surviving

SPECIAL ADAPTATIONS
A camel is well suited to desert conditions because it can go for days without water. Its body temperature can rise many degrees before the animal starts to sweat, conserving moisture. It also uses the fat stores in its hump. The fat is gradually used up if it does not eat enough, and as the fat is depleted, the hump shrinks.

Nature is a finely tuned balancing act and no one living thing can survive without some dependence on, or ability to affect, another. All animals and plants need energy and materials from the environment, and they survive despite the precarious nature of food chains and difficult environments, even coping with the additional problems of bad weather, disease, and pollution. The adaptability of life on Earth is endlessly ingenious. For example, in cold places where there are few insects to pollinate, many plants reproduce from small pieces of themselves, such as runners or bulbils. Some animals, such as the polar bear and the fox, have even benefited from the creation of towns and cities, changing their diets and scavenging on human refuse.

Northen fleabane
Erigeron borealis

LIVING FOSSIL
Some species survive for millions of years. The coelacanth is a fish that was thought to be extinct; all the known fossils were more than 200 million years old. Then, in 1938, a live coelacanth was fished out of the ocean. If such a creature can survive for 200 million years without leaving any fossils, it is not surprising that some steps in the evolution of life on Earth are not recorded.

Coloring very similar to coral snake

MISLEADING COLORS
Many creatures have evolved ways of protecting themselves from predators. This harmless Sinaloan milk snake looks like the highly venomous coral snake. This happy chance may deter quite a few predators from trying to make a meal of the snake. Milk snakes are so-called because of a mistaken belief that they steal milk from cows.

Sinaloan milk snake
Lampropeltis doliata

HARDY PLANTS
In order to survive, many plants have evolved in special ways. Low cushions of northern fleabane flower in the Arctic summer when the tundra lands become waterlogged. The plant grows in a low, compact tussock to keep out of the freezing, drying wind, to trap available moisture, and to avoid being crushed by snow and ice.

Krill are omnivores, eating phytoplankton, other crustaceans, and other krill

Krill sieve food from water with their feathery feeding apparatus

At night, the luminescent organs of krill shimmer in the darkness

Bulbous eyes

Female krill spawn twice a year, laying 2,000–3,000 eggs, which sink into deep water

Krill are just 2 in (5 cm) long, but sometimes occur in such vast numbers they turn the sea red

CAREFUL PARENTING
Survival of a species is dependent on the species' ability to produce young. This female leaf beetle, guarding her family, produces relatively few young, but by protecting them in early life, she increases their chances of survival. Some animals produce very few young and invest considerable time and energy in raising them. Others produce huge numbers of offspring, but do nothing to look after them. A female cod, for example, lays more than a million eggs, but nearly all are eaten before they have a chance to grow into adults.

FOOD SOURCES
The shrimplike crustacean krill is the basis of most of the Antarctic food chains, forming a vital food source for whales and seals, as well as penguins and seabirds. A blue whale needs more than 0.9 tons (900 kg) of krill to feel full! The reduction in whale numbers caused by human hunting in the past has made krill numbers increase. Other krill-eating species such as penguins and fur seals have increased in number to exploit the extra food source. This has upset the balance of existing food webs. The long-term repercussions of this kind of change are as yet unknown.

Glossary

ALGAE Simple plants that do not have true stems, roots, or leaves, but contain chlorophyll. Most are found in water.
See also CHLOROPHYLL.

AMOEBA A tiny, simple animal that has no fixed shape and lives in water.

AMPHIBIAN Cold-blooded and smooth-skinned vertebrate that begins life in the water, but can live on land when it is adult; for example, a frog, toad, or salamander.
See also VERTEBRATE.

ANTENNA One of a pair of flexible feelers on the head of some animals, such as insects or crustaceans.
See also CRUSTACEAN.

ANTHER The upper part of the stamen of a flowering plant.
See also STAMEN.

ARTHROPOD Creature with segmented covering and jointed limbs, such as an insect, crustacean, arachnid, and centipede.
See also CRUSTACEAN.

BACTERIUM (pl. bacteria) Microorganism that brings about decomposition; or a parasite, many of which cause disease.

BAROMETER Instrument for measuring atmospheric pressure, used in weather forecasting.

BIOSPHERE Regions of the Earth and its atmosphere in which living things are found.

BIVALVE A mollusk with a shell consisting of two hinged parts. Bivalves include oysters, cockles, clams, scallops, and mussels.
See also MOLLUSK.

BYSSAL THREADS Mass of threads that bivalves use to attach themselves to rocks.
See also BIVALVE.

CAECILIAN Legless, burrowing amphibian found in tropical regions.
See also AMPHIBIAN.

CAMOUFLAGE Color, marking, or shape of an animal or plant that enable it to hide in its surroundings.

CARNIVOROUS Meat eating.

CARPEL The central, female part of a flower, consisting of an ovary, style, and stigma.

CELL The smallest unit of an organism that can exist on its own.

CEPHALOPOD Mollusk with a beaked head and tentacles. Cephalopods include the octopus and nautilus.
See also MOLLUSK.

CHELONIAN Belonging to the Chelonia, a group of reptiles that includes turtles.

CHLOROPHYLL Green pigment found in plants that traps energy from sunlight.
See also PIGMENT.

CHLOROPLAST Tiny body in some plant cells that contains chlorophyll.
See also CHLOROPHYLL.

CHRYSALIS The stage of life between caterpillar and adult butterfly or moth.

CILIA Hairlike growths from the surface of a cell or organism.
See also CELL.

COCOON Covering of silk spun by the larvae of moths and other insects to protect them in their pupa stage.
See also LARVA.

COELENTERATE Invertebrate animal with sacklike internal cavity. Includes jellyfish, sea anemones, and cords.

COMPOUND EYE Eye of most insects, made up of separate lenses that work as individual eyes, each forming a part of the image.

CROSS-POLLINATION The transfer of pollen from the stamens of one plant to the stigma of another.
See also STAMEN.

CRUSTACEAN Any of a usually aquatic group of animals with a segmented body and paired, jointed limbs. Includes lobsters, crabs, shrimps, and sow bugs.

DECOMPOSER Something that breaks down dead organic matter, such as a bacterium or fungus.
See also BACTERIUM, FUNGUS.

DIAPAUSE A period during which certain insects do not grow or develop.

DIATOM Minute, single-celled algae.
See also ALGAE.

ECHOLOCATION A way of finding objects by sending out sounds, then listening for the echo. Bats use echolocation to navigate.

ECOSYSTEM A complete area in the biosphere that contains living things, such as a forest.

ELEMENT A substance that cannot be broken down into more simple substances by chemical reactions.

ENDOSPERM The tissue that surrounds and feeds the embryo of a flowering plant.

ENVIRONMENT The surroundings of plants or animals – the environment affects the way they live.

EPIDERMIS The outer layer of the skin.

EVAPORATION The changing of a liquid into a vapor by the escape of molecules from its surface.

EXOSKELETON The hard, outer skin of arthropods.
See also ARTHROPOD.

FOSSIL The ancient remains of a plant or animal, usually found in rocks. A fossil may be the actual bones of an animal or the shape left by the animal's body in the rock.

FOSSIL FUEL Flammable material that comes from the remains of animals and plants that lived millions of years ago. Includes coal and oil.

FUNGUS One of a group of organisms that lack chlorophyll and are usually parasitic.
See also CHLOROPHYLL.

GASTROPOD A mollusk with a coiled shell and a large, muscular foot that it uses to move.
See also MOLLUSK.

GERMINATION In plants, when seeds or spores sprout.

GILLS Parts of a fish used for breathing underwater.

HABITAT A place where an animal or plant usually lives; woodlands, grasslands, and mountains are examples of different habitats.

HERBIVOROUS Plant eating.

HIBERNATE To sleep deeply or remain still through the winter in order to conserve energy and survive the winter.

INCUBATION The warming of eggs by bodily heat or other means to encourage the growth and hatching of young.

INVERTEBRATE An animal with no backbone.

LARVA The second stage in the life of an insect, which occurs between the egg and the emergence of the adult. Tadpoles and caterpillars are larvae.

LAVA Hot, liquid rock that flows from deep inside the Earth. The lava cools and hardens when it reaches the surface.

MAGMA Melted rock beneath the Earth's crust.

MAMMAL Warm-blooded animal that gives birth to live young that feed on the mother's milk.

MANDIBLE Jaw or sharp, hard part of an insect's mouthparts. Most insects have two mandibles.

MANTLE The layer of the Earth that lies beneath the surface and the center.

MARSUPIAL A mammal that has a pouch on the outside of its body in which its young develop.

METAMORPHOSIS The transformation of an animal during growth. Includes the emergence of an adult fly from a maggot, a butterfly from a caterpillar, and a frog from a tadpole.

METEOROLOGIST Scientist who studies weather and weather conditions.

MICROBE Tiny, living organism that can only be seen with a microscope.
See also ORGANISM.

MIGRATION Moving from one place to another. Animals migrate to find food, produce young, or escape from cold weather.

MOLLUSK An animal with a soft body that usually lives in a shell. Snails, limpets, and slugs are mollusks.

MONOTREME One of a group of egg-laying animals that lives in Australia and New Guinea. Includes the platypus and the echidna.

MUTUALISM Relationship between two or more animals, in which all benefit.

NECTARY Glandlike organ at the base of a flower in which nectar is stored.

NEMATOCYST Stinging organ in coelenterates such as jellyfish.
See also COELENTERATE.

NUCLEUS The center of an atom, a nucleus is made up of electrically charged protons and of neutrons.

NYMPH A young insect. A nymph looks like its parents, but does not have any wings.

OCELLUS A small, simple eye found in many vertebrates.
See also VERTEBRATE.

ORGANISM Any living plant or animal.

PALEONTOLOGIST Scientist who studies fossils and ancient life forms.
See also FOSSIL.

PARASITE An organism that grows and feeds on or in another organism, but does not contribute to the survival of the host.
See also ORGANISM.

PHOTOSYNTHESIS The way that plants make food, using energy from sunlight and turning carbon dioxide and water into sugars.

PHYTOPLANKTON Minute, floating aquatic plants.

PIGMENT A substance, such as chlorophyll, that produces a particular color in plant or animal tissue.
See also CHLOROPHYLL.

PLACENTAL Having a placenta, the organ that develops in female mammals during pregnancy to provide the fetus with the nutrients that it needs.

PNEUMATOPHORE A gas-filled sac that serves as a float for colonies such as the jellyfish Portuguese man-of-war.

POLLINATOR The animal that carries pollen from one flower to another to help make seeds. Insects are the most common pollinators.

POLYP A coelenterate with a cylindrical body and tentacles, such as coral.

PREDATOR An animal that lives by hunting and eating other animals.

PREY An animal that is hunted and eaten by another animal.

PRIMATE A member of the mammal group that includes gorillas, monkeys, chimpanzees, and human beings.
See also MAMMAL.

PROBOSCIS A tube in some insects used for feeding and sucking.

PROMINENCE A bright spout of gas reaching out from the Sun's surface into space.

PUPA The last stage in the life of some young insects. The pupa is the resting stage during which the adult takes shape.

RADICLE The part of the plant that develops into the primary root.

REPTILE One of a group of animals with dry, scaly skin that usually lay eggs with shells. The group includes snakes, turtles, and crocodiles.

RESPIRATION The process of inhaling and exhaling; the process by which an organism takes in oxygen, releasing carbon dioxide and energy.
See also ORGANISM.

RODENT An animal with long, front teeth that are used for gnawing. Includes mice, rats, and squirrels.

STAMEN The pollen-producing part of the plant.

SUCCULENT A thick-leaved plant such as a cactus that stores water in its stems and leaves.

SWIM BLADDER Part of the body of a fish that can be filled with air. It stops the fish from sinking.

THERMAL Hot air current that blows upward.

THORAX The central part of an insect's body. The wings and legs are fixed to the thorax, which contains all the muscles that the insect uses to move them.

TUBER Swollen, usually underground stem or root, such as the potato.

TUNDRA Frozen treeless plain found close to the Arctic.

ULTRAVIOLET Color or light with a short wavelength that the human eye cannot see. To insects, it is a pale shade of blue.

VERTEBRATE Animal with a bony skeleton and a backbone. Fish, amphibians, reptiles, birds, and mammals are all vertebrates.
See also MAMMAL, REPTILE.

ZOOPLANKTON Microscopic crustaceans, fish larvae, and other aquatic animals.

Index

A

Acknowledgments

DK would like to thank

Susila Baybars and Marion Dent for editorial assistance; Ivan Finnegan, Cormac Jordan, Sailesh Patel, and Susan St. Louis for design assistance; and Alex Arthur, David Burnie, David Carter, Jack Challoner, Dr. Barry Clarke, Brian Cosgrove, John Farndon, Theresa Greenaway, William Lindsay, Dr Miranda MacQuitty, Colin McCarthy, Laurence Mound, Vassili Papastavrou, Steve Parker, Steve Pollock, Ian Redmond, Scott Steadman, Barbara Taylor, Dr. Paul D. Taylor, Susanna van Rose, and Paul Whalley for contributing to the book

Special Photography
Peter Anderson, Geoff Brightling, Jane Burton, Peter Chadwick, Andy Crawford, Geoff Dann, Philip Dowell, John Downes, Neil Fletcher, Steve Gorton, Frank Greenaway, Colin Keates, Dave King, Cyril Laubscher, Mike Linley, Andrew McRobb, Karl Shone, James Stevenson, Clive Streeter, Harold Taylor, Kim Taylor, Andreas von Einsiedel, Spike Walker, Jerry Young

Illustrators
Simone End, Andrew Macdonald, Richard Orr, Sallie Alane Reason, Colin Salmon, Richard Ward, John Woodcock, Dan Wright

Model makers
David Donkin, John Downes, Peter Griffiths, Graham High and Jeremy Hunt/Centaur Studios, John Holmes

Index
Marion Dent

Picture research
Lorna Ainger, Katie Bradshaw, Liz Cooney, John Stevenson

Picture credits
t=top b=bottom c=center l=left r=right

DK would like to thank the following for their kind permission to reproduce the photographs

Aldus Archive 33ca
Alison Anholt-White 102cb
Bryan & Cherry Alexander 94bl, 111br
American Museum of Natural History 168-9c
Ardea 62bc, 63br, 67cr, 126c, 152c
Biofotos/Heather Angel 62bl, 137tr, 154tr
Bridgeman Art Library 111tl/Prado, Madrid 161tr/Uffizi Gallery, Florence 68tl
A. Buckland 150cl
Caroline Cartwright 118tl, 119br
©Casterman 84tr
John Clegg 135tl
Bruce Coleman Ltd. 102tr, 102-3c, 103tl, 104cla, 112bc/Jane Burton 28tl, 91bl/Bob & Clara Calhoun 73c/J. Cancalosi 97tr/A. Compost 98bl/Eric Crichton 158tl/G.Dove 142tr/ Michael Fogden 178c/Jeff Foott 17c, 181tr/ L. C. Marigo 136bl/Carl Roessler 162c/Rod Williams 121tl/G. Zeisler 85clb
Brian Cosgrove 102cl, c, 103tr, cra, cr, crb, br
E. T. Archive 60tl
Mary Evans Picture Library 14bl, 32tl, 72tl, c, 84cl, 106tl, 113tr, 132tl, 158c, 166tl, 167br
Forschungsinstitut und Naturmuseum Senckenberg, Frankfurt 34-5c
Geological Survey of Greenland, Copenhagen/A. A. Garde 21br
Ronald Grant Archive 172bl
Greenpeace/Rowlands 179t
Sonia Halliday 64cl
Robert Harding Picture Library 20c, 107tr, cr
Bruce C. Heezen & Marie Tharp, 1977/ ©MarieTharp: 171tr
Illustrated London News 174cr
The Image Bank 150-1c, 151tr
Jacana/F. Gohier 168cl
Japan Meterological Agency/ Meterological Office 167t
Frank Lane Picture Agency 20tr, 166bl/ Hannu Hautala 129tc/Silvestris 98tr/ Tony Wharton 129tl/Roger Wilmshurst 139tr, cra
Mike Linley 81tr, 87tc
Barbara Lofthouse 59tr
Mansell Collection 64tl, bl
Simon Conway Morris 24tr
Musée Nationale, Paris/ Gallimard-Jeunesse 169bl
NASA 12tl
NHPA 166cl/Anthony Bannister 118cl/ G. I. Bernard 41tr/Stephen Dalton 48tr/ D. Frazier 156tr/Pavel German 157crb/ Peter Johnson 86cra, 175c/Jany Sauvanet 83cr/Lady Phillipa Scott 175bl/John Shaw 38tr
Natural History Museum 35bl
Oxford Scientific Films 17br, 181cl, bl/Doug Allan 126tl, 128bl/Kathie Atkinson 81tl, tc/Anthony Bannister 119cr/Fred Bavendam 173tl/Mike Birkhead 33bc/Jim Fraser 81cr/ Z. Leszczynski 85c/Ben Osbourne 174bl, 175cl/ S. Osolinski 178bl/Partridge Films, C. Farneti 99tr
K. Pilsbury 104cr, crb
Planet Earth Pictures 105cl, 113tr, 150b, 170tr/Gary Bell 95tl, 163br/Steve Bloom 77c/ Conlin 76br/Larry Madin 173br/ Peter Scoones 145tl, 161tl/Seaphot 122bl/ M.Snyderman 168cr/D.Weisel 107br

Roger-viollet 169t
Royal Meterological Society 102tl
Science Photo Library 39tr/John Walsh 41tl
Frank Spooner Pictures 106cr, 107tl, 112-3c
Tony Stone Images/R.Everts 108cr
Wildlife Matters 104tr, 105tr
ZEFA 76cla, 174cla

Every effort has been made to trace the copyright holders and we apologize in advance for any unintentional omissions. We would be pleased to insert the appropriate acknowledgment in any subsequent edition of this publication